READING THE GOSPELS TODAY

McMaster New Testament Studies

The McMaster New Testament Studies series, edited by Stanley E. Porter, is designed to address particular themes in the New Testament that are of concern to Christians today. Written in a style easily accessible to ministers, students, and laypeople by contributors who are proven experts in their fields of study, the volumes in this series reflect the best of current biblical scholarship while also speaking directly to the pastoral needs of people in the church today.

Reading the Gospels Today

Edited by

Stanley E. Porter

WILLIAM B. EERDMANS PUBLISHING COMPANY
GRAND RAPIDS, MICHIGAN / CAMBRIDGE, U.K.

Wm. B. Eerdmans Publishing Co.
255 Jefferson Ave. S.E., Grand Rapids, Michigan 49503 /
P.O. Box 163, Cambridge CB3 9PU U.K.

Printed in the United States of America

09 08 07 06 05 04   7 6 5 4 3 2 1

Library of Congress Cataloging-in-Publication Data

Reading the Gospels today / edited by Stanley E. Porter.
p.   cm.   — (McMaster New Testament studies)
Papers presented at the eighth H. H. Bingham Colloquium in New Testament,
McMaster Divinity College, Hamilton, Ontario, 2002.
Includes bibliographical references and index.
ISBN 0-8028-0517-5 (alk. paper)
1. Bible. N.T. Gospels — Criticism, interpretation, etc. — Congresses.
I. Porter, Stanley E., 1956-   II. H. H. Bingham Colloquium in New Testament
(8th: 2002: McMaster Divinity College)   III. Series.

BS2555.52.R43   2004
226'.06 — dc22
2004040941

www.eerdmans.com

Contents

110156

CONTENTS

Preface

The papers in this collection represent the well-considered and reconsidered thoughts of the contributors to the 2002 H. H. Bingham Colloquium in New Testament at McMaster Divinity College in Hamilton, Ontario, Canada. The Colloquium, the eighth in a continuing series, was entitled Reading the Gospels Today, and it attracted not only the speakers whose papers are included here, but a healthy gathering of those interested in hearing and responding to the papers.

The Bingham Colloquium at McMaster Divinity College provides an opportunity for selected scholars to present their perspectives on a contemporary New Testament theme of relevance to the larger community of both students and laity alike. The 2002 Colloquium focused on both understanding the text of the New Testament and interpreting it in today's context. We hope that this volume will be of interest to general readers and serve as a useful textbook for issues in contemporary Gospels study.

The Bingham Colloquium is named after Dr. Herbert Henry Bingham, who was a noted Baptist leader in Ontario. However, his leadership abilities were recognized by Baptists across Canada and around the world. His qualities included his genuine friendship, dedicated leadership, unswerving Christian faith, tireless devotion to duty, insightful service as a preacher and pastor, and visionary direction for congregation and denomination alike. These qualities endeared him both to his own church members and to believers in other denominations. The Colloquium has been endowed by his daughter as an act of appreciation for her father. We are pleased to be able to continue this tradition.

I am also very pleased to be able to thank William B. Eerdmans Publishing of Grand Rapids, Michigan, for undertaking the publication of the McMaster New Testament Studies series, of which this volume is the sixth to appear. Previous colloquia published in this series include *Patterns of Discipleship in the New Testament* (1996), *The Road from Damascus: The Impact of Paul's Conversion on His Life, Thought, and Ministry* (1997), *Life in the Face of Death: The Resurrection Message of the New Testament* (1998), *The Challenge of Jesus' Parables* (2000), and *Into God's Presence: Prayer in the New Testament* (2001). We anticipate future volumes in the series as well.

Lastly, I would like to thank the individual contributors for their efforts to translate difficult and challenging insights and concepts into presentations through spoken and written word that can communicate to a range of hearers and readers. The Colloquium was, I believe, a signal success in bringing important issues to light for both scholars and students. I think that I speak for all of the contributors in hoping that this printed volume does likewise.

STANLEY E. PORTER
McMaster Divinity College
Hamilton, Ontario, Canada

Abbreviations

AB	Anchor Bible
ABRL	Anchor Bible Reference Library
AGJU	Arbeiten zur Geschichte des antiken Judentums und des Urchristentums
ANF	Ante-Nicene Fathers
ATR	*Anglican Theological Review*
BBR	*Bulletin for Biblical Research*
Bib	*Biblica*
BibInt	*Biblical Interpretation*
BR	*Biblical Research*
CBQ	*Catholic Biblical Quarterly*
EBC	Expositor's Bible Commentary
ÉBib	Études bibliques
ECF	Early Christian Fathers
ET	English translation
ExpT	*Expository Times*
FS	Festschrift
GBS	Guides to Biblical Scholarship
GNS	Good News Studies
H.E.	Eusebius, *Historia Ecclesiae*
HNT	Handbuch zum Neuen Testament
ICC	International Critical Commentary
JBL	*Journal of Biblical Literature*

JES	*Journal of Ecumenical Studies*
JSNT	*Journal for the Study of the New Testament*
JSNTSup	*Journal for the Study of the New Testament* Supplement Series
JSOTSup	*Journal for the Study of the Old Testament* Supplement Series
JSPSup	*Journal for the Study of the Pseudepigrapha* Supplement Series
LCL	Loeb Classical Library
LJ	Lives of Jesus Series
LXX	Septuagint
m.	Mishnah
NAC	New American Commentary
NCBC	New Century Bible Commentary
NHC	Nag Hammadi Codices
NICNT	New International Commentary on the New Testament
NICOT	New International Commentary on the Old Testament
NIGTC	New International Greek Testament Commentary
NIV	New International Version
NovT	*Novum Testamentum*
NovTSup	*Novum Testamentum* Supplements
NRSV	New Revised Standard Version
NTL	New Testament Library
NTS	*New Testament Studies*
NTTS	New Testament Tools and Studies
OGIS	W. Dittenberger, ed., *Orientis graeci inscriptiones selectae* (Leipzig, 1903-05)
POxy	Oxyrhynchus papyri
RGG	*Religion in Geschichte und Gegenwart*
SBG	Studies in Biblical Greek
SBLMS	Society of Biblical Literature Monograph Series
SBT	Studies in Biblical Theology
SJT	*Scottish Journal of Theology*
SNTSMS	Society for New Testament Studies Monograph Series
TDNT	G. Kittel and G. Friedrich, eds., *Theological Dictionary of the New Testament,* trans. G. W. Bromiley (Grand Rapids: Eerdmans, 1964-76)
TSK	*Theologische Studien und Kritiken*
WBC	Word Biblical Commentary
WUNT	Wissenschaftliche Untersuchungen zum Neuen Testament
ZNW	*Zeitschrift für die neutestamentliche Wissenschaft*
ZTK	*Zeitschrift für Theologie und Kirche*

Contributors

Craig A. Evans, Payzant Distinguished Professor of Biblical Studies, Acadia Divinity College, Wolfville, Nova Scotia, Canada

Michael Knowles, George F. Hurlburt Associate Professor of Preaching, McMaster Divinity College, Hamilton, Ontario, Canada

Andrew T. Lincoln, Portland Professor of New Testament, University of Gloucestershire, UK

Lee Martin McDonald, Principal and Dean of the Faculty of Theology and Professor of Biblical Studies, Acadia Divinity College, Wolfville, Nova Scotia, Canada

Allan Martens, Adjunct Lecturer in New Testament, McMaster Divinity College, Hamilton, Ontario, Canada

Stanley E. Porter, President, Dean and Professor of New Testament, McMaster Divinity College, Hamilton, Ontario, Canada

Al Wolters, Professor of Religion and Theology/Classical Languages, Redeemer University College, Ancaster, Ontario, Canada

Yong-Eui Yang, Associate Professor of New Testament Studies, Kukje Theological Seminary; and Dean, Ezra Bible Institute, Seoul, Korea

INTRODUCTION

Reading the Gospels
as a Hermeneutical Issue

Stanley E. Porter

One Jesus and four Gospels. This realization is the challenge and opportunity presented by the New Testament canon. This situation has been addressed in varying ways over much of the history of the church, and continues to be a challenge for contemporary Gospels scholarship. The Bingham Colloquium in New Testament for 2002 gathered scholars who were interested in pursuing this topic further by addressing their particular areas of expertise. In this age of interpretation, New Testament scholars are concerned with how to read and understand the biblical text. The particular challenge of the Gospels is that they introduce differing, some would even say competing, pictures of Jesus, but in a canonical context that pushes towards harmonization and unity. Scholars, like other readers of the Bible, are also concerned with how these differing yet coexisting pictures are to be understood in our contemporary interpretive and expositional contexts. Thus, in a very real sense, this book is concerned both with the content of the Gospels and — perhaps even more importantly — with addressing the issues of how to interpret these Gospels in relation to each other and in terms of the world in which we live. As a result, some of the papers concentrate on vexing issues that surround Gospel criticism in an attempt to bring clarity to these important topics. The task is not simply to bring clarity for its own sake, but to attempt to open up understanding of the Gospels in our contemporary situation. Other papers concentrate on the interpretive issues themselves, showing how one's immediate interpretive context helps to raise and shape the issues and the answers that are found when we read the Gospels. These issues are important for those with a lay interest in the Bible, and at least as important for those who are more vocationally oriented to the Gospels, whether as pastors or students.[1]

The first paper is by Craig Evans on the Synoptic Problem. In his paper, Evans points out that source criticism of the Gospels, which is especially concerned with the Synoptic problem — or how the three Gospels that reflect similar accounts of Jesus relate to each other — and the question of the literary relationship of these writings, and the older form and redaction criticisms, have in recent years fallen out of vogue. Instead, a new literary criticism has emerged on the interpretive scene, proffering a variety of approaches often focused upon "close readings" of the text. Evans wishes to point out that this new literary criticism is not necessarily bad, since no doubt many fresh insights have been gained through such readings. The old comparative method, with one eye on source and the other eye on redaction, still has much to offer in his mind, however. What it has to offer, he believes, is not limited to the scholar — it has much to offer the busy pastor and the student of Scripture whether in seminary or personal study as well. Evans takes the opportunity to utilize a synoptic approach, where the texts of Matthew, Mark, and Luke are set in parallel columns. To illustrate, he considers several pertinent examples. These include examples that illustrate the priority of Mark: Matt 4:1-2; Mark 1:12-13; and Luke 4:1-2 and Matt 8:18-27; Mark 4:35-41; and Luke 8:22-25. He also considers examples that illustrate Matthean dependence on Mark: Matt 16:5-12 and Mark 8:14-21 and Matt 16:13-18; Mark 8:27-30; and Luke 9:18-21. He also examines instances that illustrate Lukan dependence on Mark: Matt 3:1-3; Mark 1:2-3; and Luke 3:1-6 and Mark 6:1-6 and Luke 4:16-30. Lastly, he treats Markan examples in light of Markan priority, such as Mark 1:1. Evans believes that time spent puzzling over why Mark reads one way and Matthew or Luke another will usually pay off exegetically, expositionally, and theologically.

In the second paper, Stanley Porter discusses the quest for the historical Jesus. In a number of ways, and at least in many recent scholars' minds, the idea of a picture or pictures of Jesus in the Synoptic Gospels competes with the notion of the historical Jesus, or the Jesus who lived in history nearly two thousand years ago. Historical Jesus research has gone through

---

1. I thank the individual contributors for providing abstracts of their own chapters, which I draw on freely in providing this brief summative introduction.

a number of developing phases in the ongoing quest to define and establish who Jesus was from the material available in the Gospels. In many respects, historical Jesus research — even by those who have wanted to establish a firm core of authentic Jesus material — has proceeded from a minimalistic or skeptical position that is at odds with the Gospel records, which present a more full-orbed picture. After questioning the standard schemata for discussing historical-Jesus research, Porter examines several of the most important concepts in recent historical Jesus research. These include the genre of the Gospels, where it is argued that the Gospels most accurately reflect the ancient biography; the language of Jesus, where recent research points to Jesus' use of Greek (including brief discussion of Luke 17:11-19 and Matthew 5–7); and the criteria that are used to establish the authenticity of Jesus material. These topics are analyzed in order to ask whether the opposition between the Jesus of the Gospels and of history can be sustained in the light of recent research.

Michael Knowles deals with reading Matthew's Gospel. In his paper, Knowles examines three kinds of reading that occur in relation to Matthew's Gospel. First, he depicts Matthew himself as reading Israel's sacred texts — and much else besides — and then proclaiming through his Gospel the results of such reading. In so doing, Knowles believes, Matthew seeks to demonstrate that Jesus is the fulfillment of Israel's Scripture, history, and covenant. The second act of reading that occurs is when we read Matthew's text. Or, to be more accurate in light of the historical situation, Matthew intends for us to hear the text read, and thus to encounter his narrative as "oral performance." In this process, the structure of the Gospel reinforces its theological content, with the literary order and symmetry of Matthew's presentation mirroring the historical and theological symmetry of divine providence. The third kind of reading, Knowles argues, takes place in the course of the Gospel being read, in which the text itself "reads" its readers. That is to say, by presenting specific material in a specific manner, the text not only determines the nature of our reading and separates interested from disinterested readers, but also bids us participate in a particular kind of reading and understanding that will characterize us as disciples of Jesus — anchored in the person of Jesus of Nazareth.

In the fourth chapter, Yong-Eui Yang offers a reading of Mark 11:12-25 from a Korean perspective. What might at first appear out of place in a volume by otherwise western European and North American readers becomes central to the task of this volume — recognizing that we read and interpret the Gospels in the midst of our own situation. Traditionally, scholars have been puzzled by the problematic story of Mark 11:12-14 and 20-25, the cursing of the fig tree, with questions being raised in relation to the source, origin, and historicity of the story. These questions are all relevant, as the story provides a sole destructive miracle by Jesus in the Gospels. Many conjectures have been put forward to meet the questions. Here, Yang analyzes the Old Testament and Jewish backgrounds of the story, its particular structure, and parallels in Matthew and other New Testament fig tree passages. The result is that Yang attempts to understand the story in its first-century socio-religious context, in which Jesus' action is seen as an acted parable in light of the Old Testament. If the fig tree signifies Israel, Jerusalem, and/or the Temple, then Jesus' action would have been understood as a message of messianic judgment, especially against the Temple. However, Yang is not only concerned with the search for meaning of the story, but with bringing his interpretation to his present church context. His goal is to make the biblical text alive in the church, in particular the Korean church to which he belongs.

Allan Martens turns to Luke's Gospel, where he begins by speculating about what Theophilus, presumably the first reader of Luke's Gospel, thought about Luke's work. Though not much can be known about Theophilus to help us interpret Luke's work, modern readers may put themselves in Theophilus's position, Martens believes, and, with the help of literary methods, be able to understand Luke's Gospel in the same way as a first-century reader probably did. In distinction to Matthew and Mark, Luke's major theological theme concerns salvation. Luke's major focus is on Jesus as Saviour, and the life of Jesus as "saving event" in the plan of God. Luke's composition and structure evidence this theme in a number of ways, as well as fitting into this overarching theme a number of other motifs that scholars have investigated as being central for understanding Luke's Gospel. Thus, the paper deals with such features as the divine plan in salvation history, Jesus' ministry as the fulfillment of the Old Testament, Jesus' ministry as characterized by saving activity, and the Jewish rejection of Jesus' salvation, which served to open the doors for the salvation of Gentiles.

In turning to John's Gospel, Andrew Lincoln draws on his recent research into this Gospel to bring out one of its distinctive features — the frequency with which it employs the word-group associated with "truth" and the claims it makes for its own truth. According to Lincoln, these claims have, however, come under severe criticism from both modern and postmodern readings of the Gospel, bringing together on the same side scholars who ordinarily would not agree in such matters. This paper provides an intriguing and provocative examination of how the issue of truth might be best understood in the context of the Fourth Gospel's narrative. It then explores critiques of its truth in the three important areas of historicity, anti-Judaism, and power. His discussion of historicity provides a valuable analysis of ancient biography in terms of John's Gospel. Lincoln rejects much of the recent discussion of anti-Judaism in the Fourth Gospel by appealing to the Gospel context of promoting Jesus as the criterion of truth. Lastly, Lincoln explores the notion of the suffering and death of Jesus as representative of the way power is exercised in Jesus' kingdom. Lincoln concludes by suggesting that this Gospel is most appropriately read in light of its own different perspective on truth, which encompasses but cannot simply be reduced to matters of historicity, ethics, or power.

Lee Martin McDonald takes our reading of the Gospels into the next stage of their transmission by showing how the Gospels were received in the early Christian church. This process began with their use and acknowledged authority in the individual churches, and subsequently their acceptance as scriptural documents. In order to show this development, the paper focuses primarily, though not exclusively, on the first- and second-century church literature, but also on the problem of definition of the literary genre of a "Gospel" during the development of the church. McDonald traces the development of the oral traditions into written memoirs about Jesus and then into the Gospels themselves. Particular attention is also given to the existence of this literature alongside other "gospel" literature that did not find acceptance in the New Testament canon. He concludes with discussion of the process by which the Gospels that we now find in our canon became sacred literature.

In the final but by no means least significant chapter, Al Wolters discusses what it means to read the Gospels canonically. In this essay, he engages in detailed discussion with the well-known canonical critic, Brevard Childs. By taking a detailed look at Childs's treatment of the parable of the wicked tenants in his *Biblical Theology of the Old and New Testaments* (1992), Wolters engages in a critical dialogue with Childs's "canonical approach" to the Gospels. In particular, though he is fundamentally sympathetic to Childs's overall aims, Wolters raises questions about the underlying assumptions regarding the faith-scholarship relationship in his approach. He then situates these assumptions within a broader philosophical and theological context. The result is that Wolters asks whether there is a tension between Childs's methodological assumptions and his theological aims, one that reveals that Childs's theological motives are compromised by his being wedded to mainline historical criticism. Wolters concludes that such an approach compromises Childs's ability to provide a model of how to read the Gospels canonically.

At the time that these papers were first presented in their oral form, they generated much stimulating discussion. At the end of the session, we had a panel discussion in which we invited interaction between both the individual contributors and the general audience. Out of these various times of discussion came a refining of our thoughts and ideas regarding our individual papers and the larger topic of how it is that we read the Gospels today. Although various approaches and assumptions are represented in these papers, I believe that they represent genuine attempts to come to terms with a number of the major issues that confront any Gospel interpreter today, and provide ways forward in such a task.

Sorting Out the Synoptic Problem: Why an Old Approach Is Still Best

CRAIG A. EVANS

Halfway through my lecture on the Synoptic problem at least one student asks what the point is: What does it matter which Synoptic Gospel was written first and how the three of them relate to one another? Seminary students are usually the quickest to raise this question. Undergraduates are a bit slower to ask, perhaps because they are less sure of themselves. However, the question is never heard from the pulpit or in the pew; evidently the question is completely irrelevant in the church.

This apparent indifference notwithstanding, the Synoptic problem is well worth pondering; its solution well worth taking into account in studying the Gospels in preparation for preaching and teaching in the church today. The exegetical and theological payoff is simply too great for us to ignore the problem and the study required to grapple with it.

What the Synoptic Problem Is and Why It Matters

The Synoptic problem becomes apparent when we observe the similarities and differences in content and order in Matthew, Mark, and Luke. The striking relationship among these three Gospels is only underscored when they are compared to the fourth Gospel, which differs at almost every point of comparison.

Two or more of the Synoptic Gospels hold in common many stories and teachings of Jesus. The verbal parallels are frequent and often quite

1

close. The words of John the Baptist ("You brood of vipers, who warned you . . . ?") are, with two or three minor exceptions, in exact agreement in Matthew and Luke. But there are also surprising divergences. All three Gospels seem to follow the same sequence, then unexpectedly Luke breaks away. There are also odd discrepancies between Matthew and Mark.

In Matthew we find a three-chapter version of the Sermon on the Mount, complete with the Lord's Prayer. But in Luke the sermon is given on a level place (hence it is called the Sermon on the Plain), is only half of one chapter (6:20-49), and does not contain the Lord's Prayer (which shows up several chapters later, in a completely different context).

Matthew's version of the infancy narrative features dreams, fulfilled prophecies, the visit of the magi, the wrath of Herod, and the flight to Egypt. None of this appears in Luke's version. Instead, we have canticles, a visit by shepherds, and visits to a relative and to the temple. Similar discrepancies occur in the Easter narratives. In Matthew the disciples meet the risen Jesus on a mountain; in Luke the risen Jesus joins the two on the road to Emmaus, appears in a house and eats food, and ascends. None of this is in Matthew.

Matthew presents Jesus' teaching in five major blocks of material; this material is scattered in Luke. In Matthew and Mark, Jesus makes his way from Galilee to Judea in two or three chapters. In Luke it takes ten. Matthew and Luke share a whole host of teaching, which is not found in Mark. At points Luke's version overlaps with Johannine tradition; at other points it overlaps with Pauline.

These are the most obvious examples that perplex interpreters. How are these phenomena to be explained? This is the Synoptic problem, and investigation of it is important for several reasons: (1) Explaining the relationship of the Synoptic Gospels will shed light on the origins and development of these most important sources for the life and teaching of Jesus; (2) resolution of the Synoptic problem is important for assessing the antiquity and value of the sources in study of the historical Jesus; and (3) study of the Synoptic problem heightens appreciation of the distinctive features of the Synoptic Gospels, which significantly aids the task of exegesis and theological study. It is this third reason that guides the present essay.

Why the Priority of Mark Is Still the Majority View

Matthean priority was almost universally held from the second-century church to the middle of the nineteenth century.[1] When modern biblical scholarship was in its infancy three books appeared — one English, the other two German — arguing not only for Matthean priority, but using this priority to explain the relationship of all three Synoptic Gospels to one another. Henry Owen and the much better known Johann Jakob Griesbach proposed that Matthew was written first, that Luke made use of Matthew, and that Mark, writing last, made use of both Matthew and Luke.[2]

Matthean priority remained the dominant solution to the Synoptic problem for more than a century. But the dominance of this position began to wane with the appearance of several studies in the nineteenth century. The middle position of Mark was observed, leading some to conclude that Mark may have been the first of the Synoptic Gospels, not second or third.[3] Heinrich Julius Holtzmann proposed the two-document hypothesis, whereby it was understood that a Mark-like source (document A) and a sayings source (document B) were utilized independently by Matthew and Luke.[4] The next two generations refined Holtzmann's hypothesis, resulting in the classic two-source theory, where it is understood that Matthew and Luke made use of Mark and the hypothetical Q (the abbreviation

1. On the great influence of Matthew in the early centuries of the church, see É. Massaux, *The Influence of the Gospel of Saint Matthew on Christian Literature before Saint Irenaeus,* 3 vols., ed. A. J. Bellinzoni (Macon: Mercer University Press, 1990, 1992, 1993).

2. H. Owen, *Observations on the Four Gospels* (London: T. Payne, 1764); J. J. Griesbach, *Fontes unde Evangelistae suas de resurrectione Domini narrationes hauserint* (Jena: J. C. G. Goepferdt, 1783); idem, *Commentatio qua Marci evangelium totum e Matthaei et Lucae commentariis decerptum esse monstratur,* I-II (Jena: J. C. G. Goepferdt, 1789-90). Although Griesbach gives no hint of being influenced by Owen's work, for three reasons it is very probable that he was acquainted with it: (1) Griesbach studied one year in England (1769-70), five years after the publication of Owen's book, which means he could probably read English and may have actually met Owen; (2) Griesbach actually possessed a copy of Owen's book, according to the catalogue of the contents of his library; and (3) comparison of their respective work suggests contact at several points. On this interesting topic, see M. C. Williams, "The Owen Hypothesis: An Essay Showing That It Was Henry Owen Who First Formulated the So-Called 'Griesbach Hypothesis,'" *Journal of Higher Criticism* 7 (2000): 109-25.

3. K. Lachmann, "De ordine narrationum in evangeliis synopticis," *TSK* 8 (1935): 570-90; partial ET in N. H. Palmer, "Lachmann's Argument," *NTS* 13 (1967): 368-78, esp. 370-76.

4. H. J. Holtzmann, *Die synoptischen Evangelien: Ihr Ursprung und geschichtlicher Charakter* (Leipzig: Engelmann, 1863).

of the German word *Quelle,* which means source).[5] The two-source theory and variations of it have come to dominate Gospels research.[6]

In recent years scholarly discussion of the Synoptic problem has intensified, with some claiming that the dominant view — Markan priority — is in danger of being overthrown. In 1964 W. R. Farmer challenged the near-consensus of Markan priority.[7] He has won a few converts (mostly in North America and in Britain; virtually no one in Germany).[8] He and his followers continue to pound away at what are considered the weak points of Markan priority. Despite their untiring efforts, however, Markan priority continues to be held by a majority of Gospel scholars.[9]

5. Among the most influential studies that favored the two-document (or two-source) hypothesis are J. C. Hawkins, *Horae Synopticae: Contributions to the Study of the Synoptic Problem,* 2d ed. (Oxford: Clarendon, 1909 [1st ed., 1898]); W. Sanday, ed., *Oxford Studies in the Synoptic Problem* (Oxford: Clarendon, 1911); and B. H. Streeter, *The Four Gospels: A Study of Origins,* rev. ed. (London: Macmillan, 1930 [orig. 1924]).

6. See J. A. Fitzmyer, "The Priority of Mark and the 'Q' Source in Luke," in *Jesus and Man's Hope,* vol. 1, ed. D. G. Buttrick and J. M. Bald (Pittsburgh: Pittsburgh Theological Seminary, 1970), 131-70; C. M. Tuckett, *The Revival of the Griesbach Hypothesis: An Analysis and Appraisal,* SNTSMS 44 (Cambridge: Cambridge University Press, 1983); R. H. Stein, *The Synoptic Problem: An Introduction* (Grand Rapids: Baker, 1987); S. E. Johnson, *The Griesbach Hypothesis and Redaction Criticism,* SBLMS 41 (Atlanta: Scholars Press, 1991).

7. W. R. Farmer, *The Synoptic Problem: A Critical Analysis* (New York: Macmillan, 1964); *idem,* ed., *New Synoptic Studies: The Cambridge Gospels Conference and Beyond* (Macon: Mercer University Press, 1983).

8. D. L. Dungan, "Mark — The Abridgement of Matthew and Luke," in *Jesus and Man's Hope,* vol. 1, ed. Buttrick and Bald, 51-97; H.-H. Stoldt, *History and Criticism of the Marcan Hypothesis* (Macon: Mercer University Press, 1980); D. B. Peabody, *Mark as Composer* (Macon: Mercer University Press, 1987).

9. The revival of the Owen-Griesbach hypothesis is not the only competing theory that is entertained by scholars these days. A more complicated version of the two-source hypothesis has been championed by M.-É. Boismard, *Synopse des quatre évangiles* (Paris: Éditions du Cerf, 1972), and *idem, L'Évangile de Marc sa préhistoire,* ÉBib 26 (Paris: Gabalda, 1994). Michael Goulder, following the lead of Austin Farrer (especially "On Dispensing with Q," in *Studies in the Gospels: Essays in Memory of R. H. Lightfoot,* ed. D. E. Nineham [Oxford: Blackwell, 1955], 55-88), has argued that Matthew is a midrashic expansion of Mark and that Luke is a reworking of both Matthew and Mark. Among Goulder's various studies, see especially *Midrash and Lection in Matthew* (London: SPCK, 1974) and *Luke: A New Paradigm,* 2 vols., JSNTSup 20 (Sheffield: JSOT Press, 1989). For a recent assessment of the Farrer-Goulder hypothesis that is at points supportive and at points critical, see M. S. Goodacre, *Goulder and the Gospels: An Examination of a New Paradigm,* JSNTSup 133 (Sheffield: Sheffield Academic Press, 1996).

Markan priority continues to prevail because it possesses much greater explanatory power than does Matthean (or Lukan) priority. Parallel after parallel is more easily explained in reference to Markan priority. Let us consider two examples briefly (with major points of comparison in bold face):

Example 1

Matthew 4:1-2	Mark 1:12-13	Luke 4:1-2
₁Then Jesus was **led up** by the Spirit into the wilderness to be tempted by the devil. ₂And he fasted forty days and forty nights, and afterward he was hungry.	₁₂The Spirit immediately **drove** him **out** into the wilderness. ₁₃And he was in the wilderness forty days, tempted by Satan; and he was with the wild beasts; and the angels ministered to him.	₁And Jesus, full of the Holy Spirit, returned from the Jordan, and was **led** by the Spirit ₂for forty days in the wilderness, tempted by the devil. And he ate nothing in those days; and when they were ended, he was hungry.

Analysis of Synoptic parallels often prompts the question that text critics usually ask: Which passage (or reading) best explains the others? Applying this question to the story of the temptation of Jesus is very suggestive.

Matthew says Jesus "was led up" *(anagein)* by the Spirit into the wilderness. Luke says Jesus "was led" *(agein)* by the Spirit in the wilderness. Mark says the Spirit immediately "drove"/"cast" Jesus "out" *(ekballein)* into the wilderness. Does Mark's reading explain the readings of Matthew and Luke? Or, do the readings of Matthew and Luke explain Mark's reading? If we assume that Mark wrote first, then Matthew and Luke replaced Mark's "drove out" with forms of "led." Or, if Mark wrote last, ignoring the forms of "led" in the two texts in front of him, then we must imagine that the Evangelist deliberately chose instead to write "drove out." Which option is the most plausible?

Approximately one half of the occurrences of *ekballein* ("to drive/ cast out") in Matthew and Luke are in reference to exorcism; and about one half of those not in reference to exorcism are in reference to violent or negative acts, such as murdering and casting the son out of the vineyard (Matt 21:39; Luke 20:15), casting Jesus out of town (Luke 4:29), casting someone out of the kingdom into hell (Matt 8:12; Luke 13:28), casting out someone's name, that is, striking a person's name from the membership of the local synagogue (Luke 6:22), or casting merchants out of the temple precincts (Matt 21:12; Luke 19:45).

If, in writing last, Mark read and made use of Matthew and Luke, which speak of Jesus being "led" by the Spirit, it is hard to see why this Evangelist would have chosen the verb *ekballein* ("drive out" or "cast out") when he would have observed that *this is the verb routinely used in the stories of exorcism,* for example, "Lord, Lord, did we not prophesy in your name, and cast out *(ekballein)* demons in your name?" (Matt 7:22), and that it is frequently used in other negative or judgmental contexts, as in the examples cited above.

Accordingly, probability favors the first option. For it is much easier to explain the appearance of "led up" and "led" in Matthew and Luke as stylistic improvements upon Mark than trying to find an explanation that would account for Mark's "drove out," if we suppose that when he wrote he had Matthew and Luke before him. But why did the Markan Evangelist use the word at all? Mark 1:12 is Mark's first use of *ekballein.* It did not occur to him that he would subsequently use this word in reference to exorcism. Had the Evangelist narrated (or *read* in Matthew or Luke, if we accept the Owen-Griesbach Hypothesis) one or two exorcisms *before* narrating the temptation, he too may have chosen a different verb, as Matthew and Luke would later do.

There are other editorial indications that Matthew and Luke are posterior to Mark. Matthew substitutes "devil," which Mark never uses, for Mark's "Satan." The devil is Matthew's preferred designation for the evil one (cf. Matt 4:1, 5, 8, 11; 13:39; 25:41), a preference perhaps prompted by the appearance of "devil" in Q, the tradition that Matthew and Luke have in common (cf. Luke 4:2, 3, 5, 13; 8:12). For his part, Luke takes the opportunity to say that Jesus was "full of the Holy Spirit," which is in step with this Evangelist's marked interest in pneumatology. And of course, both Matthew and Luke omit Mark's somewhat cryptic reference to Jesus' being "with the wild beasts." All of these differences are easier to explain on the assumption of Markan priority, not posteriority.

Example 2

Matthew 8:18-27	Mark 4:35-41	Luke 8:22-25
18Now when Jesus saw great crowds around him, he gave orders to go over to the other side. . . . 23And when he got into the boat, his disciples followed him. 24And behold, there arose a great storm on the sea, so that the boat was being swamped by the waves; but he was asleep. 25And they went and woke him, saying, "**Save, Lord**; we are perishing." 26And he said to them, "Why are you afraid, **O men of little faith**?" Then he rose and rebuked the winds and the sea; and there was a great calm. 27And the men marveled, saying, "What sort of man is this, that even winds and sea obey him?"	35On that day, **when evening had come**, he said to them, "Let us go across to the other side." 36And leaving the crowd, **they took him** with them in the boat, **just as he was**. And other boats were with him. 37And a great storm of wind arose, and the waves beat into the boat, so that the boat was already filling. 38But he was in the stern, asleep **on the cushion**; and they woke him and said to him, "**Teacher, do you not care** if we perish?" 39And he awoke and rebuked the wind, and said to the sea, "Peace! Be still!" And the wind ceased, and there was a great calm. 40He said to them, "Why are you afraid? Have you **no faith**?" 41And they were filled with awe, and said to one another, "Who then is this, that even wind and sea obey him?"	22One day he got into a boat with his disciples, and he said to them, "Let us go across to the other side of the lake." So they set out, 23and as they sailed he fell asleep. And a storm of wind came down on the lake, and they were filling with water, and were in danger. 24And they went and woke him, saying, "**Master, Master**, we are perishing!" And he awoke and rebuked the wind and the raging waves; and they ceased, and there was a calm. 25He said to them, "**Where is your faith?**" And they were afraid, and they marveled, saying to one another, "Who then is this, that he commands even wind and water, and they obey him?"

We have here one of the most vivid, exciting stories of the Synoptic Gospels. Every child who has attended Sunday School has heard this story, has seen it illustrated in picture books or on flannel boards, and perhaps has even acted it out in a skit.

Once again, if we ask which reading best explains the others, logic favors Markan priority. Commentators have rightly observed that the phrase "when evening had come" is from Markan redaction and serves as Mark's way of either bringing a discrete episode to a conclusion or of introducing a new one (cf. Mark 1:32; 6:47; 11:19; 14:17; 15:42). But in adding it here, Mark creates a bit of a redundancy, if not an anomaly (is it "day" or is it "evening"?). But even more problematic, the phrase stands in tension with the story of the demoniac, which follows in Mark 5:1-20 and gives every impression of taking place on the same day. Evidently Matthew senses this problem, electing to replace "On that day, when evening had come" with "Now when Jesus saw great crowds around him." Thus, it is not the end of the day that prompts Jesus to relocate; it is the crowds. Luke removes the difficulty by simply saying, "One day. . . ."

But Mark goes from the redundant and inconsistent to the strange, when he says the disciples "took him with them in the boat, just as he was." What on earth does the Evangelist mean by this? Is Jesus in some way incapacitated? Is he perhaps in a trance, so that his disciples have to pick him up and place him in the boat? No, probably not; it seems that Mark is only harking back to Mark 4:1-2, where Jesus got into the boat and commenced his teaching. That is, when the disciples departed from the shore, they took Jesus with them, already seated in the boat ("just as he was"). But it must be admitted that the text reads oddly. Not surprisingly, Matthew replaces the Markan verse with "And when he got into the boat, his disciples followed him." Not only is the problem mitigated, Jesus is properly cast as the leader and his disciples as the followers. Luke again takes the simplest course, by dropping all reference to going aboard: "So they set out."

The real rub comes when the storm frightens the disciples. Mark says Jesus "was in the stern, asleep on the cushion." Matthew and Luke see no point in these details, so omit them. Does it matter where Jesus was sleeping, or on what? But far more problematic is the way the disciples address Jesus: "Teacher, do you not care if we perish?" Even with due allowance for their terror, their question borders on disrespect. Matthew and Luke provide much more respectful cries for help: "Save, Lord; we are perishing" (Matthew); "Master, Master, we are perishing!" (Luke). Both Matthew and Luke preserve Mark's verb for "perish," but each significantly alters the manner in which the disciples address Jesus.

The various forms of Jesus' reply to the frightened disciples also recommend Markan priority. In Mark Jesus says, "Why are you afraid? Have you no faith?" What, the future apostles and leaders of the church "have no faith"? No, not exactly, says Matthew; they are "men of little faith" (a Matthean favorite; cf. Matt 6:30; 14:31; 16:8); presumably their faith will

8

grow and become stronger. Taking a different approach, but accomplishing the same thing, Luke says that Jesus asked, "Where is your faith?" That's right; the disciples do indeed have faith, but they have suffered a momentary lapse. They have misplaced their faith, as it were.

It is details such as these, in passage after passage, that have led most Gospel scholars to embrace Markan priority. In the passages that will be examined below we shall again find that it is always easier to explain Mark as the source of Matthew and Luke than to try to explain things the other way around. But our purpose will not be to offer yet more evidence in support of Markan priority; it will be to show in what ways a horizontal reading of the Synoptic Gospels aids the task of exegesis, theology, and preaching.

We shall begin with examples of how we understand Matthew and Luke in light of Markan priority. Historically, interpretation of Matthew and Luke has been easier because of our confidence in Markan priority. The two-source hypothesis provides interpreters with the sources of Matthew and Luke, thereby greatly aiding the task of interpretation. Because we have their sources and can observe what they have done with them, we are in a position to understand much better the messages they wish to communicate.

Interpreting Matthew in Light of the Priority of Mark

What interpretive insight may we gain if we approach Matthew as a revision and expansion of the Gospel of Mark? As it so happens, the interpretive payoff is quite significant. Matthew has a lot to say. Although this Evangelist was fond of Mark, retaining some 90% of its contents, he found it necessary to rewrite the story, revising and expanding and in a few places expurgating a Gospel that the Matthean Evangelist read and reread and probably taught from many times before replacing it with his new, revised edition.[10]

The messianic credentials of Jesus are much emphasized in the Gospel of Matthew. But Jesus emerges as no Messiah of popular, militant ex-

---

10. For the classic treatment of Matthew from a redaction-critical perspective, see G. Bornkamm, G. Barth, and H. J. Held, *Tradition and Interpretation in Matthew* (Philadelphia: Westminster, 1963). Cf. G. N. Stanton, *A Gospel for a New People: Studies in Matthew* (Edinburgh: Clark, 1992; Louisville: Westminster/John Knox, 1993).

pectations. We shall find a didactic, almost scribal Messiah, portrayed as master teacher. Here are two examples:

Example 1

Matthew 16:5-12	Mark 8:14-21
5When the disciples reached the other side, they had forgotten to bring any bread. 6Jesus said to them, "Take heed and beware of the leaven of the Pharisees and **Sadducees**." 7And they discussed it among themselves, saying, "We brought no bread." 8But Jesus, aware of this, said, "O men of little faith, why do you discuss among yourselves the fact that you have no bread? 9Do you not yet perceive? Do you not remember the five loaves of the five thousand, and how many baskets you gathered? 10Or the seven loaves of the four thousand, and how many baskets you gathered? 11**How is it that you fail to perceive that I did not speak about bread? Beware of the leaven of the Pharisees and Sadducees."** 12**Then they understood that he did not tell them to beware of the leaven of bread, but of the teaching of the Pharisees and Sadducees.**	14Now they had forgotten to bring bread; and they had only one loaf with them in the boat. 15And he cautioned them, saying, "Take heed, beware of the leaven of the Pharisees and the leaven of **Herod**." 16And they discussed it with one another, saying, "We have no bread." 17And being aware of it, Jesus said to them, "Why do you discuss the fact that you have no bread? Do you not yet perceive **or understand? Are your hearts hardened?** 18**Having eyes do you not see, and having ears do you not hear?** And do you not remember? 19When I broke the five loaves for the five thousand, how many baskets full of broken pieces did you take up?" They said to him, "Twelve." 20"And the seven for the four thousand, how many baskets full of broken pieces did you take up?" And they said to him, "Seven." 21And he said to them, **"Do you not yet understand?"**

Comparison of Mark 8:14-21 and Matt 16:5-12 reveals several interesting differences. According to Mark, Jesus warns his disciples: "Take heed, beware of the leaven of the Pharisees and the leaven of Herod." In Matthew the warning is nearly identical, but there is one important difference; Jesus speaks of "the leaven of the Pharisees and Sadducees." Matthew apparently is troubled by Mark's linking of the Pharisees and Herod. In what sense can their "leaven" (whatever that is supposed to mean) have something in common? It is not surprising that Matthew replaces "Herod" with "the Sadducees." Nor is it surprising that scribes after the time of Matthew the scribe make changes in Mark's text. Some scribes read "Herodians" (cf. P[45]

W and other manuscripts), which at least provides a more sensible parallel with the plural "Pharisees" and also takes the reader back to Mark 3:6, where we first hear of the Herodians (see also Mark 12:13 = Matt 22:16).

However, it is still not clear what this "leaven of the Pharisees and Herod" is. Contextually, we are probably to think that the Markan Evangelist has in mind either unbelief (in Jesus himself or in his message) or antagonism (to Jesus or to God). The Pharisees have just asked Jesus for a sign, "to test him" (Mark 8:11-13). And a bit earlier Mark narrated Herod's malevolent interest in and fear of Jesus (Mark 6:14-29). But for Matthew the "leaven" of the Pharisees and the Sadducees is their "teaching." Such an identification is more in step with Matthew's severe criticism of Israel's religious teachers, whose unbelief and opposition to God and his messengers will lead to national disaster. We shall return to this point later.

The disciples misunderstand the import of Jesus' warning, taking his reference to leaven (or yeast) literally and so acknowledge that they have "no bread." In Mark's version Jesus appears quite exasperated with his disciples: "Do you not yet perceive or understand? Are your hearts hardened? Having eyes do you not see, and having ears do you not hear? And do you not remember?" Jesus' reference to hardened hearts ominously alludes to the very language of obduracy earlier applied to Jesus' enemes (cf. Mark 3:5: "he looked around at them with anger, grieved at their hardness of heart") and to "outsiders" (cf. Mark 4:11-12), language that echoes the harsh criticism voiced by Israel's classical prophets (cf. Isa 6:9-10; Jer 5:21; Ezek 12:2). After reviewing the results of the two feeding miracles, where the disciples recall how baskets of leftover scraps were collected, Jesus brings the discussion to a close with a question that must have made the disciples wince: "Do you not yet understand?" Mark's readers are left wondering if the disciples ever understood.

In Matthew's version, however, the disciples fare much better. They are addressed as men of "little faith," an epithet that has already been noticed. But the series of rhetorical questions is abridged; Matthew has Jesus only ask: "Do you not yet perceive? Do you not remember. . . ?" Gone are the allusions to hardened hearts, unseeing eyes, and unhearing ears. Even more importantly, Matthew's form of the story ends on a much more promising note. After having Jesus repeat the original warning about the leaven of the Pharisees and Sadducees, the Matthean Evangelist assures his readers that then the disciples "understood that he did not tell them to beware of the leaven of bread, but of the teaching of the Pharisees and Sadducees."

Matthew's revision of Mark points to a significant concern on the part of this Evangelist. Jesus is the master teacher and master disciple-maker, who warns his disciples of the false teaching of their rivals in the Jewish community. In the aftermath of the destruction of the Jewish Temple and Jerusalem the holy city, the Jewish faithful are regrouping and retrenching. Increasingly there is less tolerance for sectarian groups like the messianists of the Matthean community.[11] There is especially no sympathy for messianism, which in the minds of many was a major cause of the disaster that overtook the Jewish nation.[12]

What kind of Messiah was Jesus anyway? Had he liberated Israel? No, he had not. He had been put to death by a Roman governor. So what if some of his followers believed that he had been resurrected? The day of judgment had not in fact arrived. Thus, Jesus is irrelevant, his message of the arrival of the kingdom of God mistimed, and the ongoing existence of his community or church pointless.

Against these criticisms the Matthean Evangelist must mount a serious defense. He must show that the advent of Jesus fulfilled Jewish prophecy, that Jesus himself fulfilled the requirements of the Law, that he taught a way of righteousness, and that his teaching was in fact superior to the teaching of his rival teachers. Jesus was and is Israel's Messiah, but he is no defeated militant Messiah, who calls fellow Israelites to arms. He will conquer Israel's enemies through the power of the kingdom proclamation. The day of judgment will surely come, but beware; not all the sons of the kingdom (viz., ethnic Jews) will enter the kingdom; some will be cast out.

Example 2

The second example focuses on Peter's famous confession at Caesarea Philippi:

11. For recent studies emphasizing Matthew's Jewish setting, see J. A. Overman, *Matthew's Gospel and Formative Judaism: The Social World of the Matthean Community* (Minneapolis: Fortress, 1990); A. J. Saldarini, *Matthew's Christian-Jewish Community*, Chicago Studies in the History of Judaism (Chicago and London: University of Chicago Press, 1994); and D. C. Sim, *The Gospel of Matthew and Christian Judaism: The History and Social Setting of the Matthean Community* (Edinburgh: Clark, 1998).

12. Josephus's avoidance of messianism and his disparagement of would-be liberators provide a first-century example of this tendency in Jewish circles.

Matthew 16:13-18	Mark 8:27-30	Luke 9:18-21
13Now when Jesus came into the **district** of Caesarea Philippi, he asked his disciples, "Who do men say that **the Son of man** is?" 14And they said, "Some say John the Baptist, others say Elijah, and others Jeremiah or one of the prophets." 15He said to them, "But who do you say that I am?" 16Simon Peter replied, "You are the Christ, **the Son of the living God.**" 17And Jesus answered him, **"Blessed are you, Simon Bar-Jona! For flesh and blood has not revealed this to you, but my Father who is in heaven. 18And I tell you, you are Peter, and on this rock I will build my church, and the powers of death shall not prevail against it. 19I will give you the keys of the kingdom of heaven, and whatever you bind on earth shall be bound in heaven, and whatever you loose on earth shall be loosed in heaven."** 20 Then he strictly charged the disciples to tell no one **that he was the Christ.**	27And Jesus went on with his disciples, to the **villages** of Caesarea Philippi; and on the way he asked his disciples, "Who do men say that I am?" 28And they told him, "John the Baptist; and others say, Elijah; and others one of the prophets." 29And he asked them, "But who do you say that I am?" Peter answered him, "You are the Christ." 30And he charged them to tell no one about him.	18Now it happened that **as he was praying** alone the disciples were with him; and he asked them, "Who do the people say that I am?" 19And they answered, "John the Baptist; but others say, Elijah; and others, that one of the old prophets has risen." 20And he said to them, "But who do you say that I am?" And Peter answered, "The Christ **of God.**" 21But he charged and commanded them to tell this to no one.

Once again Mark begins a narrative somewhat clumsily. The Evangelist situates this famous story of Peter's confession of Jesus as Messiah in "the villages of Caesarea Philippi." This is odd, because Caesarea Philippi is a city, not a territory. So in what sense can we speak of being in the villages of a given city? Matthew understands what Mark is trying to say, changing the text to read "the district of Caesarea Philippi." (Luke sees no point to the geographical reference, so omits it altogether; however, mention is made of Jesus in prayer, a popular theme in Luke.)

According to Mark's version, Jesus asks his disciples, "Who do men say that I am?" (which Luke modifies slightly, with "Who do the people say that I am?"). But Matthew has Jesus refer to himself as "the Son of man": "Who do men say that the Son of man is?" The Evangelist does this in order to link "Son of man" with "Christ," thereby defining the former in reference to the latter. In Mark the disciples reply, "John the Baptist, and others say Elijah, and others one of the prophets" (which again is essentially followed by Luke). But Matthew takes the opportunity here to add the name of the prophet Jeremiah, evidently as part of a typology by which Jesus and his fate are compared to the famous prophet of old.[13]

But the two most important differences between Matthew and Mark concern Peter's confession and Jesus' reply. According to Mark, Peter simply declares: "You are the Christ." Matthew's version, however, enhances Jesus' identity: "You are the Christ, the Son of the living God." (Luke also expands the confession, but more modestly: "The Christ of God.") Neither Mark nor Luke tells us what Jesus said in reply, apart from the injunctions to keep the confession quiet. But in Matthew, Jesus says: "Blessed are you, Simon Bar-Jona! For flesh and blood has not revealed this to you, but my Father who is in heaven." The idiom "flesh and blood" is Semitic (= Hebrew *bāśār we-dām*), occurring often in rabbinic literature, and simply refers to a human being as opposed to an angel, a demon, or God himself. No, the Matthean Jesus avers, Peter's insight had no human origin; it came as divine revelation. But this is not all; Simon son of John is now called *Peter*, which means "rock," and on this rock Jesus will build his church, an assembly of faithful, against which the gates of Hades cannot prevail.

13. Matthew, more than the other Gospel writers, is especially interested in the prophet Jeremiah. It has been suggested that the Evangelist has presented the rejection of Jesus in the light of the suffering and rejection that Jeremiah experienced. Jesus' appeal to Jer 7:11 ("cave of robbers") in the temple action (cf. Mark 11:17; Matt 21:13) encouraged this typology. The prophecies of Jeremiah are explicitly cited in Matt 2:17-18 (Jer 31:15) and 27:9-10 (Jer 19:1-13; cf. Zech 11:12-13). For discussion of this Matthean theme, see M. Knowles, *Jeremiah in Matthew's Gospel: The Rejected Prophet Motif in Matthaean Redaction*, JSNTSup 68 (Sheffield: JSOT Press, 1993).

Here we have the well-known wordplay on Peter (Greek: *Petros;* Aramaic: *kepha'*), whose name means "rock" (Greek: *petra*). It has been suggested that the naming of Simon and the declaration that he was the foundation of a new people of God follow an Old Testament pattern. Abram and Jacob are the only persons in the Hebrew Bible whose names are changed (Gen 17:1-8; 32:22-32). Of special interest is that the change of their names was related to their role as founders of a new nation. Of the two, only Abraham is later associated with a rock foundation. According to Isa 51:1-2, "Listen to me, you who pursue righteousness, who seek the LORD: Look to the rock from which you were hewn, and to the quarry from which you were dug. Look to Abraham your father, and to Sarah who gave birth to you in pain; when he was one I called him, then I blessed him and multiplied him." The parallel suggests that Jesus foresees founding a new people, his church, on the bedrock of Peter's confession and leadership. (See also the comment in Matt 3:9, where John the Baptist links Abraham with stones.)

Jesus' promise to build his church recalls God's promises in Jer 31:4, "Again I will build you, and you shall be rebuilt, O virgin of Israel!" and Amos 9:11, "In that day I will raise up the fallen booth of David, and wall up its breaches; I will also raise up its ruins, and rebuild it as in the days of old" (cf. Acts 15:15-18). The word translated "church" (Greek *ekklēsia*) means "assembly" or "congregation" and is the equivalent of Hebrew *qahal,* which occurs frequently in the Old Testament (often in reference to the "assembly of God" or "assembly of the Lord"; cf. Num 16:3; 20:4; Deut 23:2, 3, 4, 9).

The "gates of Hades" are the powers of evil that attempt to overwhelm the church. They are not the realm of the dead (Job 38:17; Ps 9:13, which speak of the "gates of death"; Isa 38:10, which speaks of the "gates of Sheol") or death by martyrdom. But because the church is built on the rock, it will withstand the attack (much as the house built on the rock withstands the storm in the parable in Matt 7:24-27). In view of this parallel, it has been suggested that the saying originally referred to "storm" (Aramaic: *sa'ar*), instead of "gate" (Aramaic: *ša'ar*), that is, the storms of Hades will not overpower the church.

Jesus promises Peter, "I will give you the keys of the kingdom of heaven." This saying is in some way related to Isa 22:22, "Then I will set the key of the house of David on his shoulder. When he opens no one will shut, when he shuts no one will open." As the representative of the "house of David" Jesus has given the key to his principal disciple Peter, who will exercise authority "on earth," even as Jesus as Son of Man exercised authority "on earth" (see Mark 2:10 = Matt 9:6 = Luke 5:24). As chief apostle, Peter will unlock the doors that will allow true Israel to enter the kingdom (be they Jews or Gentiles), a role we see him play at Pentecost (Acts 2) and later with respect to the salvation of Gentiles (Acts 10–11).

To have the "keys of the kingdom" is to have power to "bind on earth" what "shall be bound in heaven," etc. The binding and loosing mentioned here clarify what was said above about the keys, especially in light of the parallel in Isa 22:22. That is, binding and loosing is the equivalent of shutting and opening, shutting the door on some, opening the door for others or, less figuratively, of deciding what is permitted and what is not permitted. A similar idea is found in the parallel in Matt 18:18, but with reference to questions of discipline within the church itself. Saying that what Peter binds "on earth" shall be bound "in heaven" is to assure the apostle that he has heaven's backing (compare Luke 11:52, where legal experts misuse their expertise and take away the "key of knowledge," shutting people out of the kingdom and not entering themselves).[14]

In the passage of the confession of Peter the theme of Jesus as master teacher is continued, but the emphasis here is on the teaching authority being passed on from Jesus to his principal disciple Simon Peter. We can only surmise what role Peter played in the Matthean community. Whether he was personally known to this community we cannot say. But it is clear that his authority is respected (or at least should be, from the Evangelist's point of view). It is vital to demonstrate that Jesus has invested this apostle with heavenly authority, so that what he binds or looses on earth is what is forbidden or permitted in heaven. In essence, Peter becomes the master teacher in the absence of Jesus.[15]

---

14. For rabbinic examples of permit/not permit (or forbid), see *m. 'Eduyyot* 4:8, "the House of Shammai permit levirate marriage between the co-wives and the surviving brothers, but the House of Hillel forbid it"; *Terumot* 5:4, "the House of Shammai declare it forbidden, but the House of Hillel permit"; and other examples in *m. Pe'ah* 7:5; *m. Demai* 2:4; *m. Ta'anit* 2:7; *m. Megillah* 1:11; *m. Temurah* 7:6.

15. To be sure, the Matthean Evangelist has augmented his Markan source with Matt 16:17-19, but one should not assume that this material has no claim to antiquity, even authenticity. On this question, see S. E. Porter, *The Criteria for Authenticity in Historical-Jesus Research: Previous Discussion and New Proposals*, JSNTSup 191 (Sheffield: Sheffield Academic Press, 2000), 153-61, 201-3, and the bibliography cited in 160 n. 90.

Interpreting Luke in Light of the Priority of Mark

Many Lukan scholars suspect that in addition to Mark and Q, imbedded in Luke is an older first draft, usually called proto-Luke. The hypothesis has much to recommend it, for in Luke we find parallel tradition that resists the explanation that it is simply edited Markan or Q tradition. But perhaps the most helpful aspect of the proto-Luke hypothesis is how it may explain a perplexing chronological dilemma that Lukan scholars face.

The problem is simply put: The Gospel of Luke is followed by a second volume, the book of Acts, which refers to the Gospel as the "first account" (compare Acts 1:1-2 and Luke 1:1-4). This second volume ends with Paul under arrest in Rome (Acts 28), probably 61 or 62 CE. But if Luke made use of Mark, which was written during the Jewish war and probably near its end (ca. 69 CE), then presumably Luke wrote some time after the conclusion of the war (and most scholars place Luke in the late 70s or 80s). Why then does Acts end where it does? Why does it not go on to narrate Paul's release, his further activities, and his eventual martyrdom? Attempts to explain why Luke chooses to conclude his narrative where he does have not been persuasive. Many wonder if the narrative of Acts ends where it does simply because there was no more story to tell. If this is true, then Acts was written in the early 60s. If this is true, then the Gospel of Luke was written at the same time, perhaps a bit earlier. But how can this be, if it has made use of the Gospel of Mark, which probably was written a few years later?

This is where the proto-Luke hypothesis may clear up the problem. What was probably written in the early 60s was proto-Luke and Acts. After the publication of Mark a few years later, the Evangelist Luke rewrote his first volume, making use of Mark and Q. Chunks of proto-Luke remain, as seen in the distinctive features of the infancy and Easter narratives, the parallel narratives (especially seen in the Passion week), and the many unparalleled stories and parables. However, the Lukan Evangelist probably did not revise or update the second volume of his work, the book of Acts.

Because we do not possess proto-Luke (any more than we possess Mark's sources), we cannot be sure what the theological perspective was in this early form of Luke's Gospel story. But we can observe what the Evangelist does with his Markan and Q sources. Several areas of interest come to light: (1) the story of Jesus stands in continuity with the story of Israel; (2) proper use of wealth is a sure sign of righteousness; (3) the good news of Jesus is for Gentiles as well as Israelites; (4) the grounds of election are not what people always think; and (5) the Holy Spirit plays an important role in the life and ministry of Jesus as much as it does in the lives and ministries of his disciples.[16]

Let us probe the themes of election and the place of the Gentiles in God's plan of redemption. The first passage looks at the use of Isaiah 40 in connection with the preaching and activity of John the Baptist:

Example 1

Matthew 3:1-3	Mark 1:2-3	Luke 3:1-6
1In those days came John the Baptist, preaching in the wilderness of Judea, 2"Repent, for the kingdom of heaven is at hand." 3For this is he who was spoken of by the prophet Isaiah when he said, "The voice of one crying in the wilderness: Prepare the way of the Lord, make his paths straight."	2As it is written in Isaiah the prophet, "**Behold, I send my messenger before thy face, who shall prepare thy way;** 3the voice of one crying in the wilderness: Prepare the way of the Lord, make his paths straight — "	1**In the fifteenth year of the reign of Tiberius Caesar, Pontius Pilate being governor of Judea, and Herod being tetrarch of Galilee, and his brother Philip tetrarch of the region of Ituraea and Trachonitis, and Lysanias tetrarch of Abilene, 2in the high-priesthood of Annas and Caiaphas, the word of God came to** John **the son of Zechariah** in the wilderness; 3and he went into all the region about the Jordan, preaching a baptism of repentance for the forgiveness of sins. 4As it is written in the book of the words of Isaiah the prophet, "The voice of one crying in the wilderness: Prepare the

---

16. For the classic treatment of Luke from a redaction-critical perspective, see H. Conzelmann, *The Theology of St. Luke* (New York: Harper and Row, 1961). Conzelmann's primary focus on temporal aspects of Luke's theology has been modified and even abandoned in more recent scholarship.

way of the Lord, make his paths straight. 5**Every valley shall be filled, and every mountain and hill shall be brought low, and the crooked shall be made straight, and the rough ways shall be made smooth;** 6**and all flesh shall see the salvation of God.**"

With quotations from Malachi and Isaiah, Mark links the incipit of his narrative (v. 1: "the beginning of the good news of Jesus Christ the Son of God") to the appearance of John the Baptist in the wilderness. Of course, Mark refers only to "Isaiah the prophet," which prompts both Matthew and Luke to delete the quotation of Mal 3:1 ("Behold, I send my messenger . . .") at this point and to use it later (Matt 11:10 = Luke 7:27). The Matthean and Lukan Evangelists make other changes as well. Matthew anticipates John's preaching of repentance and proclamation of the arrival of the kingdom, while Luke prefaces his account of John's preaching with a remarkably elaborate synchronism, from Emperor Tiberius to the high priests Annas and his son-in-law Caiaphas.

But the most interesting feature in Luke's version is the extension of the quotation of Isa 40:3 to include vv. 4 and 5 as well. It is probable that the Evangelist has done this so that he might end his quotation with the words "and all flesh shall see the salvation of God" and so that he might thus underscore the coming mission of the church, as portrayed in the book of Acts. This mission will begin in Jerusalem (Acts 1), to be sure, but it will reach Rome itself (Acts 28). The gospel of Messiah Jesus is not limited to the faithful of Israel, but is to be preached to all nations (cf. Luke 4:16-30). Recall Simeon's praise: "my eyes have seen your salvation, which you have prepared in the presence of all peoples" (Luke 2:30-31). Simeon was among the first to see God's salvation; there will be many more.

Example 2

The second passage depicts Jesus' preaching in Nazareth.

Mark 6:1-6

1He went away from there and came to his own country; and his disciples followed him. 2And on the sabbath he began to teach in the synagogue; and many who heard him were astonished, saying, **"Where did this man get all this? What is the wisdom given to him? What mighty works are wrought by his hands! 3Is not this the carpenter, the son of Mary and brother of James and Joses and Judas and Simon, and are not his sisters here with us?"** And they took offense at him. 4And Jesus said to them, **"A prophet is not without honor,** except in his own country, and among his own kin, and in his own house." 5And he could do no mighty work there, except that he laid his hands upon a few sick people and healed them. 6And he marveled because of their unbelief. And he went about among the villages teaching.

Luke 4:16-30

16And he came to Nazareth, where he had been brought up; and he went to the synagogue, as his custom was, on the sabbath day. And he stood up to read; 17and there was given to him the book of the prophet Isaiah. He opened the book and found the place where it was written, 18"The Spirit of the Lord is upon me, because he has anointed me to preach good news to the poor. He has sent me to proclaim release to the captives and recovering of sight to the blind, to set at liberty those who are oppressed, 19to proclaim the **acceptable** year of the Lord." 20And he closed the book, and gave it back to the attendant, and sat down; and the eyes of all in the synagogue were fixed on him. 21And he began to say to them, "Today this scripture has been fulfilled in your hearing." 22And all spoke well of him, and wondered at the gracious words which proceeded out of his mouth; and they said, **"Is not this Joseph's son?"** 23And he said to them, "Doubtless you will quote to me this proverb, 'Physician, heal yourself; what we have heard you did at Capernaum, do here also in your own country.'" 24And he said, "Truly, I say to you, **no prophet is acceptable** in his own country. 25But in truth, I tell you, there were many widows in Israel in the days of Elijah, when the heaven was shut up three years and six months, when there came a great famine over all the land; 26and Elijah was sent to none of them but only to Zarephath, in the land of Sidon, to a woman who was a widow. 27And there were many lepers in Israel in the time of the prophet Elisha; and none of them was cleansed, but only Naaman the Syrian." 28When they heard this, all in the synagogue

> were filled with wrath. 29And they rose
> up and put him out of the city, and led
> him to the brow of the hill on which
> their city was built, that they might
> throw him down headlong. 30But pass-
> ing through the midst of them he went
> away.

Mark's version provides no actual content of what Jesus said apart from the pithy saying, "A prophet is not without honor, except in his own country, and among his own kin, and in his own house." Oddly, the Markan Evangelist relates more words of Jesus' critics than of Jesus himself: "Where did this man get all this? What is the wisdom given to him? What mighty works are wrought by his hands! Is not this the carpenter, the son of Mary and brother of James and Joses and Judas and Simon, and are not his sisters here with us?"

Luke's version of the visit to Nazareth is essentially in agreement with Mark's version. The major difference is that in Luke we have a re-markably detailed account of the content of Jesus' preaching. Jesus is handed the scroll of Isaiah, he reads from Isaiah 61, and he then expounds on the meaning of the text through appeal to the examples of the prophets Elijah and Elisha.

Jesus reads most of Isa 61:1-2 ("The Spirit of the Lord is upon me, be-cause he has anointed me to preach good news to the poor . . ."), notably omitting the final clause, "and the day of vengeance of our God." Luke's quotation is from the Septuagint (the Greek translation of the Hebrew) and is actually a combination of various parts of Isa 61:1-2 and 58:6 (61:1a, b, d; 58:6d; 61:2a, with 61:1c and 61:2b, c omitted). Isaiah 61 and 58 are linked by common words and ideas: *dektos,* "acceptable," in 61:2 and 58:5, *aphesis,* "release"/"forgiveness," in 61:1 and 58:6. Luke may understand *aphesis* in both senses of forgiveness (of sins) and release (from prison). Another noteworthy detail is the replacement of the verb meaning "to call for" in Isa 61:2a with a verb meaning "to proclaim," thus suggesting that the Anointed One, or Messiah, does more than merely "call for" the ac-ceptable day of the Lord; he actually "proclaims" its arrival, which lends it-self very well to the idea of the preaching of Jesus.

Jesus declares, "Today this Scripture has been fulfilled in your hear-ing." This assertion is very significant. It is to this passage that he appeals when a doubting, discouraged, and imprisoned John the Baptizer sends

21

word, asking Jesus, "Are you he who is to come, or do we look for another?" (cf. Matt 11:2-6 = Luke 7:18-23). It is this passage that in all probability has shaped Jesus' understanding of mission more than any other. Jesus believes that the Spirit of God is upon him. This claim is well supported by the healings and exorcisms that Jesus is able to perform "by the finger of God" (cf. Luke 11:20). In the Lukan narrative, of course, the foundation for such a claim has been convincingly laid: Jesus was generated by the Spirit, was baptized by the Spirit in great power, was full of the Spirit when he entered the wilderness to be tested, and then emerged from the wilderness "in the power of the Spirit." The reader has been well prepared for the claim that the words of Isa 61:1-2 are fulfilled in Jesus.

The reaction to Jesus is more nuanced in Luke's version than in Mark. Initially, the synagogue congregation seems pleased: "Is not this Joseph's son?" We should not read Luke through a Markan lens. The people of Nazareth are pleasantly surprised, as if to ask, "Could this be true? Could we be so fortunate that the one anointed of the Lord is one of our own?" The mood of the congregation changes when Jesus recites the proverb, "Physician, heal yourself," warning them, "Truly, I say to you, no prophet is acceptable in his own country." He goes on to appeal to the examples of Elijah and Elisha, implying that the awaited messianic blessings are not the exclusive privilege of Israelites, but will be extended to Gentiles, even to enemies. Enraged, the congregation throws Jesus out of the synagogue. It seems that the prophet who proclaims the "acceptable" year of the Lord is not himself acceptable.

Most interpreters rightly recognize that Luke has taken the opportunity to lay out Jesus' program, emphasizing the central role of election in Jesus' message and theology. The expansive rewriting of the visit to the Nazareth synagogue is consistent with the expansion of the quotation from Isaiah 40. Both revised passages contribute to the Lukan Evangelist's interests in the Gentile mission, a mission that becomes a central theme in the book of Acts.

Interpreting Mark in Light of the Priority of Mark

It has already been acknowledged that we do not possess Mark's sources. Therefore, we cannot easily identify precisely those places where the Evangelist has made changes in order to develop themes of interest to him, the way we can when we study Matthew and Luke. We must infer from the whole of Mark the message that the Evangelist hopes to convey. But there are a few key places that we may be sure will reward investigation.[17]

When studying a book from late antiquity a good place to begin is with the book's beginning, or what we have called the incipit. Mark's incipit echoes the Roman imperial cult: "The beginning *(archē)* of the good news *(euangelion)* of Jesus Christ, Son of God *(huiou tou theou)*" (Mark 1:1). We immediately think of the birthday inscription in honor of Caesar Augustus: ". . . since Providence, which has ordered all things and is deeply interested in our life, has set in most perfect order by giving us Augustus, whom she filled with virtue that he might benefit humankind, sending him as a savior *(sōtēr),* both for us and for our descendants, that he might end war and arrange all things, and since he, Caesar, by his appearance (excelled even our anticipations), surpassing all previous benefactors, and not even leaving to posterity any hope of surpassing what he has done, and since the birthday of the god *(tou theou)* Augustus was the beginning *(archein)* of the good news *(euangelion)* for the world that came by reason of him . . ." (*OGIS* 458, primarily based on the Priene Inscription; ca. 9 BCE).

The parallels between Mark's opening verse and the birthday inscription are obvious. The appearance of the god, or Son of God, is the beginning of the good news for the world. We hear this idea expressed in a papyrus in reference to Nero (reigned 54-68 CE): "The good god of the inhabited world, the beginning of all good things" (POxy 1021). Mark's Gospel was written at the very end of Nero's rule or shortly after his death (probably ca. 69 CE). Mark's incipit should be seen as a direct challenge to the cult of the emperor. In essence, the Evangelist is saying that Julius Caesar and his descendants are not divine sons; Jesus Christ is; the good news for the world does not begin with Caesar; it begins with Christ.

Mark's bold challenge to the cult of the emperor is not limited to his opening, thematic verse. It appears from time to time throughout the narrative. The Evangelist tells us that Jesus acted with great authority *(exousia),* an authority that the Son of Man possessed on earth. At the very beginning of Jesus' ministry we are told: "And they were astonished *(ekplēssein)* at his teaching, for he taught them as one who had authority *(exousian),* and not as the scribes" (Mark 1:22). In many places in the Greek Bible *exousia* is used

---

17. For the classic treatment of Mark from a redaction-critical perspective, see W. Marxsen, *Mark the Evangelist* (Nashville: Abingdon, 1956). Few today share Marxsen's optimism in distinguishing source from redaction.

in reference to a king's authority. But consider what happens to Heliodorus, agent of the tyrant Antiochus IV Epiphanes (reigned 175-164 BCE), who hoped to loot the temple at Jerusalem: "But when he arrived at the treasury with his bodyguard, then and there the Sovereign of spirits and of all authority *(pasēs exousias)* caused so great a manifestation that all who had been so bold as to accompany him were astounded *(kataplēssein)* by the power of God, and became faint with terror" (2 Macc 3:24).

The linkage of authority *(exousia)* and astonishment *(kataplēssein/ ekplēssein)* in Mark may well call to mind such stories and traditions (see also Mark 11:18 [astonished] + 11:27-33 [authority]). More interesting is the comment of the shaken disciples after Jesus stills the storm: "Who then is this, that even wind and sea obey him?" (4:41). The language of this question very probably alludes to the hated Antiochus, of whom it is said after he is stricken with a fatal illness: "Thus he who had just been thinking that he could command the waves of the sea, in his superhuman arrogance, and imagining that he could weigh the high mountains in a balance, was brought down to earth and carried in a litter, making the power of God manifest to all" (2 Macc 9:8). The idea that the emperor was master of land and sea, indeed, could even command the elements, is echoed in later imperial traditions applied to Caesar Augustus, as we see in a marble inscription from Pergamum: "The Emperor, Caesar, son of a god *(theou huion)*, the god Augustus, the overseer of every land and sea," or in the poetry of a sycophantic Virgil: "Yes, and you, O Caesar, whom which company of the gods shall claim before long is not known . . . watch over cities and care for our lands, so that the great world may receive you as the giver of increase and lord of the seasons . . . whether you come as god *(deus)* of the boundless sea and sailors worship your deity alone . . . or whether you add yourself as a new star to the lingering months . . . learn even now to hearken to our prayers!" (*Georgics* 1.24-42).

Jesus heals by touching (Mark 1:41; 8:22) or being touched (3:10; 5:27, 28, 30, 31; 6:56); he even uses his spittle to heal and restore sight (7:33; 8:22-26). These healing acts also parallel expectations of the imperial cult, as we see in stories told of the newly enthroned Vespasian: "A man of the people, who was blind, and another who was lame, together came to him as he sat on the tribunal, begging for the help for their disorders, which Serapis had promised in a dream; for the god declared that Vespasian would restore the eyes, if he would spit upon them, and give strength to the leg, if he would deign to touch with his heel" (Suetonius, *Vespasian* 7.2-3).

Details in Jesus' mockery and execution are probably modeled after the Roman imperial triumph. Jesus is dressed in purple, given a reed for a scepter and thorns for a laurel wreath, and is saluted by kneeling soldiers, with the words, "Hail, king of the Jews!" (Mark 15:16-20).[18] And of course, at the very moment of Jesus' death, the Roman centurion proclaims, "Truly this man was the Son of God!" (Mark 15:39), language that specifically alludes to the identity of Augustus and his successors.[19]

Thus, from beginning to end the Markan Evangelist narrates the story of Jesus with words and images calculated to evoke thoughts of the imperial cult in the minds of readers and hearers of the Roman Empire. Implicit is an invitation to the reader to consider who really is Lord — Caesar or Christ?

Conclusion

Old-fashioned redaction-critical, comparative analysis of the Synoptic Gospels yields a great deal of exegetical nuance. Only a few themes have been treated in the examples above. The newer forms of literary criticism rightly emphasize wholistic readings and "close" readings of the narrative. But in those cases where we have good reason to believe that we possess the sources that the Evangelists used (such as in the cases of Matthew and Luke, particularly), we do well to engage in the task of redaction criticism. The new methods run the risk of being overly subjective, if the results of comparative analysis are overlooked.

Redaction criticism has been around much longer than we realize, though we tend to think it was invented in Germany half a century ago. Church Fathers and medieval scholars employed the method long ago (albeit in a much more limited way), with some remarkable insights, some of which we think were discovered only recently.[20]

Redaction criticism serves the busy pastor well. It requires little more

18. For discussion of these details and others, see T. E. Schmidt, "Mark 15.16-32: The Crucifixion Narrative and the Roman Triumphal Procession," *NTS* 41 (1995): 1-18.

19. T. H. Kim, "The Anarthrous υἱὸς θεοῦ in Mark 15,39 and the Roman Imperial Cult," *Bib* 79 (1998): 221-41.

20. On this point, see the intriguing study by R. W. Herron Jr., *Mark's Account of Peter's Denial of Jesus: A History of Its Interpretation* (Lanham/New York/London: University Press of America, 1991).

than a Gospel synopsis (a.k.a. a Gospel harmony). Knowing Greek is a plus, of course, but even if limited to the English Bible, the student of Scripture can see many of the tendencies, preferences, and emphases of the respective Evangelists. Careful comparative analysis, always asking how the Evangelist has edited (or "redacted") his source or sources, will result in interesting and insightful exegesis, which will in turn translate into better sermon content and more stimulating Bible lessons.

It will also impress on the student that the Evangelists are theologians in their own right. We tend to think of Jesus, Paul, and John as the theologians of the New Testament. But we thus overlook the vital contributions of the Synoptic Evangelists. Luke, author of nearly twenty-five percent of the New Testament, is a profound theologian, whose themes contribute significantly to pneumatology, soteriology, and community life. The Evangelist Matthew grapples with the place of the Law of Moses, with prophetic fulfillment, with ethics, and with the salvation of Israel. And finally, who is bolder than the Markan Evangelist, who dares to challenge the political correctness of his day, denying the divinity and priority of Caesar in favor of the true Son of God, Jesus?

Each Synoptic Evangelist in his own way makes important contributions to New Testament theology and to the faith and practice of Christianity. It is up to each of us to unpack these contributions, and the comparative approach of redaction criticism, which presupposes the Synoptic problem and its solution, will greatly assist us in this task of unpacking.

Reading the Gospels and the Quest for the Historical Jesus[1]

STANLEY E. PORTER

What a lot of big dull books have been written about "the Sources of the Gospels," the "Synoptic Problem," the "lesser historical value of the Fourth Gospel," and all the rest! Those books are learned no doubt — they probably have enough of learning in them to sink a ship. But everyone knows that a hundred years from now those books will not be read. They will all be forgotten. And everyone knows that a hundred years from now the four Gospels, Matthew, Mark, Luke, and John, will be read. They will not be forgotten. They were written nearly nineteen hundred years ago, yet they still hold their own. They are interesting, arresting, vital, as those other books are not.

> C. R. Brown, former Dean, Yale Divinity School, in
> Fondren Lectures for 1936, published in *The Master's
> Influence* (Nashville: Cokesbury, 1936), 17-18.

1. The format of these papers necessitates that only a small sample of the literature available be cited. Those wishing for more complete references are referred to S. E. Porter, *The Criteria for Authenticity in Historical-Jesus Research: Previous Discussion and New Proposals*, JSNTSup 191 (Sheffield: Sheffield Academic Press, 2000), and C. A. Evans, *Life of Jesus Research: An Annotated Bibliography*, rev. ed., NTTS 24 (Leiden: Brill, 1996), both of which refer to the original publications in their original languages, where possible.

The "quest for the historical Jesus" is firmly entrenched as one of the dimensions of Gospel study today. This is plainly seen in the fact that a number of important books have recently been written that deal with this particular issue, often tracing the history of discussion of this quest.[2] This is further seen by the fact that discussion of the quest for the historical Jesus has become a standard item in many recent general introductions to New Testament study.[3] Nevertheless, the issues surrounding the quest for the historical Jesus remain either largely unknown or highly stigmatized in many circles, including some scholarly ones. Many lay people simply are not aware of the discussion that has developed over the last over two hundred years, even if they have been exposed to the products of this discussion in the form of books about Jesus. For those who know something about the quest, a few associate it with the public face that it has assumed as a result of the Jesus Seminar. The Jesus Seminar purports to represent the confident results of the latest in scholarly discussion, while at the same time doing so by recording for television cameras a bizarre ritual of voting with colored beads — something rarely seen in the best scientific laboratories. Such posturing invites, indeed welcomes, ridicule, with the result that a number of people simply dismiss the validity of the quest for the historical Jesus as another pointless episode in the history of scholarship, in which scholars find themselves talking to themselves, again, about something of little intrinsic worth and even less widespread application for the church. Before we readily agree, however, I believe that it is worth examining some of the issues suggested here in more detail. I will begin by examining the history of the quest for the historical Jesus and then suggest three areas that I see of potential productivity in the ongoing quest. I note right at the outset that these are three areas I find of potential interest.

The Quest for the Historical Jesus

Despite the tendency in some circles to dismiss the quest for the historical Jesus, the Gospels themselves push us to ask the question of the relation-

---

2. E.g., N. T. Wright, *Jesus and the Victory of God* (Minneapolis: Fortress, 1996), 13-124. Others will be cited below as pertinent.

3. E.g., R. E. Brown, *An Introduction to the New Testament* (New York: Doubleday, 1997), 817-30; L. M. McDonald and S. E. Porter, *Early Christianity and Its Sacred Literature* (Peabody: Hendrickson, 2000), 100-115.

ship between the Gospel accounts and the historical figure of Jesus. They do this in a number of ways. For example, the differences in the language of Jesus in the Synoptics and John's Gospel raise the question of whether we have the authentic voice of Jesus in any of our accounts. Differences in chronology between John and the Synoptics beg for explanation, for instance whether Jesus in the course of his ministry made one or three or four trips to Jerusalem,[4] or whether the cleansing of the Temple took place at the beginning of Jesus' ministry, as John's account would have it (2:14-18), or at the end, as the Synoptics record it (Matt 21:12-16; Mark 11:15-18; Luke 19:45-46), or whether Jesus' crucifixion took place the day before or on Passover, and the like. There are also numerous differences within the Synoptic accounts themselves that invite explanation. For example, a birth account is not found in Mark's Gospel, while two highly divergent accounts are found in Matthew's (ch. 2) and Luke's Gospels (1:5–2:52), or there are different orderings of some events in the Synoptic accounts of Jesus' ministry, or there are noteworthy differences in accounts within the Synoptics, such as whether it was the centurion himself or elders of the Jews on his behalf who came to Jesus (Matt 8:5-13 and Luke 7:1-10), or there are differences in the events surrounding the death of Jesus, such as whether he entered the Temple and left again (Mark 11:11) or cleansed it upon entering (Matt 21:12 and Luke 19:45), and the like. These are a few of the more obvious episodes that elicit comment.

These kinds of discrepancies — grantedly, encouraged by the Enlightenment philosophical orientation — are what has given rise to what has come to be known as the quest for the historical Jesus. Not only scholars, but laity alike, have noted such passages, and have tried to understand them in terms of each other and in terms of their contemporary world. Larger questions have thereby been raised, regarding such things as the birth (where, when, how?), actions (e.g., miracles), teachings (e.g., kingdom), and death and resurrection (can such a thing happen?) of Jesus and what he thought or knew about these things, that is, his self-consciousness. The results have usually focused on two inextricably interwoven areas — history and theology.[5] These issues have raised questions regarding the

---

4. Cf. Matt 26:17; Mark 14:1; Luke 22:1; and John 2:13, 23; 6:4; 11:55.

5. I believe that J. H. Charlesworth is being either incredibly optimistic, or possibly naive, when he contends that he can keep history and theology apart. See "The Historical Jesus: Sources and a Sketch," in *Jesus Two Thousand Years Later*, ed. J. H. Charlesworth and W. P. Weaver (Harrisburg: Trinity Press International, 2000), 84-128, especially 115-16.

historicity and historical veracity of the individual Gospel accounts. For example, such a blatant example as the cleansing of the Temple occurring at the outset of Jesus' ministry in John's Gospel and just after his entry into Jerusalem for the last time in the Synoptics raises historical questions. Did Jesus cleanse the Temple at the outset or the end of his ministry, or did he do it twice? And if he did it twice, why is it recorded only once in each Gospel? What do his actions imply regarding who he thought he was? The attempt to differentiate the historical from the ahistorical (I use this term consciously, rather than using a more prejudicial term such as unhistorical or nonhistorical) is fundamental to the quest for the historical Jesus. Similarly, these same passages, with their differing wording, ordering, and the like, have invited speculation on the theological motives of the authors, that is, whether and how the changes and differences among the accounts reflect theological interpretations of Jesus by his earliest followers. Jesus has been seen to be depicted, even in recent times, by the Gospel writers as any number of differing things, from a Jewish rabbi and teacher to an exorcist and healer to a wandering cynic philosopher.[6] This too is central to the quest for the historical Jesus. In other words, the defining feature of the quest for the historical Jesus has been the attempt to understand and interpret the figure of Jesus within his larger historical and theological context. That is, there has been a differentiation between the Jesus of history and the Christ of faith, a bifurcation that posits the historical Jesus on the one hand, to be differentiated from the Christ worshipped by the church. The former supposedly lurks behind the Gospels while the latter is uncomfortably embedded within them.

The result is that there is a standard scenario that is often related regarding the quest for the historical Jesus. It is found in most books that write upon it.[7] It goes something like this. The story begins in the eighteenth century, and what is often called now the first quest for the historical Jesus. This Life-of-Jesus Research began with Hermann Samuel Reimarus's fragments (1778), edited by Lessing, and led to the works of

6. See B. Witherington, *The Jesus Quest: The Third Search for the Jew of Nazareth* (Downers Grove: InterVarsity Press, 1995).

7. The number of works is too many to mention, but besides several mentioned above (e.g., Wright, McDonald and Porter, Witherington), note W. R. Telford, "Major Trends and Interpretive Issues in the Study of Jesus," in *Studying the Historical Jesus: Evaluations of the State of Current Research*, ed. B. Chilton and C. A. Evans, NTTS 19 (Leiden: Brill, 1994), 34-74. Cf. Porter, *Criteria*, 30-31 n. 6.

such well-known scholars as David Friedrich Strauss (1835), Ernst Renan (1863), and Adolf Harnack (1900).[8] Reimarus made a fundamental distinction between the historical Jesus and the Jesus of the Gospels, claiming that much of the Gospel material was confessional and contradicted the historical facts. Others followed suit, often renouncing supernaturalism in trying to depict the human Jesus who was full of high-minded thoughts and ideals. After literally thousands of such accounts were written, so the story is told, Albert Schweitzer published a now famous work in 1906 that recounted such attempts and showed that these lives of Jesus were as much autobiographical of their authors as they were accounts of Jesus.[9] The force of Schweitzer's analysis and critique brought the first quest for the historical Jesus to an abrupt end. This begins the so-called no-quest period, epitomized perhaps in the work of Rudolf Bultmann.[10] It was not, by this accounting, until 1953 and a public lecture by Ernst Käsemann that the second or new quest for the historical Jesus was begun.[11] Käsemann asked whether in fact there was not still historical information about Jesus that could be gleaned from the Gospel sources. This act of direct challenge of his teacher, Bultmann, supposedly engendered a rejuvenation of questing after the historical Jesus, a questing that has continued to this day. Many are even saying that at some time in the 1980s a third quest was introduced, characterized in different ways by various scholars, but perhaps seen as interested in the Jewishness of Jesus, determining the motivation for Jesus' crucifixion, concerned about political and theological issues, and bringing various scholars together.[12] So, to summarize, there have been four periods

8. H. S. Reimarus, *Reimarus: Fragments,* ed. C. H. Talbert, trans. R. S. Fraser (Philadelphia: Fortress, 1970); D. F. Strauss, *The Life of Jesus, Critically Examined,* trans. G. Eliot (London: Chapman, 1846); E. Renan, *The Life of Jesus* (London: Trübner, 1864); A. Harnack, *What Is Christianity?* trans. T. B. Saunders, CThL (London: Williams and Norgate, 1900).

9. A. Schweitzer, *The Quest of the Historical Jesus: A Critical Study of Its Progress from Reimarus to Wrede,* trans. W. Montgomery (London: Black, 1910).

10. E.g., R. Bultmann, *Jesus and the Word,* trans. L. P. Smith and E. Huntress (New York: Scribner, 1934); *Theology of the New Testament,* trans. K. Grobel (2 vols.; London: SCM, 1951, 1955).

11. E. Käsemann, "The Problem of the Historical Jesus," in his *Essays on New Testament Themes,* trans. W. J. Montague, SBT 41 (London: SCM Press, 1964), 15-47. Cf. J. M. Robinson, *A New Quest of the Historical Jesus,* SBT 25 (London: SCM Press, 1959).

12. See S. Neill and T. Wright, *The Interpretation of the New Testament, 1861-1986,* 2d ed. (Oxford: Oxford University Press, 1988), 379, in an appendix written by Wright, who labeled the third quest.

in the quest for the historical Jesus, a first quest from the eighteenth century to 1906, a no-quest period from 1906 to 1953, a new or second quest from 1953 to say 1988, and a third quest from around 1988 to the present.

There is only one major problem with this depiction, and that is that, I believe, it is wrong.[13] I don't mean wrong in the sense that all brief generalizations are wrong, but wrong in the sense that — even if it accurately reflects certain facts — it seriously misrepresents a whole lot more of them. Let me enumerate some of these briefly. (1) The quest for the historical Jesus, in fact, clearly began soon after Jesus' death and is reflected in the writings of the early church. Often neglected in the discussion is that there are numerous apocryphal Gospel accounts that attempt to interpret the life of Jesus, some of which are thought by some scholars (mistakenly, I believe) to be as early as the canonical accounts. The church Fathers too engaged in early forms of questing after the historical Jesus in their attempts to depict Jesus.[14] However, even if we agree that a quest for the historical Jesus is something that only an Enlightenment or post-Enlightenment person can engage in (I have my doubts, but will let this stand for now), the standard depiction is sorely inadequate. (2) Standard characterizations of the first quest strongly emphasize those who fostered the agenda of their scheme and bifurcate the Jesus of history from the Christ of faith, at the expense of dismissing numerous seriously scholarly attempts to affirm the depiction of Jesus during the first quest period. Such scholars as Frederic W. Farrar (1874), Bernhard Weiss (1882), Alfred Edersheim (1883), and William Sanday (1899), among others, cannot be dismissed so easily.[15] They were clearly comfortable with modern critical methods but still believed that the Gospel sources could be reliably used to discuss the historical Jesus. (3) The depiction of the first quest coming to a halt with the writing of Schweitzer is wrong in at least two regards. The first is that many of the

13. See Porter, *Criteria*, 17-62, where I provide the major support for my contention.

14. See, e.g., J. K. Elliott, *The Apocryphal New Testament* (Oxford: Clarendon Press, 1996), 3-225; J. Pelikan, *Jesus through the Centuries: His Place in the History of Culture* (New Haven: Yale University Press, 1985); R. M. Grant, *Jesus after the Gospels: The Christ of the Second Century* (London: SCM, 1990). The classic example, perhaps, is Marcion.

15. F. W. Farrar, *The Life of Christ*, 2 vols. (London: Cassell, Petter, and Galpin, 1874); B. Weiss, *The Life of Christ*, 3 vols., trans. J. W. Hope (Edinburgh: Clark, 1883-84); A. Edersheim, *The Life and Times of Jesus the Messiah*, 2 vols. (London: Longmans, Green, 1883); W. Sanday, "Jesus Christ," in *A Dictionary of the Bible*, 5 vols., ed. J. Hastings (Edinburgh: Clark, 1898-1904), 2.603-53.

things that Schweitzer had said had already been written and entered into the discussion of the historical Jesus at least 15 or 20 years earlier by other writers. For example, many of the ideas attributed to Schweitzer were introduced by such writers as Martin Kähler (1882), Johannes Weiss (1892), and William Wrede (1901), who by such an accounting would have been writing during the first quest period, when according to the standard scheme they are making the comments of a no-quester.[16] The fact that these authors enter into Schweitzer's critique certainly shows that he did not see the schema in the way later scholars do. The second way in which such a depiction is wrong is that it simply is not true that this became a period in which there was no questing after the historical Jesus. Some would say that Schweitzer introduced a period of no questing in German circles, but even this is not true — not when you have such authors as Heinrich Soden (1909), Adolf Schlatter (1921), K. L. Schmidt (1929), Joachim Jeremias (1935), Martin Dibelius (1939), and even Rudolf Bultmann (1926) writing during this period.[17] It is often overlooked that despite Bultmann's oft-cited protests in his New Testament theology regarding knowledge of Jesus,[18] he himself wrote a book on Jesus in 1926.[19] Authorship in English-

16. M. Kähler, *The So-Called Historical Jesus and the Historic, Biblical Christ*, trans. C. E. Braaten (Philadelphia: Fortress, 1964); J. Weiss, *Jesus' Proclamation of the Kingdom of God*, trans. R. H. Hiers and D. L. Holland, LJ (Philadelphia: Fortress, 1971); W. Wrede, *The Messianic Secret*, trans. J. C. G. Greig (Cambridge: J. Clarke, 1971). I also note the following sources, not noted in my previous work: G. B. Stevens, *The Teaching of Jesus* (New York: Macmillan, 1902); F. G. Peabody, *Jesus Christ and the Christian Character* (New York: Macmillan, 1905); O. Schmiedel, *Die Hauptprobleme der Leben-Jesu-Forschung*, 2d ed. (Tübingen: Mohr Siebeck, 1906).

17. H. F. Soden, *Die wichtigsten Fragen im Leben Jesu*, 2d ed. (Leipzig: Hinrichs, 1909); A. Schlatter, *The History of the Christ: The Foundation for New Testament Theology*, trans. A. J. Köstenberger (Grand Rapids: Baker, 1997); K. L. Schmidt, "Jesus Christ," in *Twentieth-Century Theology in the Making*, I. *Themes of Biblical Theology*, ed. J. Pelikan, trans. R. A. Wilson (London: Collins, 1969), 93-168 (translated from *RGG*, 2d ed.); J. Jeremias, *The Eucharistic Words of Jesus*, trans. A. Ehrhardt (Oxford: Blackwell, 1955); *idem, The Parables of Jesus*, 3d ed., trans. S. H. Hooke (London: SCM Press, 1972); *idem,* "Characteristics of the *Ipsissima Vox Jesu*," in *The Parables of Jesus*, trans. J. Bowden, C. Burchard, and J. Reumann, SBT 2.6 (London: SCM Press, 1967), 108-15; *idem, Unknown Sayings of Jesus*, trans. R. H. Fuller (London: SPCK, 1957); M. Dibelius, *Jesus*, trans. C. B. Hedrick and F. C. Grant (Philadelphia: Westminster, 1949).

18. *Theology of the New Testament*, 1.3: "The Message of Jesus is a presupposition for the theology of the New Testament rather than a part of that theology itself."

19. Even here, however, he wanted to minimize our knowledge: "I think that we can

speaking circles during this time included such luminary figures as A. T. Robertson (1908), T. R. Glover (1917), A. C. Headlam (1923), T. W. Manson (1931), F. C. Burkitt (1932), C. H. Dodd (1932), R. H. Lightfoot (1935), C. J. Cadoux (1941), W. Manson (1943), G. S. Duncan (1947), A. M. Hunter (1950), Vincent Taylor (1950), and E. J. Goodspeed (1950), to name only a few. Those writing in other languages include also J. Klausner (Hebrew 1925), M.-J. Lagrange (French 1928), M. Goguel (French 1932), A. Loisy (French 1933)[20] (the last two skeptical, but writing, nonetheless), and H. Daniel-Rops (French 1945).[21] It is hardly a period of no questing after the historical Jesus. Even those who are skeptical are clearly questing!

now know almost nothing concerning the life and personality of Jesus, since the early Christian sources show no interest in either, are moreover fragmentary and often legendary; and other sources about Jesus did not exist" (*Jesus*, 8). Nevertheless, his book was 182 pages and appeared in the German series Die Unsterblichen, on the spiritual heroes of humanity in their life and work, as volume 1.

20. See also A. Loisy, *The Gospel and the Church* (1903; reprint, Philadelphia: Fortress, 1978).

21. See Porter, *Criteria*, for bibliography on these. In the course of subsequent work, I have noted the following further writings during this period, several of which are not in the standard bibliographies (note some of the titles, hardly skeptical or not questing): J. Denney, *Jesus and the Gospel: Christianity Justified in the Mind of Christ* (London: Hodder and Stoughton, 1908); H. C. King, *The Ethics of Jesus* (New York: Macmillan, 1910); C. F. Kent, *The Life and Teachings of Jesus According to the Earliest Records* (New York: Scribner, 1913); F. C. Conybeare, *The Historical Christ* (London: Watts, 1914); S. Mathews, *The Social Teaching of Jesus: An Essay in Christian Sociology* (New York: Macmillan, 1915); A. Deissmann, *The Religion of Jesus and the Faith of Paul*, trans. W. E. Wilson (London: Hodder and Stoughton, 1923); J. Moffatt, *Everyman's Life of Jesus: A Narrative in the Words of the Four Gospels* (London: Hodder and Stoughton, 1924); A. Steinmann, *Jesus und die soziale Frage. Ein Beitrag zur Leben-Jesu-Forschung und zur Geschichte der Karitas*, 2d ed. (Paderborn: Schöningh, 1925); A. C. Headlam, *Jesus Christ in History and Faith* (London: John Murray, 1925); W. E. Bundy, *The Religion of Jesus* (London: Cassell, 1929 [the title is similar to that of a book by Vermes published in 1993]); W. R. Bowie, *The Master: A Life of Jesus Christ* (New York: Scribner, 1930); J. MacKinnon, *The Historic Jesus* (London: Longmans, Green, 1931); J. S. Stewart, *The Life and Teaching of Jesus Christ* (London: Church of Scotland Committee, 1933); C. E. Raven and E. Raven, *The Life and Teaching of Jesus Christ* (Cambridge: Cambridge University Press, 1934); C. R. Brown, *The Master's Influence* (Nashville: Cokesbury, 1936); I. R. Beiler, *Studies in the Life of Jesus* (New York: Abingdon-Cokesbury, 1936); S. P. Carey, *Jesus* (London: Book Club, 1940); A. T. Olmstead, *Jesus in the Light of History* (New York: Scribner, 1942); J. W. Bowman, *The Intention of Jesus* (Philadelphia: Westminster, 1943); H. A. Fosdick, *The Man from Nazareth as His Contemporaries Saw Him* (New York: Harper, 1949); H. E. W. Turner, *Jesus, Master and Lord: A Study in the Historical Truth of the Gospels* (London: Mowbray, 1953).

(4) One of the major factors that does come into play in Jesus research in the twentieth century, however, is form and later redaction criticism. Form criticism has become the predominant method utilized in much historical Jesus research, especially in German circles, so much so that a scholar such as Jeremias who did not widely embrace the method could be cavalierly dismissed by such a scholar as Käsemann.[22] One might be tempted to use the introduction of form criticism as a way of segmenting Jesus research. However, the use of form and redaction criticism has also distinguished much of the research in the new or second quest and the third quest, and lies at the very heart of the so-called criteria for authenticity so widely discussed and endorsed in historical Jesus research. So, this cannot be used as a way of segmenting the quest into various periods. (5) A number of recent scholars, especially those aligned with the third quest, have wanted to characterize the recent quest as asking new and unique questions that distinguish it as a period. Such claims can and have been made for any of the periods, but are belied, I believe, by the facts. For example, I have already mentioned how Schweitzer's criticisms and distinguishing features were already part of the first quest for much of the preceding 15 or 20 years. When Käsemann wrote his important essay in 1953, he was a firm advocate of form criticism, which had been developed during much of the no-quest period. Every period has asked questions in terms of the social environment of the first century. Lastly, one of the supposed hallmarks of the third quest is the emphasis upon the Jewishness of Jesus. One of the major scholars invoked in this discussion is Jeremias, who first wrote during the no-quest period and continued to be important in the second or new quest. Also, the Jesus Seminar is a part of the third quest, and its orientation is toward the Mediterranean and Hellenistic world of the New Testament, a perspective emphasized by those of the history of religions school who wrote around the turn of the nineteenth and twentieth centuries. (6) Lastly, it is worth noting that a number of other recent scholars have come to question the standard schema for talking about the quest for the historical Jesus. In fact, once one is able to take off the normal quest glasses, one is able to see that a number of scholars have pointed out problems in the scheme, such as Robert Banks, William O. Walker, Stephen

---

22. See E. Käsemann, "Blind Alleys in the 'Jesus of History' Controversy," in his *New Testament Questions of Today*, trans. W. J. Montague (London: SCM Press, 1969), 23-65, especially 24.

Fowl, and Colin Brown.[23] There are three recent works besides mine, however, that go further. The first is by Colin Marsh, who offers a New Historicist perspective on the quests of the historical Jesus, and who contends that there have always been numerous quests of the historical Jesus taking place simultaneously. He cites, for example, several positivist quests, a romantic quest, form-critical and traditio-historical quests, a non-Jewish Jesus quest, an existentialist quest, a Jewish-Christian quest, and a postmodern quest.[24] In a recent work by Walter Weaver, who surveys in great detail work on the historical Jesus for the first fifty years of the twentieth century, he states: "The impression that remains with me after completing this work is that our usual views of the 'Quests' of the historical Jesus do not do justice to the actual history. We have grown accustomed to appealing to the 'old Quest–No Quest–New Quest–third Quest,' but we may have to reconsider, for the common language represents a distinctively German perspective for the most part."[25] He goes on to note that the Americans, French, Dutch, and Scandinavians have also made contributions that merit notice. I would go even further and say that I am not convinced that the old schema even accurately reflects German scholarship, but perhaps one oversimplified version of German scholarship, one that was itself theologically motivated in the light of the Jewishness of Jesus. Lastly, Tom Holmén points out that there are numerous overlaps in method and approach among the so-called quests.[26]

As a result, rather than saying with Marsh that there are numerous quests — although I think that there is some validity in what he says, especially when one sees that certain questers are well outside the mainstream

23. W. O. Walker, "The Quest for the Historical Jesus: A Discussion of Methodology," *ATR* 51 (1969): 38-56, especially 52; R. J. Banks, "Setting 'The Quest for the Historical Jesus' in a Broader Framework," in *Gospel Perspectives: Studies of History and Tradition in the Four Gospels*, II, ed. R. T. France and D. Wenham (Sheffield: JSOT Press, 1981), 61-82, especially 61; S. E. Fowl, "Reconstructing and Deconstructing the Quest of the Historical Jesus," *SJT* 42 (1989): 319-33; C. Brown, "Historical Jesus, Quest of," in *Dictionary of Jesus and the Gospels*, ed. J. B. Green, S. McKnight, and I. H. Marshall (Downers Grove: InterVarsity Press, 1992), 326-41, especially 334-35.

24. C. Marsh, "Quests of the Historical Jesus in New Historicist Perspective," *BibInt* 5 (1997): 403-37.

25. W. P. Weaver, *The Historical Jesus in the Twentieth Century, 1900-1950* (Harrisburg: Trinity Press International, 1999), xi-xii.

26. T. Holmén, *Jesus and Jewish Covenant Thinking* (Leiden: Brill, 2001), especially 346-47.

of plausibility — I believe that we can see a single yet multi-faceted quest, certainly since the eighteenth century, but perhaps even since the earliest reflection upon Jesus. These attempts to understand Jesus continue to develop in perspective and in method, with the result that we think that we know more about the historical figure of Jesus today than we did before. However, the quest has had common motivations, similar assumptions at least since the Enlightenment, common methods despite their ongoing development, and similar types of results. By similar results, I mean that since its inception scholars and lay interpreters alike have sensed that there are questions that need to be raised about the depiction of Jesus that raises further historical and theological questions. There have been extremes on both sides. On the one hand, very conservative interpreters have come up with harmonized Bibles that eliminate all tensions in the Synoptic accounts while, on the other hand, other scholars have gone to the extreme of dismissing the very existence of Jesus as a myth. Thankfully, the vast bulk of interpreters have been somewhere in the middle, attempting to reconcile apparent discrepancies in the Gospel accounts with their understanding of history and the theological interpretation of the early church.

What Can We Learn from the Quest for the Historical Jesus for Reading the Gospels Today?

In the light of this discussion, I think that the next question to ask is what we can learn from the quest for the historical Jesus for reading and understanding the Gospels today. I have selected several issues that I think are of importance. They do not necessarily reflect the standard questions asked by others in historical-Jesus research. One of the possible reasons for this is that a number of these scholars have a very different perspective on the development of the discussion, as I have outlined above, and this inevitably leads them in different directions than it does me. A larger list of such issues would concern the philosophical and theological presuppositions of historical Jesus research (note that some scholars believe that the Jesus of the church is the only Jesus worth discussing),[27] Jesus' own self-consciousness as a

27. See L. T. Johnson, *The Real Jesus: The Misguided Quest for the Historical Jesus and the Truth of the Traditional Gospels* (San Francisco: HarperCollins, 1996), reviewed in *BBR* 7 (1997): 225-54.

prophet, sage or messiah (clearly a theme that goes back to the first quest), questions of method concerning sources and the criteria by which they are assessed, social and political contexts, Jesus' relation to Judaism, and Jesus' relation to earliest Christianity.[28] Others choose to differentiate between the deeds and the words of Jesus.[29] In any case, I wish to explore three areas — the question of genre, the language of Jesus, and criteria for authenticity.

The Genre of the Gospels

The first area of interest and concern is that of the genre of the Gospels. This is often not an area of explicit discussion in historical Jesus research but one that I think merits further discussion. It is usually not included, I believe, because it seems to relate more directly to the individual Gospels, rather than to the question of the historical Jesus revealed through those Gospels. However, I think that the question of the genre of the Gospels has been a misunderstood and misguided one that has had an unfortunate influence upon historical Jesus research. What will become clear is that even though some of the methods of New Testament study, and in particular Gospel study, have changed over the course of the last several centuries, the implications of these changes did not always become integrated into other areas of New Testament study, especially historical Jesus research. Here I wish to trace briefly the history of discussion of genre research in regard to the Gospels, and then show how it has implications for historical Jesus research.

It appears that those who were part of the first quest for the historical Jesus believed that the Gospels were biographies.[30] This assumption, how-

---

28. For summaries of the issues in recent Jesus research, see Telford, "Major Trends," 61-74, and G. Theissen and A. Merz, *The Historical Jesus: A Comprehensive Guide*, trans. J. Bowden (London: SCM, 1998), 10-11.

29. The most recent major treatments of these topics are B. Chilton and C. A. Evans, eds., *Authenticating the Words of Jesus*, NTTS 28.1 (Leiden: Brill, 1998) and *Authenticating the Activities of Jesus*, NTTS 28.2 (Leiden: Brill, 1998). See C. A. Evans, "Authenticating the Activities of Jesus," in *Authenticating the Activities of Jesus*, 4-29, where he discusses the eight or nine activities Jesus probably did!

30. For this and much of what follows, I am reliant upon R. A. Burridge, *What Are the Gospels? A Comparison with Graeco-Roman Biography*, SNTSMS 70 (Cambridge: Cambridge University Press, 1992), here 4 and *passim*.

ever, led to difficulty, because the definition of biography that was used was the one current in the nineteenth century. The notion of biography during this time seemed to entail the requirement of a thorough treatment of the life of the subject, which included beginning with the events surrounding the birth and infancy of the subject, then describing in detail the education and upbringing of the subject in the light of the surrounding environment, before proceeding to a detailed treatment of the adult life, and concluding with an evaluation and assessment of this life. Right away one can tell that there are going to be problems with such an analysis. First, the Gospels clearly do not have many of the features required, which are transferred directly from the contemporary biography of the time, which often involved massive multi-volume treatments of the subject. The result was that the material that fit this chronological and evaluative schema constituted the historical part, while the other part was labeled with various names, such as mythology, to use the words of Strauss. Secondly, the literature that was seen to follow the schema of the contemporary biography was found in lives of the saints, philosophers, and other heroes, which literature was full of legendary material. As has been shown, much of this material, though similar in some ways, is quite different in fundamental respects. Thirdly, there was a clear failure to understand the characteristics of ancient genres,[31] and to define the Gospels in terms of the literature of the time.

As a result of the failure to find the Gospels conforming to this type of biographical literature, the important work of Eduard Norden (1898) and Paul Wendland (1912) further distanced the Gospels from contemporary literature. Norden thought that the Gospels were exceptional with regard to the literature of the time, and Wendland thought that the Gospels did not have literary pretensions, as did the biographies of the Greco-Roman world.[32] This work anticipated the development of form criticism, which latched onto this distinction between the Gospels and ancient biography. In the work of the major form critics, such as Schmidt, Dibelius, and Bultmann,[33] the Evangelists were seen to lack the intentionality of lit-

---

31. This is not to say that there was such a thing as ancient literary theory. There was not. See D. A. Russell, *Criticism in Antiquity* (Berkeley: University of California Press, 1981), 158.

32. E. Norden, *Die antike Kunstprosa* (Stuttgart: Teubner, 1995), 2:480-81; P. Wendland, *Die urchristlichen Literaturformen*, 2d/3d ed. (Tübingen: Mohr Siebeck, 1912), 266.

33. K. L. Schmidt, *Der Rahmen der Geschichte Jesu. Literarkritische Untersuchungen*

erary authors, but were seen merely as compilers who brought together individual units of oral tradition, much like stringing beads on a string. They therefore posited that the Gospels were unliterary writings that fell into their own singular category. This viewpoint has had an important effect on subsequent Gospel criticism, even to the present. Nevertheless, it is subject to further scrutiny. First, it neglects work done outside of German circles. This form-critical opinion regarding the uniqueness of the Gospels may represent developments in twentieth-century German scholarship on the Gospels, but it does not necessarily mean that everyone concluded in this way. There was important work done by such scholars as Clyde Weber Votaw (1915) who argued that the Gospels were a form of common person's ancient biography, C. H. Dodd (1936) who argued for a kerygmatic outline into which the stories of the Gospels were placed, and even Vincent Taylor (1930) — the English-language proponent of form criticism — who believed that form criticism did nothing to detract from the biographical nature of the Gospels.[34] Secondly, this position has itself been rendered indefensible by the rise of redaction criticism. Redaction criticism, which began taking shape in 1948 in German circles,[35] contends that the Gospel authors are in fact intentional in their literary work. However, this important observation — crucial to redaction criticism and much subsequent Gospel scholarship — did not seem to influence much German-inspired genre criticism of the Gospels until around 1983 or 1984, when the work of a

zur ältesten Jesusüberlieferung (Berlin: Trowitzsch, 1919); M. Dibelius, From Tradition to Gospel, trans. B. Woolf (London: Ivor Nicholson and Watson, 1934); R. Bultmann, History of the Synoptic Tradition, 2d ed., trans. J. Marsh (Oxford: Blackwell, 1968); idem, "The Gospels (Form)" (1928), in Twentieth Century Theology in the Making, 86-92.

34. C. W. Votaw, The Gospels and Contemporary Biographies in the Greco-Roman World (Philadelphia: Fortress, 1970); C. H. Dodd, The Apostolic Preaching and Its Developments (London: Hodder and Stoughton, 1936); V. Taylor, The Gospels: A Short Introduction (London: Epworth, 1930), 13-19; idem, The Formation of the Gospel Tradition (London: Macmillan, 1933), especially vi ("Form-Criticism seems to me to furnish constructive suggestions which in many ways confirm the historical trustworthiness of the Gospel tradition").

35. G. Bornkamm, "The Stilling of the Storm in Matthew," in G. Bornkamm, G. Barth, and H. J. Held, Tradition and Interpretation in Matthew, trans. P. Scott, NTL (London: SCM Press, 1963), 52-57, along with other essays; and developed further in H. Conzelmann, The Theology of St. Luke, trans. G. Buswell (New York: Harper, 1960); W. Marxsen, Mark the Evangelist: Studies on the Redaction History of the Gospel, trans. J. Boyce et al. (Nashville: Abingdon, 1969); and E. Haenchen, Der Weg Jesu: Eine Erklärung des Markus-Evangeliums und der kanonischen Parallelen (Berlin: Töpelmann, 1966).

number of scholars worked to overthrow the one-hundred-year German consensus.[36] If its full effect had been realized, redaction criticism would have rendered much of the form-critical agenda and its resultant conclusions obsolete. However, despite some who favored the position,[37] much English-language scholarship appears never to have fully swallowed the form-critical conclusions regarding the genre of the Gospels, since English forms of redaction criticism, in anticipation of the full-blown German form, had begun to appear as early as 1935[38] and were never as categorical in their generic analysis.

The result was that there was ongoing discussion of the genre of the Gospels especially in English-language scholarship that continued to define it in terms of the biographical genre. The key works in this discussion include the following. Graham Stanton's book on New Testament preaching noted that Greco-Roman biographies lacked a number of characteristics associated with modern biographies, such as chronological development and attention to character development.[39] Charles Talbert and Philip Shuler tried to create alternative models that challenged the form-critical consensus, especially represented by Bultmann. They have not been entirely convincing in their accounts, since they have not necessarily shown that there was such a genre, merely that Bultmann may have been wrong.[40] David Aune provided a clear defense of the biographical theory by illus-

36. W. Beilner and M. Ernst, *Unter dem Wort Gottes. Theologie aus dem Neuen Testament* (Thaur: Kulturverlag, 1993), 419, citing A. Dihle, K. Berger, D. Dormeyer, H. Frankemölle, and G. Theissen.

37. These include many of the followers of form criticism, and are as recent as R. H. Gundry, "Recent Investigations into the Literary Genre 'Gospel,'" in *New Dimensions in New Testament Study*, ed. R. N. Longenecker and M. C. Tenney (Grand Rapids: Zondervan, 1974), 97-114; R. Guelich, "The Gospel Genre," in *The Gospel and the Gospels*, ed. P. Stuhlmacher (Grand Rapids: Eerdmans, 1991), 173-208; and M. A. Tolbert, *Sowing the Gospel: Mark's World in Literary-Historical Perspective* (Minneapolis: Fortress, 1989).

38. E.g., R. H. Lightfoot, *History and Interpretation in the Gospels* (London: Hodder and Stoughton, 1935); N. B. Stonehouse, *The Witness of Matthew and Mark to Christ* (London: Tyndale Press, 1944); A. M. Farrer, *A Study in St. Mark* (London: Dacre Press, 1951).

39. G. N. Stanton, *Jesus of Nazareth in New Testament Preaching*, SNTSMS 27 (Cambridge: Cambridge University Press, 1974).

40. C. H. Talbert, *What Is a Gospel? The Genre of the Canonical Gospels* (Philadelphia: Fortress, 1977); P. L. Shuler, *A Genre for the Gospels: The Biographical Character of Matthew* (Philadelphia: Fortress, 1982). Besides criticism in Burridge, see D. E. Aune, "The Problem of the Genre of the Gospels: A Critique of C. H. Talbert's *What Is a Gospel?*" in *Gospel Perspectives* II: 9-60.

trating similarities in form and content between the New Testament and ancient material.[41] Eugene Lemcio showed how the Gospel writers exceeded the standards of veracity of biographical and historical writers of the ancient world.[42] The most important recent attempt to establish the genre of the Gospels is by Burridge. He argued that the Gospels are a form of ancient biography, by first establishing a means of evaluating such a genre in terms of its opening, subject matter, and internal and external features. He then conducted extensive analysis to show that the Gospels fit the patterns found in Greco-Roman biographies.[43]

In terms of historical Jesus research, the study of the genre of the Gospels seems to have at least the following implications. One of the obvious observations is that genre theory is often neglected or misunderstood by Jesus scholars. The level of discussion of much historical Jesus research is in terms of individual pericopes. These form the basic units for comparison among Gospels and analysis in relation to extra-canonical sources. However, this level of analysis assumes the form-critical agenda, but fails to consider the Gospels in terms of the kinds of family resemblances that are relevant to biographies or, to use the terms of genre theory, in terms of intrinsic generic characteristics.[44] This is not to deny that biographies have individual units, such as stories, sayings, and speeches, but that these are not the basic units of analysis. When the larger patterns are considered, the Gospels are seen to reflect biographical literature in most if not all essential features.

The recognition of the biographical character of the Gospels does not necessarily determine their interpretation. The use of the notion of intrinsic genre is not meant to be determinative but to constitute the beginning point for interpretation in terms of the structure and characteristics

41. D. E. Aune, *The New Testament in Its Literary Environment* (Philadelphia: Westminster, 1987), 17-76.

42. E. E. Lemcio, *The Past of Jesus in the Gospels*, SNTSMS 68 (Cambridge: Cambridge University Press, 1991), especially 28-29.

43. See Burridge, *What Are the Gospels?* for discussion of other scholars who are part of this consensus.

44. This is the terminology of E. D. Hirsch Jr., *Validity in Interpretation* (New Haven: Yale University Press, 1967), especially 76; cf. 86-89, cited and applied to New Testament studies in B. W. R. Pearson and S. E. Porter, "The Genres of the New Testament," in *Handbook to Exegesis of the New Testament*, ed. S. E. Porter, NTTS 25 (Leiden: Brill, 1997), 131-65. Cf. Burridge, *What Are the Gospels?* 26-69, 109-27.

of a book.[45] At numerous points, however, much of the study of the historical Jesus in terms of the Gospels still seems to be bound by the kind of disjunctive definition of genre that was found in the nineteenth century, in which the historical and the mythological were played off against each other. Study of ancient biography has shown that the ancient biography does not necessarily conform to what might have been expected in the nineteenth and twentieth centuries, in which extrinsic genres were brought to bear in a determinative way. Ancient biographies — even if they maintained an overall chronological sequence — often did not pay attention in the same way and in the same proportion to such things as the ancestry, birth, or education of the subject, but often paid more attention to the deeds, virtues, and especially death of the subject. This is directly in keeping with the Gospel accounts, in which a rough though not necessarily fixed chronological sequence is followed, in which such material as discourses (e.g., Matthew 5–7) or parables (e.g., Matthew 13) can be grouped together and inserted. There is also much less attention to character analysis and much more to displaying the character of the subject through actions and words. This also implies the author's latitude in choosing to include or exclude episodes and edit these sources in his biography in order to depict the subject as the author wishes.[46] This further indicates that the author of the Gospel had particular intentions for the writing that was created. These intentions, so far as they are able to be determined, should first of all be seen in terms of the conventions of ancient biographical writing. There has been a distinctive tendency by many historical Jesus researchers to take a minimalist view of the evidence, with the result that in those places where it is possible to determine that Jesus may have done (or said) something, this is a minimal core event. The acknowledgment that the Gospels are ancient biographies, and that they should be evaluated in terms of the conventions of this literary genre, should create a presumption towards a maximalist view of assessing the evidence, in which the burden of proof rests with those who wish to dismiss the stories, and there is no constraint to prove that they happened.[47] The latter, it seems to me, is a virtually impossible task. In weighing probabilities regarding "what really

---

45. See Pearson and Porter, "Genres," 161.
46. Burridge, *What Are the Gospels?* 192-219.
47. See Charlesworth, "Historical Jesus," 101.

happened" (to use Ranke's phrase) — so far as that is even conceivable — one cannot speak in terms of absolutes but only in terms of probabilities.

The Language of Jesus

The emphasis for the last fifty or so years in historical Jesus research has been upon the Jewishness of Jesus and in particular his use of Aramaic. Research such as has been put forward by such scholars as Jeremias, Matthew Black (1946), and most lately Maurice Casey (1998) has been widely and readily accepted by many if not most historical Jesus scholars.[48] The logic seems to function along the lines that, despite the Gospels appearing in Greek, the original language of Jesus and the early church was Aramaic. Aramaic was the language of the Jews after their return from exile, and reflects their ethnic and religious heritage and their socially oppressed distinctiveness from the occupying Romans. Therefore, if we are able to find material in the Gospels that reflects this Aramaic background, both in terms of linguistic and cultural features, then this gives a solid basis for asserting the historical reliability of the event involved.[49] This view has been put forward and held to for so long that in many circles it has become a commonplace and developed into a distinct criterion for authenticity (see below). It is only with the recent work of John Meier, followed in principle by a few other scholars, that this criterion has been seriously questioned.[50] I will return to the other criteria for authenticity below, but will treat the one of Aramaic language phenomena here as it has a bearing on Greek language. Nevertheless, despite the questioning of this criterion, it is still widely used in fact in much Gospel research, whereby scholars note a particular Aramaic or other Semitic feature and draw the conclusion that this must constitute primitive and perhaps even authentic Jesus material.

48. See above on Jeremias; M. Black, *An Aramaic Approach to the Gospels and Acts,* 3d ed. (Oxford: Clarendon Press, 1967); M. Casey, *Aramaic Sources of Mark's Gospel,* SNTSMS 102 (Cambridge: Cambridge University Press, 1998).

49. In fact, some have argued, the language of the Jews reflects their way of thinking as distinct from that of the Greeks. On this issue, see S. E. Porter, "The Greek Language of the New Testament," in *Handbook to Exegesis,* 99-130, especially 124-29.

50. J. P. Meier, *A Marginal Jew: Rethinking the Historical Jesus,* ABRL (New York: Doubleday, 1991-), 2:179-80; E. Schillebeeckx, *Jesus: An Experiment in Christology,* trans. H. Hoskins (New York: Seabury, 1979), 98-99; and now Porter, *Criteria,* 89-99.

This approach to historical Jesus research also is in need of serious correction. One of the major features of this position is that it relies upon a nineteenth-century romantic stereotype of Jesus as a poor unilingual Galilean peasant for its major foundation. This romanticized view has formed the basis for much of the social gospel movement, as Jesus meek and mild was seen to be one of those for whom he was an advocate. Recent research into the social setting of early Christianity has clearly called into question this nineteenth-century portrait, even though some of the ramifications, especially in terms of language, have not yet been affected. The major hindrance seems to be the failure to recognize that what it meant to be Jewish in the Greco-Roman world of the first century was to be someone who had to some degree been Hellenized, including speaking Greek.[51] Despite this fairly recent change in orientation, there have been a number of scholars who for over a century have maintained that there is a chance that Jesus may on occasion have spoken Greek, even if they cannot identify the particular passages or exact wording.[52] This position is too weak, I believe. The preponderance of the evidence is that in fact Jesus clearly did speak Greek, the only question being how much and on what occasion.[53] Jesus was from Galilee, not Jerusalem, and Galilee was a center of Greco-Roman influence and culture, as indicated by epigraphical and literary evidence. A person wanting to do business in Galilee — whether as a carpenter or a fisherman — would have been required to speak Greek. One need not even agree that Jesus spent his first several years in Egypt to create the presump-

51. See, especially, V. Tcherikover, *Hellenistic Civilization and the Jews*, trans. S. Applebaum (New York: Atheneum, 1975), especially 347 and *passim;* M. Hengel, *Judaism and Hellenism: Studies in Their Encounter in Palestine during the Early Hellenistic Period,* trans. J. Bowden (Philadelphia: Fortress, 1974); *idem* with C. Markschies, *The "Hellenization" of Judaea in the First Century after Christ,* trans. J. Bowden (London: SCM Press, 1989); cf. Porter, *Criteria,* 138-39.

52. See S. E. Porter, *Studies in the Greek New Testament: Theory and Practice,* SBG 6 (New York: Lang, 1996), 139-71, especially 139-60 and the lists in 139-40 n. 1, 141-42 n. 11, 143-44 n. 17; cf. also Porter, *Criteria,* 127-41, 164-80.

53. Besides those cited in the note above, to be added to the list are Stewart, *Life and Teaching,* 21; R. N. Longenecker, *Biblical Exegesis in the Apostolic Period* (Grand Rapids: Eerdmans, 1975), 64; Wright, *Jesus and the Victory of God,* 147; and especially R. O. P. Taylor, *The Groundwork of the Gospels* (Oxford: Blackwell, 1946), especially 91-95 (written by G. A. Smith) and 96-105, whose discussion is directly drawn upon below, besides my previous research. Cf. also J. L. Reed, *Archaeology and the Galilean Jesus: A Re-Examination of the Evidence* (Harrisburg: Trinity Press International, 2000), 134.

tion that he spoke in Greek.[54] Presumably — if this episode did take place — Joseph and Mary visited a Jewish settlement in Egypt, but this does not mean that the settlers spoke Aramaic. In fact, the evidence from Egypt, and now from the papyri found in the eastern Mediterranean, is that certainly in Egypt but also in the eastern Mediterranean Greek had become firmly established as the *lingua franca*. This was true for official business, but in many cases extended to daily usage as well. Some of the most convincing evidence of this is the fact that the Septuagint (the Greek translation of the Hebrew Bible) was the Bible of the early church, for most of Judaism outside of Palestine, and even for some inside it, as the Greek Bible documents from Qumran help to establish. The vast majority of the quotations of the Old Testament in the New follow the Septuagint.[55] There are also other Greek documents, such as the Bar Kokhba letters, Babatha archive, and other Greek papyri, as well as a range of inscriptional evidence, to be considered as well.[56] This then makes good sense of why all of the Gospels and literature of the Apostolic Fathers were written in Greek, and not only these but most of the apocryphal and pseudepigraphal Jewish literature as well (even those written in a Semitic language usually found their way into Greek). The few places in the Gospels where Aramaic is used are provided with translations, not necessarily as guides to translation difficulties but to help the readers to understand. There is some evidence that an early form of Matthew's Gospel was written in Aramaic — Papias says that logia of Matthew were written in "Hebrew" (see Eusebius, *H.E.* 3.39.16) — but Papias also says that everyone translated as best he could, which indicates that there was no demand for such a document in Aramaic.[57] Further, within the Gospels themselves, there are numerous incidents where Jesus is plausibly depicted as speaking Greek, often to people who appear to have been Greek speakers. In some instances, there may have been a translator present (since few learned the occupied language), but there is no record of such.

The results of such an analysis for historical Jesus research are several. First, it indicates that historical Jesus research may be closer to finding

---

54. This argument is introduced by Taylor/Smith, *Groundwork*, 91.

55. Taylor/Smith, *Groundwork*, 92.

56. See S. E. Porter, "The Greek Papyri of the Judaean Desert and the World of the Roman East," in *The Scrolls and the Scriptures: Qumran Fifty Years After*, ed. S. E. Porter and C. A. Evans, JSPSup 26 (Sheffield: Sheffield Academic Press, 1997), 293-316.

57. Taylor/Smith, *Groundwork*, 92-93.

the original words of Jesus *(ipsissima verba Jesu)* than was once thought, although in a way that has its own problems. When Aramaic linguistic evidence was thought to be determinative, there was much talk of authenticity when various linguistic features were uncovered — such as particular supposed Semitic constructions, or particular wording — but the result was the belief that an approximation of the voice of Jesus had been found *(ipsissima vox Jesu)*. When it is realized that Jesus may have spoken Greek, and that we may have such instances in the Gospels, we then may have direct access not only to the voice but to the actual words. However, these actual words must be found among all of the other Greek words of the Gospels, uttered by Jesus and others, as well as the narrative voice. This has led me to propose a new criterion — the criterion of Greek language and its context — to aid in discovering those passages that might provide a basis for ascertaining authentic Jesus material.[58]

Secondly, this issue refocuses the discussion of the social environment of the world out of which the Gospels emerged. There are many longstanding stereotypes regarding the world of the Gospels, including issues regarding the purity of Judaism of the time. Recent research has helped us to realize that there were many Judaisms of the time, and that none of them was untouched by Hellenism, including that of those who went off into the desert at Qumran. Galilee, surrounded by the cities of the Decapolis, was in the midst of Hellenistic culture. Even Jerusalem was thoroughly Hellenistic.[59] If this is the case, and I believe that it is, then it opens up a larger number of social and environmental factors for consid-

---

58. Porter, *Criteria*, 126-64.

59. The evidence for Jerusalem includes the fact that it was a cosmopolitan city that attracted people, especially Jews, who lived all over the Mediterranean world, and whose common language would have been Greek. The Pentecost episode of Acts 2 may well show this (Taylor/Smith, *Groundwork*, 94). There is also inscriptional and literary evidence that attests to the widespread use of Greek (e.g., roughly fifty percent of epitaphs are in Greek). Episodes such as the capture of Jerusalem, and Josephus's writing of his *Jewish War* in Aramaic (but probably not his *Antiquities*), are not best explained as supporting the Aramaic hypothesis, but as indicating that politics and linguistics have always gone together. In other words, the variety of rebels in Jerusalem were resistant to speaking Greek in defiance of Rome. Further, Josephus prepared his *Jewish War* in Aramaic for those barbarians in Parthia, Babylonia, and Arabia, and the Jews beyond the Euphrates, and those in Adiabene, but the Greek version for those within the empire, certainly including Jerusalem, which had been completely vanquished (see Josephus, *War* 1:3, 6). See Taylor, *Groundwork*, 98-99; Porter, *Criteria*, 169-71, 176-78.

eration. One of the problems with much social-scientific analysis of the Jesus movement has been that it has been done in isolation from the major issues in historical-Jesus research. With language, the single most important social tool, as the basis, this creates links between the two areas that have increased promise of providing useful insights into the world that created the Gospels, including the world in which Jesus lived and taught.

I have argued that there are eight episodes in which Greek might have been used by Jesus. These include John 12:20-28, Jesus' discussion with certain Greeks; Matt 8:5-13 = John 4:46-54, Jesus' conversation with the centurion or commander; John 4:4-26, Jesus' conversation with the Samaritan woman; Mark 2:13-14 = Matt 9:9 = Luke 5:27-28, Jesus' calling of Levi/Matthew; Mark 7:25-30 = Matt 15:21-28, Jesus' conversation with the Syrophoenician or Canaanite woman; Mark 12:13-17 = Matt 22:16-22 = Luke 20:20-26, Jesus' conversation with the Pharisees and Herodians over the Roman coin; Mark 8:27-30 = Matt 16:13-20 = Luke 9:18-22, Jesus' conversation with his disciples at Caesarea Philippi; and Mark 15:2-5 = Matt 27:11-14 = Luke 23:2-4 = John 18:29-38, Jesus' trial before Pilate. The example in John 12 does not actually have words for examination, but all of the rest, I believe, have at least some probability (and some reasonably high probability) that words of Jesus are recorded, quite possibly with the actual words of Jesus in the episode with Pilate.[60]

I would like to add two further episodes that I think are worth entering into such a discussion. The first is the episode in Luke 17:11-19, the episode of the cleansing of the ten lepers, in which one, a Samaritan, speaks to Jesus. The Samaritans had been a multilingual people since the third century BCE, with Greek serving as a *lingua franca* (a language for economic and administrative purposes). In fact, Greek may also have been the religious language of some of these people, since the Isis and Serapis cult flourished there until Roman times, replaced by the cult of Kore in Roman times, which continued to use Greek.[61] The second episode is no doubt more controversial, and is the Sermon on the Mount itself. I will bypass questions of whether this was a single sermon delivered on one occasion, a composite, or the core of what were larger remarks, and will not examine the language of the Sermon itself, but instead wish to look at the descriptive context in which it is delivered. Matthew's Gospel has Jesus traversing

60. See Porter, *Criteria*, 141-63.
61. See Porter, *Criteria*, 153 n. 72.

Galilee, teaching and preaching, so much so that his reputation spread to Syria. As a result crowds gathered around him, and Matthew's Gospel says that these crowds were from Galilee and the Decapolis and Jerusalem and Judea and the other side of the Jordan (Matt 4:23-25). Luke 6:17 adds to those from Judea and Jerusalem the coast of Tyre and Sidon. It is in the light of seeing these crowds that, in Matthew, Jesus delivers the Sermon. I believe that it is arguable that only one language could serve as the common language of these various peoples, and that was Greek. Galilee and the Decapolis have already been mentioned as thoroughly Hellenized areas, the extent of Judea might well include heavily Greek-speaking areas if it is delimiting the boundaries of the Roman province (such as Samaria), and the other side of the Jordan could include places that papyri from the early second century indicate were also highly influenced by Greek as well. Tyre and Sidon were clearly Gentile and Greek-speaking establishments.[62] Greek language — assuming that communication took place — is clearly the common basis. One might be picky and say that the Sermon is delivered only to the disciples, but that would be an odd situation if Jesus had this large crowd around him and then chose to speak to his disciples in Aramaic, thus excluding what was probably the majority of the people from understanding what he was saying. In fact, this argues that, so far as we can establish it, Jesus probably spoke the Sermon in Greek to his disciples, allowing the others to overhear as well.[63]

The Criteria for Authenticity

The criteria for determining authenticity are the third and final area that I wish to discuss. The criteria themselves began to be explicitly developed at the beginning of the last century, and continue to be discussed up to the present. Of course, there were criteria used in discussion before that time, especially those related to naturalistic cosmology, as a result of the Enlightenment, but it was with the rise of form criticism that these became systematically expressed. As noted above in discussing form criticism, con-

---

62. On these Hellenized cities, see A. H. M. Jones, *Cities of the Eastern Roman Provinces* (Oxford: Clarendon Press, 1998), 227-95 *passim*.

63. Cf. A. Roberts, *Greek: The Language of Christ and His Apostles* (London: Longmans, Green, 1888), 145-57; Taylor/Smith, *Groundwork*, 93.

certed and explicit efforts to develop the criteria corresponded with the growth of form criticism. This is understandable, since the theory of form criticism — that individual units of tradition developed according to set rules of transmission — required criteria by which they could be evaluated as to their form and development. These criteria are varied in number, depending upon the scholar who is using them. I have already briefly discussed the criterion of Semitic language phenomena. It actually dates back to the seventeenth century and was used by a number of scholars dismissed by Schweitzer (e.g., A. Meyer [1896] and Gustav Dalman [1898]).[64] Nevertheless, the work of such scholars as Charles Cutler Torrey (1912), C. F. Burney (1925), and Jeremias, followed by such scholars as Black and Joseph A. Fitzmyer (1970), has kept it alive.[65] In the recent revival by Casey, he regresses to a form of retroversion found in nineteenth-century scholarship,[66] and Bruce Chilton (1984) posits two forms of coherence, dictional and thematic (see below).[67] Meier has dismissed this criterion as dubious, as noted above, since all it can do is place the tradition in Palestine and possibly in the Aramaic-speaking church.[68]

Similarly, all of the criteria have been proposed, modified, and criticized through the centuries, and to some extent do not offer more now than they did in the past.[69] (1) The criterion of double dissimilarity,[70]

64. A. Meyer, *Jesu Muttersprache. Das galiläische Aramäisch in seiner Bedeutung für die Erklärung der Reden Jesu und der Evangelien überhaupt* (Freiburg: Mohr Siebeck, 1896); G. Dalman, *The Words of Jesus: Considered in the Light of Post-biblical Jewish Writings and the Aramaic Language*, trans. D. M. Kay (Edinburgh: Clark, 1909); cf. *idem, Jesus-Jeshua: Studies in the Gospels*, trans. P. P. Levertoff (London: SPCK, 1929).

65. Besides those noted above, see C. C. Torrey, "The Translations Made from the Original Aramaic Gospels," in *Studies in the History of Religions*, FS C. H. Toy, ed. D. G. Lyon and G. F. Moore (New York: Macmillan, 1912), 269-317; *idem, Our Translated Gospels: Some of the Evidence* (Cambridge: Harvard University Press, 1916); C. F. Burney, *The Poetry of Our Lord* (Oxford: Clarendon Press, 1925); J. A. Fitzmyer, *A Wandering Aramean: Collected Aramaic Essays*, SBLMS 25 (Missoula: Scholars Press, 1979).

66. See Porter, *Criteria*, 95-97.

67. B. Chilton, *A Galilean Rabbi and His Bible: Jesus' Use of the Interpreted Scripture of His Time*, GNS 88 (Wilmington: Glazier, 1984), especially 70-71, 90-137. This criterion has been expanded by Evans to include exegetical coherence. (See his introduction to Black's *Aramaic Approach to the Gospel and Acts* [Peabody: Hendrickson, 1998], v-xxv, especially xii-xiii, xv-xvii.)

68. Meier, *Marginal Jew*, 1:179-80.

69. See Porter, *Criteria*, 58 n. 71 for bibliography and 63-123.

70. See Porter, *Criteria*, 70-76.

which dates back to the Renaissance and found major proponents in Bultmann, Käsemann, and Norman Perrin (the redaction critic!),[71] argues that authentic material must be dissimilar to that found in the Judaism of the time and in the early church. This has been the most enduring of criteria, but it is also minimalistic, since it creates a Jesus who was unlike everyone else. One wonders who even understood him at all. This criterion has been reformulated by Tom Wright in terms of a criterion of double similarity, that is, authentic material is credible in terms of ancient Judaism and the early church.[72] Whether this actually does what a criterion should do, that is, distinguish this material from other material, is a big question, but it does reverse the minimalistic tendencies of the criterion. This criterion, despite trenchant criticism along the way, has persisted in both form-critical and redactional circles and remains widely used by many.

Similarly, (2) the criterion of least distinctiveness,[73] which grew directly out of the form-critical agenda, argues that a particular literary form follows particular laws of style, and by knowing these one can distinguish original from secondary tradition. This criterion, however, has been seriously challenged by observing the complexity of change in traditions in extra-biblical literature[74] and, more importantly, by detailed study of the Synoptics by E. P. Sanders that shows that there are no such clear-cut laws.[75] (3) The criterion of coherence is to some extent a secondary criterion,[76] since it asserts that material that coheres with previously established authentic material should also be regarded as authentic. Of course, this begs the question of what is authentic material. (4) The criterion of multiple attestation has taken two forms.[77] One of those is to examine which units of tradition appear in the major Gospel sources (Mark, Q, M, or L), while the other is to examine which units appear in multiple literary forms (e.g., parables, miracles stories, etc.). The latter,

---

71. N. Perrin, *What Is Redaction Criticism?* GBS (Philadelphia: Fortress, 1970).

72. Wright, *Jesus and the Victory of God*, 131-33.

73. Porter, *Criteria*, 77-79.

74. E.g., see C. L. Blomberg, "Historical Criticism of the New Testament," in *Foundations for Biblical Interpretation*, ed. D. S. Dockery, K. A. Mathews, and R. B. Sloan (Nashville: Broadman/Holman, 1994), 414-33, especially 421-22.

75. E. P. Sanders, *The Tendencies of the Synoptic Tradition*, SNTSMS 9 (Cambridge: Cambridge University Press, 1969).

76. Porter, *Criteria*, 79-82.

77. Porter, *Criteria*, 82-89.

developed by Dodd (1935),[78] has not been widely used, while the former, put forward by Burkitt as early as 1906,[79] assumes a particular theory of Gospel source criticism, that is, Markan priority. (5) The criterion of embarrassment or movement against the redactional tendency[80] was originally proposed by Paul Schmiedel around 1900,[81] but was developed by Käsemann (1954) and especially promoted by Meier.[82] It states that material that would have embarrassed the early church but was left in the tradition is presumably authentic. Again, this is a difficult criterion, since the presumed stable core of authentic material would be the embarrassing Jesus, unless this criterion simply adds secondary material to a core determined by another means. (6) The criterion of rejection and execution,[83] which dates back to the late 1960s and 1970s,[84] has been put forward in two different and perhaps competing ways. One is as a form of the criterion of coherence, in which the death of Jesus at the hands of the Romans becomes central to a network of coherent facts against which other words and actions can be judged.[85] Another is as a stipulation that draws attention to the centrality of Jesus' death, even if it cannot be used to adjudicate individual actions and words of Jesus.[86] It is unclear how exactly this criterion functions. (7) Lastly, Gerd Theissen (1996) has posited the criterion of historical plausibility.[87] Rejecting the criterion of double dissimi-

78. C. H. Dodd, *The Parables of the Kingdom* (London: Nisbet, 1935), 26-29; *idem, History and the Gospel* (London: Nisbet, 1938), 91-102.

79. F. C. Burkitt, *The Gospel History and Its Transmission,* 3d ed. (Edinburgh: Clark, 1911), especially 147-68.

80. Porter, *Criteria,* 106-110.

81. P. Schmiedel, "Gospels," in *Encyclopaedia Biblica: A Critical Dictionary of the Literary, Political, and Religious History, the Archaeology, Geography, and Natural History of the Bible* (London: Black, 1899-1907), 2:1761-898, especially 1881-83.

82. Käsemann, "The Problem of the Historical Jesus," in his *Essays on New Testament Themes,* 15-47, especially 37; Meier, *Marginal Jew,* 1:168.

83. Porter, *Criteria,* 110-13.

84. Schillebeeckx, *Jesus,* 97; Walker, "Quest for the Historical Jesus," 55.

85. C. A. Evans, *Jesus and His Contemporaries: Comparative Studies,* AGJU 25 (Leiden: Brill, 1995), 13-15.

86. Meier, *Marginal Jew,* 1:176-77.

87. G. Theissen, "Historical Scepticism and the Criteria of Jesus Research *or My Attempt to Leap across Lessing's Yawning Gulf,*" *SJT* 49 (1996): 147-76; *idem* and D. Winter, *The Quest for the Plausible Jesus: The Question of Criteria,* trans. M. E. Boring (Louisville: Westminster John Knox Press, 2002), especially 172-259; *idem* and Merz, *Historical Jesus,* 115-18. Cf. Porter, *Criteria,* 113-22, especially 119-22.

larity, although accepting the two-dimensional perspective in terms of the early church and Judaism, Theissen effects a shift more in emphasis than in method, since he relies upon the same traditional criteria as his sub-criteria in order to establish plausibility.

This brief synopsis of the criteria, including several recent developments, illustrates one of the major limitations of recent historical Jesus research that wishes to establish itself as new, independent, and significant — its failure to develop its own set of criteria. Even if we concede that there is greatly increased knowledge of the social, linguistic, and cultural environment in which Jesus lived, the criteria by which these data are evaluated reflect much earlier periods in the discussion. This may be acceptable, but it certainly does not promote or support the idea that we have entered a new period of Jesus research if we use the same criteria to evaluate the evidence. As a result, several further points need to be noted with regard to reading the Gospels. First, this critique does not mean that one should abandon the development of criteria by which the data are assessed. However, it does raise the question of the origin of the criteria that are used, their relation to other historical and literary disciplines, and the results gained from their use. Many have expressed skepticism regarding these criteria, because some of them developed in the pre-Enlightenment era, while others developed under the influence of other factors, such as form criticism. As a result, there are some like Johnson who believe that the Jesus of the church is the Jesus of the Gospels, and that for all intents and purposes this is the only Jesus to be known. One can be sympathetic to what is being said here, in the sense that the kind of criteria that are often brought to bear on the discussion reflect interests antithetical to those of the church, and were developed for other purposes than those for which they are being used. There is the further issue of how these criteria relate to similar disciplines. Many are skeptical that the kinds of criteria used in historical Jesus research are reflected in modern linguistic and historical disciplines.[88] Some of the differences might be seen in the lack of acknowledgment of the linguistic (or literary) nature of the Gospels, as conscious creations, rather than simply as the results of unintentional compilation. As a result, there have been some attempts to develop more linguistic criteria but these are in their incipient stages.[89] Others are advocating a wholesale abandonment of the task of de-

---

88. See P. W. Barnett, *Jesus and the Logic of History* (Grand Rapids: Eerdmans, 1997).
89. Porter, *Criteria*, 210-37.

veloping criteria altogether, since the result is often a disjunctive thinking that categorizes the results as either authentic or inauthentic. Instead, they have proposed that the terminology be shifted from discussion of criteria to the notion of an index in an attempt to appreciate the influence of various factors that might influence a judgment one way or another.[90] The debate has tended to resist the language of probabilities, since so many theological issues have been linked to discussion of the historical Jesus.[91]

Conclusion

The relation of the Gospels to questions regarding the historical Jesus is a complex one. As I have tried to show, it involves discussion of two dimensions. The first is the dimension of scholarly involvement in the course of trying to come to terms with the Jesus of the Gospels. Many scholars have seen segmented periods in this discussion, while a few others have seen this as one continuing, developing quest after understanding more and more about the Jesus Christ who is both the figure who lived two millennia ago and the figure of the church's worship and adoration. I wish to argue that how one depicts the enterprise makes a difference in how one perceives it. I believe that there has been — and I think that there will continue to be — a seeking after the deeds and words of Jesus of Nazareth. The second is the dimension of how it is that one goes about trying to undertake such an endeavor. I have tried to shift the focus somewhat in this essay. Rather than undertaking a standard investigation, in which I attempt to offer a number of events that I think that Jesus performed, I have raised questions that push the discussion outside of the traditional boundaries, in an attempt to renew debate through the consideration of often neglected or overlooked factors.[92] Two things are certain, however, regarding the quest for the historical

90. E.g., B. F. Meyer, *The Aims of Jesus* (London: SCM Press, 1979), 86; S. McKnight, *Interpreting the Synoptic Gospels,* Guides to New Testament Exegesis (Grand Rapids: Baker, 1988), 66-69; R. Riesner, *Jesus als Lehrer: Eine Untersuchung zum Ursprung der Evangelien-Überlieferung,* 4th ed., WUNT 2:7 (Tübingen: Mohr Siebeck, 1994), 86-87.

91. Nevertheless, issues regarding burden of proof must be raised, and have been in S. C. Goetz and C. L. Blomberg, "The Burden of Proof," *JSNT* 11 (1981): 39-63.

92. Two other attempts to do so are B. Chilton, "Assessing Progress in the Third Quest," 15-26, and B. J. Malina, "Criteria for Assessing the Authentic Words of Jesus: Some Specifications," 27-46, both in *Authenticating the Words of Jesus.*

Jesus. One is that it will continue, probably without widespread agreement on a number of either methodological issues or significant conclusions. The other is that the Gospels as transmitted to us will continue to be central to the discussion, and knowledge and appreciation of them must remain paramount, for without them we have cut ourselves off from any direct link to the foundations of the investigation.

Reading Matthew:
The Gospel as Oral Performance

MICHAEL KNOWLES

Introduction: "Have You Not Read?"

As a teacher of preaching with a background in English literature and a particular interest in early English drama, I find myself all too often reading texts that were never intended simply to be read. For example, like the sermon texts that I compel my students to interpret, the Corpus Christi pageants of the Wakefield, York, or Chester cycles are meant to be performed, not perused on a page. Modern sermons and medieval guild plays are equally intended as performances, to be encountered and experienced by audiences and congregations rather than dissected and discussed within the relative safety of the classroom or study.

Along the same lines, Graham Stanton has advanced the provocative, yet curiously obvious proposal that Matthew's Gospel was originally intended as oral performance, to be read aloud to gathered listeners.[1] Provocative, because it forces us to question unexamined assumptions about how we encounter Matthew's text (or how it encounters us), yet in retrospect obvious given a probable literacy rate of ten to fifteen percent of adult males in the first-century Mediterranean world and less than five percent of women.[2] Ob-

---

1. G. N. Stanton, *A Gospel for a New People: Studies in Matthew* (Louisville: Westminster/John Knox, 1993), 73-75.
2. W. V. Harris, *Ancient Literacy* (Cambridge: Harvard University Press, 1989), 248-84, 328-30.

vious too in that centuries later no less a scholar than St. Augustine was amazed at the ability of Ambrose, bishop of Milan, to read without speaking (*Confessions* 6.3.3).[3] As Martin Jaffee observes with regard to the literature of the Second Temple period, "For most people and for most of the time, a book was a commodity that one 'heard' through the medium of another human voice; 'reading' was the activity of declaiming a text before an audience in a social performance approaching the gravity of ceremonial ritual."[4] The point emerges more clearly elsewhere in the New Testament, for example in the contrast of Rom 2:13 and Jas 1:22-25 between "hearers" of God's word — not "readers" — and "doers."[5]

Although orality is a familiar consideration with regard to the pre-textual, pre-canonical transmission of gospel traditions, post-literary orality presents us with a new set of questions and concerns. If Stanton is correct, we must come to terms with the difficulty that few if any in our day will experience Matthew's Gospel as the author first intended it. The fact that we read silently and individually is not the real problem: audio recordings of the New Testament are widely available, and a public recitation of Matthew's text would not be difficult to stage. The real problem is that our limited linguistic abilities prevent us from experiencing the text both aloud and *in Greek*. Were we able to accomplish even that much, the chances are slimmer yet that we could bring to such a hearing a lifelong aural familiarity with the text of the Old Testament — at least in Greek, if not in Hebrew also. But that is precisely the kind of familiarity that many in Matthew's audience would likely have brought with them, insofar as the Evangelist writes for believers of Jewish origin, as well as for those of Gentile descent. As part of their religious upbringing, many in his audience would have listened to and absorbed the cadences of Scripture from infancy onward. The best we

---

3. Granted, however, silent reading was not unknown in the ancient world: see B. M. W. Knox, "Silent Reading in Antiquity," *Greek, Roman, and Byzantine Studies* 9 (1968): 421-35.

4. M. S. Jaffee, *Torah in the Mouth: Writing and Oral Tradition in Palestinian Judaism, 200 BCE–400 CE* (New York: Oxford University Press, 2001), 17. So, more generally, W. H. Kelber, *The Oral and the Written Gospel: The Hermeneutics of Speaking and Writing in the Synoptic Tradition, Mark, Paul, and Q* (Philadelphia: Fortress, 1983), 17: "Because the vast majority of people were habituated to the spoken word, much of what was written was meant to be recited and listened to." Kelber does not, however, explore the full implications of this observation for early Christian literature.

5. Compare the NRSV rendering of Rev 1:3, "Blessed is the one who *reads aloud (ho anaginōskōn)* the words of the prophecy, and blessed are those who hear."

can do, by comparison, is to hunt for clues to Matthew's method, hoping to uncover secondary echoes of the original experience.

This is not to suggest, however, that Matthew's theological purpose and meaning are now inaccessible — generations of faithful readers would rise up to prove such a contention wrong. It is simply to assert, first, in terms of structure and literary method, that Matthew's text will have been shaped by the writer's expectations as to how it would be disseminated and received. Modern scholars, literate all, have traditionally concentrated on literary relationships among Synoptic texts. Yet while Matthew is demonstrably dependent upon textual antecedents, his editorial strategies and interests are undoubtedly prospective as well as retrospective; that is, concerned with his audience as much as with his sources. Again, Jaffee states the matter succinctly: "Precisely because texts were composed under the assumption that they would be read in the setting of oral performance, their compositional styles drew deeply upon habits of speech and rhetorical traditions that had their living matrix in oral communication."[6] Second, with regard to content, it is altogether likely that what came to those first hearers naturally — fluently — by virtue of common linguistic, social, and religious circumstances can now be recovered only by dint of hard labor and the sweat of our collective brow. In order, therefore, to appreciate this particular text in its full dimensions, we must learn anew what it means (in the etymological, Latinate sense) to be Matthew's "audience": that is, "those who hear."

Such qualifications notwithstanding, it is fair to say that at least three kinds of reading take place in relation to Matthew's Gospel, in more or less the following order. First, Matthew himself reads Israel's sacred texts — and much else besides — then proclaims through his own text the results of such reading. In so doing, he seeks to demonstrate that Jesus is the fulfillment of Israel's Scripture, Israel's history, and Israel's covenant. Second, we read Matthew's text, or — as is more likely to have been the case — Matthew expects that we will *hear* it read. In this process, various structures in the text serve to reinforce its theological content, with the literary order and symmetry of Matthew's presentation mirroring the historical and theological symmetry of divine providence. Third, it is neither sophistry nor scholarly artifice to insist that in the course of being read and proclaimed, the text itself "reads" its readers. That is to say, by presenting specific material in a specific manner, the text not only determines the

---

6. Jaffee, *Torah in the Mouth*, 18.

content of our reading, not only separates interested from disinterested readers, but also bids us participate in a particular kind of reading and understanding that potentially characterizes us as disciples of Jesus.

Matthew as Reader

Matthew's role as both reader and author is already fully evident in his first chapter. The narrative opens with a selective interpretation of sacred history, schematized as three consecutive series of fourteen generations each between Abraham and David, David and the Babylonian exile, and the Babylonian exile and the Messiah (1:1-17). Israel's historical destiny is fulfilled, it would seem, in the *genesis* (which can mean both "genealogy" [1:1] and "birth" [1:18]) of "Jesus the Messiah." "All this took place," Matthew tells us, "to fulfill what had been spoken by the Lord through the prophet [Isaiah], 'Behold, a virgin shall conceive'" (1:22-23).

Several forms of reading are in evidence here. First, Matthew reads the Scriptures of Israel, interpreting them with respect to Jesus of Nazareth. Although concentrated in the infancy and Passion narratives, fourteen "fulfillment" citations throughout this Gospel (together with a host of non-formulaic references and allusions) provide an outline of sorts for Jesus' life, indicating that the major contours of his life and ministry are divinely guided, conforming to God's plan.[7] In reading Scripture this way, Matthew follows the example of Jesus, who, himself a prophet (13:57; 21:11, 46, etc.), reinterprets the teaching of Moses (5:21-48) and applies the words of both prophets and psalms to his own ministry (e.g., 22:41-45; 26:31, 54, 56, 64).

Matthew reads the history of Israel in much the same manner, seeking to discern its fulfillment in the life of the Messiah. Accordingly, the Evangelist repeatedly depicts Jesus as an "antitype" — or historical fulfillment — of revered figures from the past: not only Abraham and David, but also Moses, Jeremiah, Jonah, and even Noah.[8] To some extent, the ful-

---

7. See 1:22-23 (Isa 7:14); 2:5-6 (Mic 5:2); 2:15 (Hos 11:1); 2:17-18 (Jer 31:15); 2:23 (Isa 11:1); 3:3 (Isa 40:3); 4:14-16 (Isa 9:1-2); 8:17 (Isa 53:4); 12:17-21 (Isa 42:1-4); 13:14-15 (Isa 6:9-10); 13:35 (Ps 78:2); 21:4-5 (Isa 62:11, Zech 9:9); 26:56 ("the Scriptures of the prophets"); 27:9-10 (Zech 11:12-13, Jer 19:1-13); cf. 15:7-9 (Isa 29:13); 21:13 (Jer 7:11, Isa 56:7); 21:16 (Ps 8:2).

8. For references and further discussion, see M. Knowles, *Jeremiah in Matthew's Gospel: The Rejected-Prophet Motif in Matthean Redaction*, JSOTSup 68 (Sheffield: Sheffield Academic Press, 1993), 223-46.

fillment of Scripture and history overlap, as in the citation of Hos 11:1 ("Out of Egypt I have called my son"), according to which Jesus recapitulates the historical experience of Israel as a whole.

All this is made possible, in fact, by a third kind of reading, whereby Matthew has rightly interpreted what Jesus calls "the signs of the times," in particular "the sign of the prophet Jonah" (16:3-4). That "sign" is Jesus himself. As was also the case for disciples of the so-called "Teacher of Righteousness" at Qumran, the advent of a messianic prophet provides Matthew with the essential clue to the "mystery" of God's purposes (cf. Matt 13:11; Eph 3:9, etc.). Because the Messiah himself represents the climax of divine revelation, his life and teaching alike reveal the hidden meaning of all that has gone before.[9] In this sense, Matthew's reading of the messianic present makes possible a new reading of Israel's pre-messianic past — scriptural prophecies and historical antecedents alike.

It also enables a new reading of Israel's religious identity. In the popular piety of Jesus' day, allegiance to the land, the law, and the Temple was the essential expression of covenant fidelity.[10] Yet in three unique Matthean passages, Jesus challenges and reinterprets each of these. At 12:6, he declares with reference to himself, "I tell you, something greater than the temple is here"; 5:17 indicates that his purpose is not to abolish but to fulfill both the precepts of Torah and the sayings of the prophets; while the wording of 5:5 echoes the language of repeated Old Testament promises: "Blessed are the meek, for they shall possess the land."[11] These passages suggest not only that Matthew has reread Israel's history and Scriptures with an eye to messianic fulfillment, but that he has done the same with Israel's covenant as well, key features of which are now reinterpreted with reference to Jesus.[12]

9. Knowles, *Jeremiah in Matthew's Gospel*, 23-25.

10. R. N. Longenecker, *Acts*, EBC (Grand Rapids: Zondervan, 1971), 337.

11. The language of Matthew's phrase, *klēronomein tēn gēn*, occurs repeatedly in the LXX with regard to inheritance or possession of the land, starting with God's promise to Abraham in Gen 15:7, but most frequently in Deuteronomy. More specifically, not only does the same phrase appear in LXX Num 14:31, 34:2; Deut 4:22; and Isa 60:21; 61:7 — in each case with reference to the "promised land" — but LXX Ps 36:11 provides an exact parallel to Matt 5:4: *hoi de praeis klēronomēsousin gēn* (Ps 37:11: "The meek will inherit the land," NIV; similarly NRSV and others).

12. Along the same lines, Robert McIver's reading of the Matthean "kingdom" as a physical metaphor for the Messianic community (that is, the church) suggests a significant redefinition of what it means to be the people of God: see R. K. McIver, "The Parable of the

Particularly if he is writing in the aftermath of Rome's destruction of Jerusalem (as seems most likely), Matthew thus joins other contemporary Jewish interpreters in seeking to reformulate Israel's religious identity. For him the key to understanding God's purposes is no longer any one of covenant, Temple, Torah, land, prophets, or history per se. Rather — and as distinct from other contemporary schools of interpretation — Matthew now reads and understands all these through the lens of messianic encounter. More to the point, as we will see later, he understands that messianic encounter to extend well beyond the historical confines of Jesus' earthly ministry and into the world of later audiences.

Matthew himself does not explicitly discuss the question, but at least two statements from elsewhere in the Christian canon commend his methodology (or something like his methodology) to subsequent readers and hearers. In the Gospel of John, Jesus is the preexistent "Logos" (John 1:1, etc.). Although it is difficult to assess the extent to which John is alluding to a Hellenistic, and more particularly Stoic, understanding of the *Logos,* the use of this term may imply that Jesus is the rational principle that makes unified intellectual sense of the cosmos.[13] More obviously, the hymn recorded in Col. 1:15-20 has as its structural and theological centerpiece the statement, "in him [that is, in Christ], all things hold together." This all-encompassing philosophical assertion implies a method of interpretation and therefore also a strategy for reading. What Matthew has done for the religious heritage of ancient Israel in particular, can, according to John the Evangelist and Paul the Apostle, be extended to the whole of human experience. The latter concur that Jesus of Nazareth holds the key to the meaning of human existence, as indeed of the entire created order. Such is the hermeneutical significance of the Messiah that, by implication, all reading — all interpretation — is illuminated by what John calls "the true light that enlightens all humanity" (John 1:9).

We turn now to the further outworking of this christological hermeneutic in the remainder of Matthew's Gospel.

Weeds among the Wheat (Matt. 13:24-30, 36-43) and the Relationship between the Kingdom and the Church as Portrayed in the Gospel of Matthew," *JBL* 114 (1995): 654-57.

13. See representative discussions in C. K. Barrett, *The Gospel According to St. John: An Introduction with Commentary and Notes on the Greek Text* (London: SPCK, 1972), 28-30, 127-28; and R. E. Brown, *The Gospel According to John I-XII: A New Translation with Introduction and Commentary,* AB 29 (Garden City, New York: Doubleday, 1966), 519-20.

Reading Matthew:
A Reader Reads Matthew for Hearers to Hear

As literate readers of Matthew's printed text, our own attention is naturally drawn to such phrases as "Let the *reader* understand" in 24:15 (//Mark 13:14) or to the several instances in which Jesus importunes his hearers, "Have you not *read?*"[14] Such admonitions need not imply that Matthew's original audience was also literate, insofar as Jesus is here addressing professional scribes on the subject of the written Torah.[15] By contrast, Jesus exhorts his wider audience, "those with ears, let them hear" (11:15; 13:9 [= Mark 4:9]; 13:43), indicating that "understanding" is a consequence of "hearing" (13:13 [= Mark 4:12], 14 [cf. Mark 8:18], 15, 19; 15:10 [= Mark 7:14]; cf. 13:16). Perhaps these latter passages would have more directly captured the attention of Matthew's audience, both because most would have heard, rather than read these words, and because they might have identified more easily with the narrative's listening crowds than with scribal opponents in particular. Thus whereas John of Revelation can insist, "Let the one with ears hear what the Spirit is saying to the churches" (Rev 2:7, etc.), Matthew makes a similar appeal by means of Jesus' own words.

Along the same lines, Matthew's proportionately frequent use of the emphatic interjections *ide* and especially *idou* (that is, "look" or "behold") reinforces the power of a direct appeal to listeners, notwithstanding the fact that such terms employ metaphors of sight rather than of hearing.[16] These words make as powerful an appeal in the Matthean narrative as does Mark's more familiar catchword "suddenly," even though their force is frequently muted by English renderings that variously translate or else leave out the word altogether. Consider, for instance, the infancy narratives: "Behold, an angel of the Lord appeared to Joseph. . . . Behold, the virgin shall conceive. . . . Behold, magi from the East came to Jerusalem. . . . Behold, ahead of them went the star that they had seen. . . . After they had left, behold, an

14. So 12:3 (par. Mark 2:25); 12:5 (not found in the Markan parallel); 19:4 (not found in the Markan parallel); 21:16 (not found in the Markan parallel); 21:42 (par. Mark 12:10); 22:31 (par. Mark 12:26).

15. See the comments of C. H. Roberts, "Books in the Graeco-Roman World and in the New Testament," *The Cambridge History of the Bible*, Volume 1: *From the Beginnings to Jerome*, ed. P. R. Ackroyd and C. F. Evans (Cambridge: Cambridge University Press, 1970), 48-49; and the response of Harris, *Ancient Literacy*, 281-82.

16. Occurrences: Matthew 66; Mark 16; Luke 57; John 19; Acts 23.

angel of the Lord appeared to Joseph" (1:20–2:13). Or the visit of Jesus' family: "While he was still speaking to the crowds, behold! His mother and his brothers were standing outside, wanting to speak to him. Someone told him, 'Behold, your mother and your brothers are outside. . . .' And pointing to his disciples, Jesus said, 'Behold my mother and my brothers . . .'" (12:46-49). Similarly, in Matthew's account of the arrest in Gethsemane Jesus declares, "'Behold, the hour has arrived. . . . Behold, my betrayer has arrived.' While he was still speaking, behold, Judas arrived. . . . Behold, one of those with Jesus drew his sword . . ." (26:45-51). The book ends on a similar note: "Behold, I am with you always" (28:20). Matthew repeatedly insists that we give heed both to his own and to Jesus' words, seeking to impress the power and immediacy of each declaration on us.

Matthew's text is replete with less direct indicators that also guide and shape the listening experience. We have already noted that Matthew is attentive to the providential symmetry whereby Israel's past is fulfilled in the messianic present. Not by accident, his compositional strategy reflects this theological preoccupation, for, like his interpretation of Israel's history, Matthew's text is characterized by order and symmetry. This can be observed in the arrangement both of the narrative as a whole and of particular passages.

So, for example, the opening designation of Jesus as a descendent of Abraham (1:1, 2, 17) anticipates the conclusion of Matthew's volume, according to which disciples are to be made of "all nations" (28:19), enabling them to inherit the blessings first promised to the patriarch.[17] This is only one of several apparent correspondences between Matthew's infancy and Passion narratives. Other examples include references to Jesus as "[God] with us" (1:23; 28:20) and "King of the Jews" (2:2; 27:11, 29, 37); the intervention of heavenly messengers ("angels": e.g., 1:24; 2:13, 19; 28:2, 5); the prominence of secondary figures named "Mary" and "Joseph" (1:18-20, etc.; 27:55-61; 28:1); and — above all — threats to the life of Jesus (2:16; 26:4, etc.) marked in both settings by collusion between religious and secular authorities and accompanied by the fulfillment of prophecies from Jeremiah (2:17-18; 27:9-10).[18]

On a smaller scale, the repetition of key phrases serves to delineate the boundaries of particular sections of the text. Thus the phrase "for theirs is

---

17. Cf. W. D. Davies and D. C. Allison, *The Gospel According to Saint Matthew*, ICC (Edinburgh: Clark, 1988-97), 1:158-59, 3:687.

18. Davies and Allison, *Matthew* 3:640, 656.

the kingdom of heaven" frames the beatitudes (5:3, 10); the declaration "by their fruits you will know them" brackets the discussion of "fruit" in 7:16-20; and the references to "the law and the prophets" in 5:17 and 7:12 mark out the central section of ethical precepts in the Sermon on the Mount.

A more complex version of this technique involves the symmetrical arrangement of material in order, apparently to highlight particular thematic or narrative concerns. So, for example, in 2:12-22 we find a concentric series of dream warnings, angelic appearances, and fulfillment citations that bracket Herod's murder of the children of Bethlehem (Figure 1). Similarly, in 4:3-10, three exchanges between Satan and Jesus refer twice each to the titles "Son of God" and "the Lord your God," with the second exchange incorporating both titles. This symmetry (which differs from Luke's presentation) reinforces the impression that the question of Jesus' identity lies at the heart of Satan's challenge to Jesus (Figure 2). A more striking instance of concentric patterning occurs in Jesus' references to God as "Father" in a range of formulations throughout the Sermon on the Mount (specifically, between 5:16 and 7:21; Figure 3). Although the correlation of elements is not perfectly uniform, we should note that all seventeen formulations are uniquely Matthean. At the center of this pattern lies Jesus' appeal to his Father in the words of the Lord's Prayer, presumably highlighting the significance of this text for Christian spirituality.

Figure 1. Concentric patterning in Matthew 2:12-22

A "Having been warned in a dream . . . [the Magi] withdrew to their own land" (2:12)

B "Behold, an angel of the Lord appeared in a dream to Joseph, saying . . ." (2:13)

C "In order to fulfill the word of the Lord through the prophet, saying . . ." (2:15)

D "Then Herod sent and killed all the children in Bethlehem and its vicinity" (2:16)

C′ "Then was fulfilled what had been spoken through the prophet Jeremiah, saying . . ." (2:17-18)

B′ "Behold, an angel of the Lord appeared in a dream to Joseph . . . saying . . ." (2:19-20)

A′ "Having been warned in a dream, [Joseph] withdrew to the region of Galilee" (2:22)

Figure 2. Symmetrical arrangement in Matthew 4:3-10

A. Stones to bread: "If you are the Son of God" (4:3) [Deut 8:3]

B. Pinnacle of Temple: "If you are the Son of God" (4:6) [Ps 91:11, 12]
                        "the Lord your God" (4:7) [Deut 6:16]

C. Kingdoms of earth   "the Lord your God" (4:10) [Deut 6:13]

Figure 3. References to God as "Father" in the Sermon on the Mount (5:16–7:21)

A   *ton patera hymōn ton en tois ouranois* (5:16 [M])

A   *tou patros hymōn tou en ouranois* (5:45 [≠ Luke])

B   *ho patēr hymōn ho ouranios* (5:48 [+ Luke])

?B   *tǭ patri hymōn tǭ en tois ouranois* (6:1 [M])

C   *ho patēr sou ho blepōn en tǭ kryptǭ apodōsei soi* (6:4 [M])

C   *tǭ patri sou tǭ en tǭ kryptǭ:*

C   *kai ho patēr sou ho blepōn en tǭ kryptǭ apodōsei soi* (6:6 [M])

D   *ho patēr hymōn* (6:8 [M])

E   *pater hymōn ho en tois ouranois: hagiasthētō to onoma sou*
         (6:9 [+ Luke])

?E'   *ho patēr hymōn ho ouranios* (6:14 [≠ Mark])

D'   *ho patēr hymōn* (6:15 [M])

C'   *tǭ patri sou tǭ en tǭ kryphaiǭ*

C'   *kai ho patēr sou ho blepōn en tǭ kryphaiǭ apodōsei soi* (6:18 [M])

B'   *ho patēr hymōn ho ouranios* (6:26 [≠ Luke])

B'   *ho patēr hymōn ho ouranios* (6:32 [+ Luke])

A'   *ho patēr hymōn ho en tois ouranois* (7:11 [≠ Luke])

A'   *tou patros mou tou en tois ouranois* (7:21 [≠ Luke])

Finally, the parables and apparent non-parables of 13:24-50 are evidently arranged in a concentric pattern (Figure 4).[19] All six are said to describe "the kingdom of heaven." But in addition, the parable of the Wheat and Weeds and the simile of the Net both feature the intermingling of

19. David Wenham ("The Structure of Matthew XIII," *NTS* 25 [1979]: 516-22) discerns a structure similar to that proposed here (albeit in less detail with regard to the specific parables in question), interpreting it to mean that parables function for Matthew "to conceal truth from some, but to reveal it to others" (522).

"good" and "bad" elements that can be sorted out only by the angels of judgment. The Mustard Seed and Pearl of Great Price both depict items whose value or effect far outweighs their insignificant physical size. The final pair concerns yeast that a woman is said — somewhat oddly — to "hide" within the flour *(enekrypsen)*, juxtaposed with a treasure "hidden" *(kekrymmenō)* in a field that a man found and "hid" *(ekrypsen)* once more. We will return later to the possible meaning of this particular structure.

Figure 4. Concentric patterns in Matthew 13:24-50

1. Jesus addresses the *crowds* outside (13:2)
   A   Seeds and Weeds (13:24-30)
   B   Mustard Seed (13:31-32)
   C   Leaven "hidden" in flour (13:33)
2. To the crowds, nothing without a parable; Ps 78:2 fulfilled (13:34-35)
3. Jesus addresses the *disciples* within the house (13:36a)
4. Explanation of the parable of the weeds (13:36b-43)
   C'   Treasure hidden in a field (13:44)
   B'   Merchant in search of fine pearls (13:45-46)
   A'   Net thrown into the sea (13:47-50)

On a different front, Matthew applies numerical patterning not only to his reading of history (as in the case of his opening genealogy) but also, frequently, to his use and arrangement of literary material.[20] Perhaps reflecting the legal requirement that a matter be established by a minimum of two or three witnesses (Deut 19:15; cf. Matt 18:16), doublets abound in Matthew's text.[21] For example, Matthew has Jesus cite LXX Hosea 6:6 ("I desire mercy, not sacrifice") twice, at 9:13 (added to Mark 2:17) and 12:7 (added to Mark 2:26), while harmonizing the wording of the heavenly attestations at Jesus' baptism (3:17) and transfiguration (17:5) more closely than is the case in his Markan source (cf. Mark 1:11; 9:7). Even more striking is the sequence in 20:20–21:32 of two brothers (20:21, added to Mark 10:37), two blind men (20:30 ≠ Mark 10:46), and two disciples (21:1 = Mark 11:1), followed by a parable about two sons (21:28).

20. Cf. U. Luz, *Matthew 1–7: A Commentary*, tr. W. C. Linss (Minneapolis: Augsburg, 1989), 38-40; Davies and Allison, *Matthew* 1:85-87.
21. For an extensive listing, see Davies and Allison, *Matthew* 1:88-92.

Further examples of numerical patterning quickly emerge. There are three tests by Satan, Jesus prays three times in Gethsemane (accompanied by three disciples), and Peter denies him thrice (26:34, 75).[22] Three times the disciples are bidden to meet Jesus in Galilee (26:32; 28:7, 10). There are five major discourses in this Gospel, the occasion of ongoing debate over possible allusions to Moses and the Pentateuch.[23] Patterns of seven are frequent: the account of Jesus' background and preparation for public ministry (1:18–4:16) focuses on the fulfillment of seven biblical texts;[24] there are seven "woes" against scribes and Pharisees (23:13-26)[25] and seven parables of judgment in the final discourse.[26] Jesus makes — arguably — seven appearances on a mountain,[27] while there are fourteen references to him as the "Christ" or "Anointed One" (of which the seventh is Peter's confession in 16:16), and — as mentioned earlier — fourteen fulfillment formulas.[28] As a final example, many commentators recognize ten miracles in the section from 8:1 to 9:34, in addition to which Matthew makes ten references to Jesus as "Son of God."[29]

---

22. Unlike Mark, however, Matthew has not three but four Passion predictions, adding 26:2 to 16:21 (par. Mark 8:31); 17:22-23 (par. Mark 9:31); and 20:18-19 (par. Mark 10:33-34). On the prevalence of triads in Matthew, see further D. C. Allison, "The Structure of the Sermon on the Mount," *JBL* 106 (1987): 423-45; Davies and Allison, *Matthew* 1:62-71.

23. In particular, the transitional formula in 7:28-29; 11:1; 13:53; 19:1; and 26:1, in three instances followed by references to Jesus' teaching, bears a significant resemblance to the formulas found in LXX Deut 31:1 and especially 31:24 (cf. also Deut 32:44-46). See further discussion in Knowles, *Jeremiah in Matthew's Gospel*, 239-40; Luz, *Matthew 1–7*, 455.

24. 1:22-23; 2:5-6, 15, 17-18, 23; 3:3; 4:14-16.

25. On the assumption that 23:14 is an interpolation: see B. M. Metzger, *A Textual Commentary on the Greek New Testament* (London: United Bible Societies, 1971), *in loc.*

26. The fig tree (24:32), the flood (24:37-42), the thief at night (24:43-44), the wise and wicked servants (24:45-51), the ten bridesmaids (25:1-13), the talents (25:14-30), the sheep and goats (25:31-46).

27. See (1) 4:8 (testing by Satan), (2) 5:1; 8:1 (seated, for the sermon "on the mount"), (3) 14:23 (praying alone), (4) 15:29 (seated, healing the multitudes), (5) 17:1, 9 (the mount of transfiguration), (6) 24:3 (seated, for the eschatological or "Olivet" discourse), (7) 28:16 (the commissioning of the disciples in Galilee).

28. 1:1, 16, 17, 18; 2:4; 11:2; 16:16, 20; 22:42; 23:10; 26:63, 68; 27:17, 22. In two further instances, the title refers to *false* claims of messianic identity (24:5, 23). Cumulatively, such evidence contradicts the assertion of Davies and Allison (*Matthew* 1:87) that the number seven "is usually from the tradition, and Matthew does not lend it any significance."

29. 4:3, 6; 5:9; 8:29; 14:33; 16:16; 26:63; 27:40; 27:43; 27:54, of which it may be significant that the fifth (14:33) and tenth (27:54) repeat the phrase *alēthōs theou huios*.

Some of these patterns may be accidental, others only emerge upon close analysis, and still others may reflect selective reading. That is, only the most arithmetically obsessive listener might notice them. Not implausibly, some such patterns may owe their origins to an earlier stage of preliterary, oral transmission.[30] But this does not absolve us of responsibility for evaluating their purpose within their present literary and theological context, which envisages the re-oralization of originally oral traditions now codified in literary form. In general, are such patterns to be viewed primarily as literary or as oral/aural phenomena? How, more specifically, does concentric patterning (chiasm) function for a listening audience? Even as a literary phenomenon, chiasm involves selective reading.[31] As an oral technique, its function is even more problematic, for by the time the chiasm is complete, its center is long gone. Similarly, with regard to numerical patterning, how many instances of a given phrase or theme can be held in memory? Did ancient listeners actually keep track of and count specific literary phenomena while listening?

Perhaps, therefore, some elements of Matthew's Gospel are intended primarily for readers, in which case his text likely has more than one audience in view.[32] Or should we account for such phenomena under the category of *compositional* technique? The least plausible explanation is that such structures functioned as mnemonic devices at an antecedent stage of oral transmission, since Matthew has unmistakably employed written texts in compiling his Gospel. On the other hand, it is not impossible that some such structures could have facilitated *subsequent* memorization on the part of later generations of illiterate or semi-literate audiences.

Given the indeterminate status of such questions, the explanation proposed at the outset still seems the most cogent, namely that the text's many literary symmetries reflect Matthew's preoccupation with theological symmetry, order, and fulfillment. Demonstrating providential order is of the essence in this Gospel, with the result that Matthew's "reading" of Scripture and history influences the form as well as the content of his own

---

30. Cf. Kelber, *The Oral and the Written Gospel*, 66 (with reference to Mark).

31. See the critique offered by S. E. Porter and J. T. Reed, "Philippians as a Macro-Chiasm and Its Exegetical Significance," *NTS* 44 (1998): 213-21.

32. Luz, for instance, understands Matthean repetitions and structural features to imply the need for repeated examination: "He wished for an intensive reading, with the possibility of reviewing . . . it becomes obvious that Matthew wishes that his book be read and meditated upon as a whole again and again" (*Matthew 1–7*, 39-40).

text. Accordingly, our experience of this text (whether as a verbal or a written literary artifact) is likely to reinforce its theological substance.

But what might listeners themselves have brought to their experience of Matthew's text? A case in point emerges from Dale Allison's proposal that the structure of the Sermon on the Mount reflects debate about the redefinition of Judaism in the aftermath of the Jewish War. Specifically, Allison suggests that Matthew's arrangement of material under the categories of Torah (5:17-48), cult (6:1-18), and social conduct (6:19–7:12) reflects the dictum of Simeon the Just that "By three things is the world sustained: by Torah, by Temple service, and by deeds of loving kindness" (*m. 'Abot* 1:2). On such a view, Matthew provides a Christian response to discussion of this saying and its implications for the religious observance on the part of contemporary rabbis such as Johanan ben Zakkai.[33] The proposal is richly suggestive, but ultimately depends for its heuristic value on our estimation of the extent of this debate and the ability of Matthew's hearers to situate the Sermon on the Mount within it — factors well outside the bounds of the text itself.

We may be on firmer ground when it comes to listeners' putative familiarity with the Scriptures of Israel, the centrality of which for Second Temple Judaism is beyond question. Here three examples will suffice, each uniquely Matthean. First, whereas according to Luke 17:4 Jesus declares that his disciples must be willing to offer forgiveness as many as seven times in a single day, Matt 18:22 multiplies this already formidable requirement to "seventy-seven," or even "seventy times seven," depending on how one interprets the Greek phrase *hebdomēkontakis hepta*. Since the time of Tertullian and Origen in the early third century, commentators have seen here an allusion to the vengeful oath of Lamech in LXX Gen 4:24, where the identical phrase appears.[34] That is to say, the Matthean Jesus apparently insists that among *his* followers, mercy and forgiveness must extend at least as far as have vengeance and retribution in the past.

In 21:14, Matthew's observation that "the blind and the lame came to him in the Temple, and he cured them" appears at first glance to be no more than an extension of Jesus' healing ministry. But for hearers familiar with the Septuagint, the statement becomes a rebuttal of King David's ha-

---

33. Allison, "Structure," 442-45; cf. W. D. Davies, *The Setting of the Sermon on the Mount* (Cambridge: Cambridge University Press, 1966), 304-8.

34. So R. H. Gundry, *The Use of the Old Testament in St. Matthew's Gospel with Specific Reference to the Messianic Hope*, NovTSup 18 (Leiden: Brill, 1967), 139-40; cf. Davies and Allison, *Matthew* 2:793 with note 29.

tred and banishment of the same *typhloi kai chōloi* from the Temple (LXX 2 Kgdms 5:8), all the more so in light of the references to Jesus as "son of David" in 21:9 and 21:15.[35]

Finally, whereas Mark simply notes that the angel at the tomb was "garbed in a white robe" (16:5), Matthew expands the description: "his appearance was like lightning and his garments white as snow" (28:3). Such language reflects that of LXX Dan 7:9, describing the "Ancient of Days" enthroned in splendor, and LXX Dan 10:6, Daniel's vision of an angelic warrior proclaiming divine victory.[36] Of course, an angel in splendor is still an angel, but recognition of such allusions can suggest to the hearer, yet again, a correspondence between the prophetic past and the messianic present, with the angelic testimony to Jesus' resurrection fulfilling the expectations of Israel's Scripture. Or perhaps we should say that such allusions fulfill the author's or audience's expectation that the events of the present should correspond to the Scriptures of the past.

In each of these instances, a reasonable case can be made for the existence of verbal correspondences between the LXX and Matthew's text. But allusions (as opposed to explicit citations) assume significance for the hearer or reader only if they are recognized as such. Similarities of wording suggest the parallels to be intended, but they depend for their effect on knowledge that the audience — rather than the author — brings to the text. The most Matthew can do is to create the possibility of meaning, but that possibility awaits actualization in the mind of the hearer. To this extent, Matthew's relation to his hearers appears directly analogous to the relationship between Jesus and his own audience. Both rabbi and writer must appeal for "those with ears" to "hear," once again collapsing into a single focus the interpretative — indeed, salvific — dynamic of "understanding" that operates both within and outside the text.

Matthew's Readers: The Text "Reads" Its Audience

Yet Matthew is far from passive in directing his audience's encounter with this text. One of the more remarkable features of his Gospel is the selective

---

35. Cf. Gundry, *The Use of the Old Testament,* 140, 210.

36. Compare Matt 28:3 with LXX Dan 7:9 and 10:6. Cf. Davies and Allison, *Matthew* 3:666.

nature of the information it provides. Matthew seems either to assume or to ignore details that might otherwise be of interest to audiences of a later day. For example, Jesus' life between his return from Egyptian exile and his emergence on the public scene years later in Galilee has provided opportunity for endless speculation. Details are similarly missing from Matthew's descriptions of John the Baptist, and of Jesus' disciples: what accounts he does provide are remarkably sparse. Comparison with the roughly contemporary, lengthy, and detail-rich histories by Flavius Josephus suggests that neither stylistic convention nor limitations of physical space in a volume of bound papyrus can account for this narrative austerity. Rather, it would appear that Matthew is more concerned with interpretation and meaning — with delineating historical, textual, and theological patterns that reveal the divine purpose — than with historical detail for its own sake.

From another perspective, Matthew's choice of subject matter implies (and to some extent selects) a particular audience. For instance, Matthew is everywhere concerned with halakah and Torah-observance, surely matters of exclusive interest to those of Jewish heritage. The Sermon on the Mount gets down to business with a declaration that Jesus intends to fulfill "the Law and the Prophets" (5:17-18), a refrain later repeated (7:12) in order to delineate the central body of teaching in this discourse (cf. 11:13; 22:40). Jesus in fact redefines Torah observance (5:21-47), while he and his contemporaries frequently debate the question of what conduct may be deemed "lawful."[37] The central role of prophetic fulfillment has already been noted. In other words, Matthew is everywhere concerned with ways in which the Scriptures of Israel both give meaning to and are given meaning by Jesus the Messiah. All this indicates (whatever subsequent qualifications may need to be added) that Matthew addresses his Gospel in the first instance to those for whom such Scriptures are antecedently authoritative.

More subtly, Matthew shapes our experience of his narrative by consistently placing the hearer in a position of privileged understanding. That is, Matthew not only explains the messianic import of Israel's prophetic past, but also makes the audience privy to everything Jesus' immediate disciples are allowed to hear. Hence the concentric arrangement of parabolic

37. Specifically, 12:2, 4, 10, 12; 14:4; 19:3; 20:15; 22:17; 27:6; occurrences: Matthew 9; Mark 6; Luke 5; John 2.

material in ch. 13. Here Jesus tells his disciples, "To you it has been given to know the secrets of the kingdom of heaven, but to [the crowds] it has not been given" (13:11). Shortly thereafter, he addresses the parables of the Wheat and Weeds, the Mustard Seed, and the Hidden Yeast to the crowds, leading Matthew to comment that "apart from parables he told them nothing" (13:34). But the three similes of the Treasure, Pearl, and Net that Jesus relates to the disciples once they have withdrawn into the house (Matthew carefully avoids calling them parables) are formally similar to the parables the crowds have heard, indicating that the teaching offered to "outsiders" and "insiders," respectively, is virtually identical. At least from the perspective of Matthew's audience, this similarity significantly reduces Jesus' apparent distinction between the two groups. Moreover, whereas the crowds are left to puzzle things out for themselves, Matthew's audience hears every explanation. However we may conceive of ourselves, the narrative treats us as equivalent to the twelve.

A third "privileging" of the hearer occurs through Matthew's use of literary irony, particularly in his account of Jesus' betrayal and passion. Over and over again, the audience possesses an awareness that lends meaning to words and events that they would not have conveyed to all the original participants. So, in the betrayal scene, Judas greets Jesus as "Rabbi" (26:25, 49), the only character in Matthew's Gospel to do so, having apparently forgotten his teacher's explicit prohibition of this form of address (23:6-8). Our recollection of Jesus' earlier ruling reinforces the sense that Judas has rejected everything this particular "rabbi" stands for. More substantively, two false witnesses testify against Jesus (26:60-61). The audience's recognition of what for Matthew is a significant legal principle, that a matter be established on the testimony of "two or three" (Matt 18:16; cf. Deut 17:6; 19:15), lends the scene a deeply ironic twist. In response to such testimony, the high priest's oath ("I put you under oath before the living God, tell us if you are the Messiah, the Son of God," 26:63) specifically echoes the language by which Peter earlier confessed Jesus' messianic sonship ("You are the Messiah, the son of the living God," 16:16). Similarly, the court officers torment Jesus for his prophetic and messianic pretensions (26:68), even as the Roman soldiers mock him with the title "king of the Jews" (27:29) and bystanders at the cross deride his claim to be "God's son" (27:40, 43; cf. 27:37, 42). Yet Matthew has already affirmed the titles "prophet," "Son of God," "King," and "Messiah" to be true of Jesus (2:2; 14:33; 16:16; 21:11, 46, etc.), with the result that his detractors speak more accurately than they know. No less telling is the fact that the bystanders' derision ("If you are the son of God, come down from the cross," 27:40) directly echoes Satan's similar taunting of Jesus in the wilderness: "If you are the son of God, command these stones . . . throw yourself down," etc. (4:3, 6). In the same vein, certain chief priests and Pharisees approach Pilate with advice on how to forestall false rumors of resurrection, lest "the last deception be worse than the first" (27:64). What they do not know is that Jesus has already used similar language to describe the state of their own "generation" (12:45), in which case their words say more about themselves than about the church and its risen Lord. Time and again, even a modest effort of memory on the part of Matthew's audience lends the words of Jesus' various opponents a meaning none of them could possibly have intended.

Nor can it escape our attention that the text makes clear distinctions in its manner of addressing those arrayed for and against the Messiah, respectively. Jesus describes his followers as members of a single family: "whoever does the will of my Father in heaven is my brother and sister and mother" (12:50).[38] Opponents, on the other hand, or those who do not follow Jesus' precepts, are "hypocrites,"[39] "Gentiles,"[40] or simply "them."[41] With few exceptions, those who take issue with Jesus and his teaching are said to do so on the basis of ulterior and hostile motives (e.g. 10:16-18; 21:23-32; 22:15; 23:1-38; 26:3-5, 55, 59-60; 27:1, etc.), leaving the audience little doubt as to where their own sympathies should lie.

Among the other Evangelists, Luke declares his intention of setting the facts straight (Luke 1:1-4) and John means to convince his audience that Jesus is the Messiah (John 20:31). While lacking such explicit statements, Matthew is no less hegemonistic or absolute, everywhere insisting that Jesus as Messiah fulfills the expectations of history, teaches and heals with *exousia* (power, authority), and ultimately suffers an unjust fate that identifies him with all God's prophets and faithful servants of the past. Matthew's entire narrative is intentionally persuasive, seeking to construe those who encounter this text on the model of the followers depicted

38. In sociological analysis, this is known as "fictive kinship." Cf. 5:22, 23, 24, 47; 7:3, 4, 5; 18:15, 21, 35; 19:29; 25:40; 28:10.

39. Cf. 6:2, 5, 16; 15:7; 22:18; 24:51; and especially 23:13, 15, 23, 25, 27, 28, 29; but, conversely, 7:5.

40. See especially 5:47; 6:7, 32; 10:5; 18:17.

41. E.g., 8:4; 10:17-18, 26.

within it. In this sense, his text may be said to "read" its audience as much as it may be read to or by them.[42]

The text likewise shapes the experience of those who are already disciples, for it offers an interpretative framework by which to understand discipleship itself. Not unexpectedly, Matthew delineates a series of parallels between the ministries of Jesus and John the Baptist. Both inaugurate their respective ministries by calling for repentance in light of God's imminent kingdom (3:2 = 4:17), both are regarded as "prophets" yet have their authority challenged by the religious authorities (11:9 = 21:11; 21:23-27), and both are martyred. More surprising, perhaps, are the parallels that Matthew consistently observes between Jesus and his disciples. Twice in this Gospel Jesus directly identifies himself with his followers: "Whoever welcomes you," he tells them, "welcomes me" (10:40); they are to be like children, he says, and "whoever welcomes one such child in my name welcomes me" (18:5).

The similarities are even more specific. All of Jesus' followers, some identified as "prophets," suffer persecution and rejection (5:11-12; 10:16-23; 23:34; cf. 13:16-17). Indeed, Jesus warns them to expect as much: "If they have called the master of the house Beelzebul, how much more those of his household" (10:25). Thus they, like Jesus, must each take up their cross and — unless our fear of such consequences causes us to hear this as mere hyperbole — give up their very lives (10:38-39; 16:24-25; 24:9-10). In words that repeat those of Jesus and John alike, the disciples (or at least the twelve) proclaim good news that "the kingdom of heaven has come near" and, like Jesus, are empowered to "cure the sick, raise the dead, cleanse the lepers, [and] cast out demons" (10:7-8). Like Jesus, they are bidden to call God "Father" (6:9 = 11:25-26). Finally, the twelve are promised that having identified with and suffered like their Lord, they will sit enthroned with him in glory (19:28), where (like Jesus already at his transfiguration, 17:2), they "will shine like the sun in the kingdom of their Father" (13:43).

At one level, such parallels serve to interpret the historical experience

---

42. Matthew's method is consistent with that of all Scripture, according to Erich Auerbach's classic formulation (*Mimesis* [Princeton: Princeton University Press, 1953], 14-15): "The Bible's claim to truth is not only . . . urgent . . . it is tyrannical — it excludes all other claims. The world of the Scripture stories . . . insists that it is the only real world, is destined for autocracy. . . . Far from seeking . . . merely to make us forget our own reality for a few hours, it seeks to overcome our reality: we are to find our own life in its world, feel ourselves to be elements in its structure of universal history."

of Jesus' immediate followers, assuring them that their own discipleship falls as much within the divine plan as did Jesus' own life. But such similarities invite subsequent generations to entertain further such comparison, as they too identify with their Lord. Indeed, the similarity is explicit at the conclusion of Matthew's Gospel, with the eleven bidden to make disciples of others just as Jesus has made disciples of them (28:19). With this last move, Matthew's interpretive program is complete. Just as Matthew highlights patterns of historical, scriptural, and theological symmetry that give meaning to the messianic present, and this preoccupation gives literary shape to his text, so the patterns of the Messiah's own life are understood to be repeated in the experience of his immediate disciples. Finally, a similar symmetry is projected forward, via Matthew's text, into the lives of future followers. From the perspective of the audience, the repeated patterns of providential ordering emerge yet again in their own experience. Matthew's reading, our reading, and the text's reading of us merge, as it were, into a single pattern of divine direction and fulfillment.

This perspective is rooted in the theological conviction that the Messiah is as powerfully present in the lives of Matthew's audience as he has once been present with the followers of his earthly ministry. For Jesus is the fulfillment of Isaiah's prophecy, "'they shall name him Emmanuel,' which means, 'God with us'" (1:23). Nothing in this passage indicates that it speaks only of the time prior to Jesus' death and resurrection. Indeed, Matthew makes it abundantly clear that Jesus remains present both in the gathered community, wherever numbers are sufficient to bear legal witness to that presence (18:20), and in the missionary outreach of the community as it makes "disciples of all nations," baptizing them and teaching them to obey all that Jesus has commanded (28:18-20).[43] Here, then, is confirmation that Matthew understands Jesus to provide the interpretive principle — perhaps we could say the spiritual, intellectual, and salvific "fulcrum" — by which each generation of disciples will subsequently interpret, even "move," their world.

This dynamic is particularly relevant for understanding the process of public reading itself, according to which the reader adopts the role —

---

43. C. H. Talbert ("Indicative and Imperative in Matthean Soteriology," *Bib* 82 [2001]: 515-38; esp. 523-28) emphasizes that by recalling the scriptural theme of God's presence with Israel, the motif of *Jesus'* enduring presence assures the audience of continued divine empowerment for succeeding generations of his disciples.

and authority — of Jesus himself.[44] Simply by rehearsing Jesus' words in the first person (e.g., "You have heard it said . . . but I say to you . . ."), the speaker strongly identifies with Jesus, implying such oral proclamation to be one of the means by which the risen Lord continues to be present among subsequent generations of disciples. This observation strongly qualifies Werner Kelber's contention that with the codification of Christian tradition, "it is the written medium, not a special contract with the Jesus of history, that reorients oral consciousness . . . [the gospel] is no longer an orally present actuality, but is now connected with the textual recapitulation of Jesus' life and above all death."[45] Rather, the re-oralization of the written text amounts to a "re-vivification" of Jesus' teaching and historical presence as a whole. In this sense, it is the medium of speech (not the written text per se) that orients the consciousness of the audience toward the historical Jesus. Indeed, insofar as the gospel tradition points to the culmination of Jesus' historical experience in the resurrection, the public reading of Scripture, by re-presenting and re-vivifying Jesus, itself both appeals and testifies to the reality of the resurrection.

Conclusion

For those whose métier is the *production* of texts, there is great virtue in originality: scholars are forever trying to say — or more precisely, to publish! — something "new" about other, more ancient texts, whether these be from the recent or from the more distant past. But for all that Matthew's own approach is truly original, he might be the first to argue that any subsequent originality risks betraying his particular text. As he sees it, all possible "newness" consists already in Christ alone, in the Messiah who has fulfilled all. Granted, all readings, all hearings are unique to the extent that

44. So Kelber (*The Oral and the Written Gospel*, 20; cf. 202), citing Jesus' dictum in Luke 10:16, "Whoever hears you hears me."

45. *The Oral and the Written Gospel*, 115, 130 (with reference to Mark's text in particular). Against the contention of Willi Marxsen (*Mark the Evangelist*, trans. R. A. Harrisville, et al. [Nashville: Abingdon, 1969], 135) that "the presence of the risen Lord is experienced in . . . proclamation," Kelber insists that a "written re-presentation of Jesus' past" presents "an *alternative* to the presence of the living Lord in oral proclamation" (*The Oral and the Written Gospel*, 210, emphasis added). But such distinctions are obviated and redefined by the phenomenon of postliterary re-oralization.

they are unavoidably constrained by the characteristic perspectives and capacities of those who receive them. Yet in the last analysis, Matthew's intent and expectation are not simply for us to "read" his text, that is, to render a judgment as to its meaning. Rather, he intends us to "understand" his Gospel, in the medieval, etymological sense of "standing under" it and being ruled by its meaning. He wants us to find our meaning not in some new way, but in a pattern already established in and hermeneutically anchored by the person of Jesus of Nazareth. Perhaps this posture comes more readily to those whose inability to read for themselves requires them to stand, both physically and intellectually, under the reading of another.

To conclude with an analogy from more recent devotional literature, Matthew's approach bears comparison with the "Apology," or prologue, to John Bunyan's 1678 bestseller, *The Pilgrim's Progress*. Granted, the latter text is distinctive both theologically (in its determinedly Calvinist sentiments) and formally (in that it is addressed to readers rather than to hearers). Nonetheless, Matthew and Bunyan share a common desire to discern the purpose of sacred texts as they relate to the encounter with Israel's Messiah, and thereby to delineate the shape of Christian experience. As to method, both combine entreaty and appeal, on the one hand, with profound theological conviction, on the other, seeking to call an audience into being by means of their respective texts. In this regard, Bunyan describes Matthew's intent as accurately as his own:

> This Book will make a Travailer of thee,
> If by its Counsel thou wilt ruled be;
> It will direct thee to the Holy Land,
> If thou wilt its Directions understand . . .
> Would'st read thy self, and read thou know'st not what
> And yet know whether thou art blessed or not,
> By reading the same lines? O then come hither,
> And lay my Book, thy Head and Heart together.[46]

---

46. J. Bunyan, *The Pilgrim's Progress from This World to That Which Is to Come*, ed. J. B. Wharey, 2d ed. rev. R. Sharrock (Oxford: Clarendon, 1960), 6, lines 33-36; 7, lines 22-25.

Reading Mark 11:12-25
from a Korean Perspective[1]

YONG-EUI YANG

One of the most enigmatic and perplexing pericopes in Mark's Gospel is certainly Mark 11:12-14, 20-25, which presents the fig tree story on either side of the Temple cleansing story (11:15-19). Scholars have long been puzzled by this problematic pericope. Questions about its origin and historicity are not irrelevant, along with the problem that the story provides a sole destructive miracle by Jesus. What is the reason and purpose of the miracle? The awkwardness of the problem is added to by Mark's perplexing comment in v. 13d: "for it was not the season for figs." Furthermore, comparison of this pericope with its parallel in Matthew raises a critical Synoptic problem, especially in relation to the chronology of the story.

Numerous approaches have been attempted to meet these problems,[2] and many of them have, though in different degrees, moved us for-

1. I would like to express my appreciation to Rev. Dr. R. T. France for reading an early version of this essay and for his valuable comments. I bear all responsibility, however, for any inaccuracies or deficiencies.

2. E. Schwartz, "Der verfluchte Feigenbaum," *ZNW* 5 (1904): 80-84; C. W. F. Smith, "No Time for Figs," *JBL* 79 (1960): 315-27; A. de Q. Robin, "The Cursing of the Fig Tree in Mark xi: A Hypothesis," *NTS* 8 (1961-62): 276-81; H.-W. Bartsch, "Die Verfluchung des Feigenbaumes," *ZNW* 53 (1962): 256-60; G. Münderlein, "Die Verfluchung des Feigenbaumes (Mark 11:12-14)," *NTS* 10 (1963): 89-104; R. H. Hiers, "Not the Season for Figs," *JBL* 87 (1968): 394-400; J. D. M. Derrett, "Fig Trees in the New Testament," *Heythrop Journal* 14 (1973): 249-65; H. Giesen, "Der verdorrte Feigenbaum. Eine symbolische Aussage? Mark 11,12–14.20f.,'" *Biblische Zeitschrift* 20 (1976): 95-111; L. A. Losie, "The Cursing of the Fig Tree:

ward into a better understanding of the story. Among them, a comprehensive study of this pericope by W. R. Telford[3] has made remarkable progress in our understanding of the story. Here I do not add a new approach but present and discuss some of the major ways of interpretation advanced to date and evaluate them in order to identify those that are most reliable and profitable in reading the Markan story today. The perspective at work will be my own Korean perspective, which is different from that of western scholars in some ways. Then in the final section, we will bring the question of the Korean perspective to the surface so as to point out those differences.

The Synoptic Problem

The literary and chronological scheme of Mark 11:12-25 is significantly different from that of Matt 21:12-22. In Mark the story is broken up into two parts (11:12-14, 20-25) and surrounds the Temple story (11:15-19), but in Matthew (21:18-22) it simply follows the Temple story (21:12-17) without separation. The literary and chronological disagreements between the two Gospels can be easily observed in the tables on page 80.

There are at least two options to account for these disagreements: (1) Those who support the two-source hypothesis of Gospel origins may argue that Matthew has deliberately rearranged Mark's three-day scheme and reduced it to a two-day scheme.[4] Matthew's redactional purpose, however, is not easy to discern. Matthew may have aimed to make the chrono-

---

Tradition Criticism of a Marcan Pericope: Mark 11:12-14, 20-25," *Studia Biblica et Theologica* 7 (1977): 3-18; W. R. Telford, *The Barren Temple and the Withered Tree: A Redaction-Critical Analysis of the Cursing of the Fig Tree Pericope in Mark's Gospel and Its Relation to the Cleansing of the Temple Tradition,* JSNTSup 48 (Sheffield: JSOT, 1980); W. J. Cotter, "'For It Was Not the Season for Figs,'" *CBQ* 48 (1986): 62-66; W. R. Telford, "More Fruit from the Withered Fig Tree," in *Templum Amicitiae,* ed. W. Horbury, FS E. Bammel, JSNTSup 48 (Sheffield: Sheffield Academic Press, 1991), 264-304; B. von Kienle, "Mk. 11:12-14, 20-25. Der verdorrte Feigenbaum," *Biblische Notizen* 57 (1991): 17-25; D. E. Oakman, "Cursing Fig Trees and Robbers' Dens," *Semeia* 64 (1993): 253-72; G. W. Buchanan, "Withering Fig Trees and Progression in Midrash," in *The Gospels and the Scriptures of Israel,* ed. C. A. Evans and W. R. Stegner, JSNTSup 104 (Sheffield: Sheffield Academic Press, 1994), 249-69; C. Böttrich, "Jesus und der Feigenbaum. Mark 11:12-14, 20-25 in der Diskussion," *NovT* 39 (1997): 328-59.

3. Telford, *Temple.*

4. Telford (*Temple,* 71-73) presents points in defense of this solution.

Table 1: Chronological Sequence according to Mark — The Three-Day Scheme

Mark 11	Matthew 21	
vv. 1-11a	vv. 1-10a	The triumphal entry and the first visit to Jerusalem
(no par.)	*(vv. 10b-11)*	*Jesus' arrival in Jerusalem; the reaction of the city*
v. 11b	**no par.**	**The first visit to the Temple; the first return to Bethany**
vv. 12-14	**(cf. vv. 18-19a)**	**The cursing of the fig tree on the second visit to the Temple**
vv. 15-17	vv. 12-13	The second visit to the Temple; the cleansing of the Temple
(no par.)	*(vv. 14-16)*	*Jesus' healing in the Temple*
v. 18	no par.	The chief priests and scribes conspire against Jesus
v. 19	v. 17	The second return to Bethany
(cf. vv. 12-14)	*(vv. 18-19a)*	*The cursing of the fig tree*
vv. 20-25 (26)	vv. 19b-22	The fig tree is found withered on the third visit to Jerusalem
vv. 27-33	vv. 23-27	The question about Jesus' authority

Matthew 21	Mark 11	
vv. 1-10a	vv. 1-11a	The triumphal entry and the first visit to Jerusalem
vv. 10b-11	no par.	Jesus' arrival in Jerusalem; the reaction of the city
(no par.)	*(v. 11b)*	*The first visit to the Temple; the first return to Bethany*
(cf. vv. 18-19a)	*(vv. 12-14)*	*The cursing of the fig tree*
vv. 12-13	vv. 15-17	The first visit to the Temple; the cleansing of the Temple
vv. 14-16	no par.	Jesus' healing in the Temple
(no par.)	*(v. 18)*	*The chief priests and scribes conspire against Jesus*
v. 17	v. 19	The first return to Bethany
vv. 18-19a	**(cf. vv. 12-14)**	**The cursing of the fig tree on the second visit to Jerusalem**
vv. 19b-22	vv. 20-25 (26)	The fig tree withers immediately
vv. 23-27	vv. 27-33	The question about Jesus' authority

Boldface type indicates chronological disagreements.

Italics indicate verses that are omitted or that appear in a different location.

logical process of the events simpler and clearer and to make Mark's looser connections between the triumphal entry and the cleansing of the Temple stronger and clearer.[5] Matthew may also have intended to enhance the marvelous character of the miracle, not only by removing the interval between Jesus' announcement (Mark 11:14) and the account of the withering (11:20-21), but also by stating that the withering took place instantaneously (Matt 21:19).[6]

(2) Those who support the Griesbach hypothesis of Matthean priority may argue that Mark has deliberately rearranged Matthew's two-day scheme and extended it to a three-day scheme.[7] Mark has done so by separating the instantaneous withering miracle (Matt 21:18-22) into two stages (Mark 11:12-14, 20-25). In that case Mark's redactional purpose is not difficult to discern. An answer is immediately found in one of Mark's most characteristic literary methods, his sandwich structure.[8] As is generally recognized, this technique is used in order to establish a relationship between the two stories. In this case Mark would have interwoven the stories so that the fig tree story is understood in the light of the Temple story. As a matter of fact, this relationship is generally agreed on, even without a hypothesis of a Markan sandwich structure (see below on "The Old Testament Background"). Mark's interweaving, then, may have been introduced to highlight the relationship even more clearly and strongly.[9]

Which best accounts for the pericope as it stands in the two Gospels

---

5. Telford, *Temple*, 74; C. A. Evans, *Mark 8:27–16:20*, WBC 34b (Nashville: Thomas Nelson Publishers, 2001), 149-50; cf. R. T. France, "Chronological Aspects of 'Gospel Harmony,'" *Vox Evangelica* 16 (1986): 38.

6. A. Plummer, *An Exegetical Commentary on the Gospel According to S. Matthew* (London: Robert Scott, 1909), 290-91; R. Bultmann, *The History of the Synoptic Tradition*, trans. J. Marsh (Oxford: Blackwell, 1963), 218; Telford, *Temple*, 74-75; cf. France, "Chronological Aspects," 38. For a critique of this view, however, see E. Klostermann, *Das Matthäusevangelium*, HNT 3 (Tübingen: Mohr, 1950), 169.

7. W. R. Farmer, *The Synoptic Problem: A Critical Analysis* (Dillsboro: Western North Carolina Press, 1976), 258-62, presents arguments for this solution; cf. C. S. Mann, *Mark*, AB 27 (New York: Doubleday, 1986), 443-44; cf. also Bultmann, *History*, 218; France, "Chronological Aspects," 39.

8. Most commentators and writers on Mark recognize this technique, and we will focus on it later in this paper. For a helpful account of it at the moment, however, see J. R. Edwards, "Markan Sandwiches: The Significance of Interpolations in Markan Narratives," *NovT* 31 (1989): 193-216.

9. For more detailed discussion see below.

depends, of course, on one's view of the literary relationship between Matthew and Mark.[10] The great majority of scholars support the two-source hypothesis, and not a few of them are ready to suggest that the sandwich structure is not original but Mark's own creation.[11] But this suggestion, regardless of its intention, can add weight to option (2). So if we argue just from this case, then option (2) seems more persuasive than option (1). Such a situation brings us into a really unsettled area. The present writer, therefore, wonders whether any decision is truly helpful or even required for the proper interpretation of the pericope. In such a situation it seems possible and even realistic to leave the Synoptic problem unsettled, but to confirm that the sandwich structure shown in Mark's Gospel is the result of Mark's redaction.

A final comment on the chronological disagreements may be needed. Either of the above options (or any other explanations of the present Synoptic problem)[12] shows clearly that at least one of the two Evangelists (and Mark for certain) has "deliberately subordinated chronological order to the effective communication in narrative form of the theological significance which he saw in the cursing of the fig tree."[13] In this case it may not be fair for an interpreter of this pericope to focus attention on chronology. Furthermore, as R. T. France points out, if "Mark was not at this point intending to write in strict accordance with chronology, it is perverse to label non-chronological order as an 'error.'"[14]

Other Problems

In addition to the Synoptic problem, the present pericope raises some other perplexing problems. One of the most apparent problems is that the withering of the fig tree is the sole miracle of destruction attributed to Jesus in the canonical Gospels.[15] It is, then, natural to ask whether such a de-

10. Or some may argue that Mark and Matthew draw on an independent source respectively; for the list of those who support this solution, see Telford, *Temple,* 71.

11. E.g., Bultmann, *History,* 218; Telford, *Temple,* 43-49, 238-39; Evans, *Mark,* 151-52.

12. E.g., the Augustinian hypothesis, Goulder's hypothesis.

13. France, "Chronological Aspects," 39.

14. France, "Chronological Aspects," 40.

15. The destruction of the swine in Mark 5:1-20 is different from this case; the incident, in fact, was the result of the action of the unclean spirits rather than that of Jesus' or-

structive miracle is consistent with Jesus' character as it is generally described in the Gospels. The two ways of dealing with the problem are to insist that Jesus really worked the miracle and then to seek his purpose for doing so or to insist that Jesus did not work this miracle and then ask why and how the story arose.

Another problem in the Markan story is the incongruity between Jesus' expectation in v. 13b: "He went to see if he could find anything on it," and Mark's comment in v. 13d: "for it was not the season for figs." The latter statement renders the former problematic, especially when it accompanies his statement in v. 14. Furthermore, if the real motive of Jesus' statement in v. 14 were his hunger (v. 12), this would aggravate the difficulty.[16] That statement ("May no one ever eat fruit from you again") adds difficulties on its own. If it is regarded as a curse, then such a response is not thought consistent with the merciful character attributed to Jesus in the Gospels and is simply unjust. Would it be possible to imagine that Jesus cursed the tree (v. 14) even though it was not the season for figs (v. 13), especially just because he was hungry (v. 12)? T. W. Manson and others have suggested, therefore, that the statement in v. 14 was not a curse, but a simple declaration that the fruit of the tree would never be eaten either by Jesus himself or perhaps by anyone else.[17] Their suggestions are by and large grounded on the ambiguity of the possible underlying Aramaic sentence. "Whatever the original meaning however," as M. D. Hooker points out, it is beyond a doubt that "Mark has understood the words as an emphatic curse,"[18] in which case the problem remains.

---

der; cf. C. E. B. Cranfield, *The Gospel According to St. Mark*, Cambridge Greek Testament Commentary (Cambridge: Cambridge University Press, 1977), 354 n. 1; J. P. Meier, *A Marginal Jew: Rethinking the Historical Jesus* (New York: Doubleday, 1991, 1994), 2:986-87, n. 69. In noncanonical Gospels, however, some destructive miracles are attributed to Jesus; e.g., *Infancy Gospel of Thomas* 3:1-3; 4:1-2; 14:2; cf. *Gospel of Pseudo-Matthew* 26, 38. It should be also noted that in the Old Testament (e.g., Exod 7:14–12:30; 14:23-31; 1 Kgs 13:1-5; 2 Kgs 2:23-24) and outside the Gospels in the New Testament (Acts 5:1-11; 9:1-9; 13:6-12) there are a number of destructive/punitive miracles; see Meier, *Marginal Jew*, 2:895.

16. Cf. Cranfield, *Mark*, 354-55. He sees Jesus' behavior as causing the moral difficulty. However, it does not seem to be proper to categorize one's treatment of a tree as a matter of "morality."

17. T. W. Manson, "The Cleansing of the Temple," *Bulletin of the John Rylands Library* 33 (1951): 271-82.

18. M. D. Hooker, *The Gospel According to St. Mark*, Black's New Testament Commentary (London: Black, 1991), 267.

Numerous understandings of the nature and origin of the story have been put forward as attempts to solve these problems, some denying the historicity of the story and attributing its origin to someone other than Jesus' words and actions. Others admit the historicity of the story and attempt to resolve the problems in different ways.

A Legend

E. Schwartz and many others regard the whole story as a legend and consequently deny the historicity of the story altogether.[19] This view is summarized well by B. H. Branscomb:

> One is tempted to conjecture that a fig tree on the road between Bethany and Jerusalem, from which the disciples and Jesus had several times gathered figs, withered either during the latter days of the ministry or subsequently, and that pious legend supplied the cause.[20]

This view, however, faces some serious objections. First, it is purely based on conjecture without any concrete evidence.[21] Second, A. de Q. Robin notes that the present form of the Markan narrative, short though it is, contains details which would be expected from "an eye-witness narrative."[22] C. E. B. Cranfield points out that the reference to Peter's memory in 11:21 "looks like a personal reminiscence."[23] Third, if the story were a created legend, such an awkward comment as "for it was not the season for figs" of v. 13d would not be included. This comment rather lends support to the historicity of the story. "All these details," Robin concludes, "re-

19. Schwartz, "Der verfluchte Feigenbaum"; J. Weiss, *Die Schriften des Neuen Testaments* (Göttingen: Vandenhoeck und Ruprecht, 1907), 1:178-79; M. Goguel, *The Life of Jesus,* trans. O. Wyon (London: George Allen and Unwin, 1933), 240-41; B. H. Branscomb, *The Gospel of Mark,* Moffatt New Testament Commentary (London: Hodder and Stoughton, 1937), 201-2.

20. Branscomb, *Mark,* 201-2.

21. Cf. H. Anderson, *The Gospel of Mark,* NCBC (London: Marshall, Morgan and Scott, 1976), 263-64. Even the supporters of this view admit that it is purely guesswork. Branscomb (*Mark,* 202) even says, "one guess is as good as another"; cf. V. Taylor, *The Gospel According to St. Mark,* 2d ed. (London: Macmillan, 1966), 459.

22. Robin, "Fig Tree," 277.

23. Cranfield, *Mark,* 355.

inforce the conclusion that the narrative rests on eye-witness testimony."[24] Finally, as M.-J. Lagrange properly points out, a withered fig tree was too common an object to give rise to a legend.[25] All these counterarguments incline us to conclude that the legend theory cannot be a satisfactory solution for the problems that the pericope raises.[26]

A Historicized Parable

A number of scholars have suggested that the fig tree story originated from a parable of Jesus, such as the parable of the fig tree in Luke 13:6-9.[27] Arguments for this view are well summarized by Telford: (1) In substance, the Lukan parable and the Markan story are similar: if the fig tree (= Israel) cannot show itself fit for the kingdom, it must perish. (2) The "disappointed search for figs" theme of the Lukan parable would have made it a ready subject for historicization through allegorization, especially when it was once connected with the disappointed result of Jesus' visit to Jerusalem. (3) In certain circumstances parabolic teaching can be converted into historical story (e.g., the widow's mite, Mark 12:41-44;[28] the stater in the fish's mouth, Matt 17:24-27[29]). (4) While Mark and Matthew have the fig tree story, they lack the fig tree parable, while Luke has the parable but lacks the story.[30]

24. Robin, "Fig Tree," 277; he points out another detail, namely "Jesus seeing the tree *apo makrothen*" (v. 13).

25. M.-J. Lagrange, *Évangile selon saint Marc*, 8th ed. (Paris: J. Gabalda, 1947), 399 n. 24; cf. A. Plummer, *The Gospel According to St. Mark*, Cambridge Greek Testament for Schools and Colleges (Cambridge: Cambridge University Press, 1915), 137.

26. For more criticism, see Telford, *Temple*, 12.

27. A. Loisy, *Les Évangiles synoptiques* (Ceffonds: Prés Montier-en-der, 1907, 1908), 2:28-29; A. E. J. Rawlinson, *The Gospel According to St. Mark*, Westminster Commentaries (London: Methuen, 1925), 154; E. Klostermann, *Das Markusevangelium*, HNT 3 (Tübingen: Mohr, 1950), 116; W. L. Knox, *Sources of the Synoptic Gospels*, vol. I: *St. Mark* (Cambridge: Cambridge University Press, 1953), 80-81; V. Taylor, *The Gospel According to St. Mark* (London: Macmillan, 1966), 458-59; Anderson, *Mark*, 263-64; E. Schweizer, *The Good News According to Mark*, trans. D. H. Madvig (London: SPCK, 1970), 230-31; and others.

28. B. T. D. Smith, *Parables of the Synoptic Gospels* (Cambridge: Cambridge University Press, 1937), 67.

29. B. W. Bacon, "Fig Tree," in *Dictionary of Christ and the Gospels*, ed. J. Hastings (Edinburgh: Clark, 1906, 1908), 2:594.

30. Telford, *Temple*, 234-35.

In reply to this view, however, some crucial counterarguments have been put forward. These are the main ones:[31] (1) A number of scholars point out that the similarities taken for granted between the parable and the story are not significant.[32] The parable and the story are different in spirit,[33] contents,[34] and style.[35] (2) The second and third arguments above are not convincing at all. In particular, the examples given for the third argument are "for the most part inappropriate or speculative."[36] (3) It seems more likely that Luke uses Mark as his source, than vice versa. It seems odd, though not impossible, then that the earlier Gospel should present the later form (i.e., the story), while the later Gospel should present the earlier form (i.e., the parable). Furthermore, as Telford properly points out, "at a redactional level, the respective presence-absence of both story and parable in either Gospel is not a sufficient reason to conclude that the one was a *source* for the other, especially when such a derivation is considered unusual."[37] Then the fourth argument above loses its ground. Considering all these counterarguments, this second view once again seems to be neither a persuasive nor a satisfactory solution for the problems raised by our pericope.

A Creation of an Early Christian Author

Another suggestion attempts to resolve the problem of discontinuity with Jesus' character by attributing the origin of the story to someone other than Jesus. J. P. Meier argues that, judging from the criteria of historicity,[38]

31. A useful list of counterarguments is found in Telford, *Barren Temple*, 235-36. I am indebted to him for most of the following list.

32. It is, of course, true that the disproof of the similarities does not necessarily imply that the story and the parable have no relation to one another; cf. Telford, *Barren Temple*, 236. Nevertheless, it cannot be denied that this disproof significantly weakens the view above.

33. Goguel, *Life*, 240.

34. Branscomb, *Mark*, 201.

35. Robin, "Fig Tree," 277; cf. Cranfield, *Mark*, 355.

36. Telford, *Barren Temple*, 236.

37. Telford, *Barren Temple*, 237. In relation to this counterargument the concluding remark of Oakman ("Fig Trees," 267-68) is noteworthy: In the course of development of the tradition, "[t]he tendency was to forget the story [of the cursing the fig tree], not to create it."

38. Scholars seem to vie with one another to show the best working criteria of histo-

that is, those of coherence and discontinuity, the fig tree story "has no claim to go back to the public ministry of the historical Jesus." Curse miracles are known to the Old Testament (Exod 7:14–12:30; 1 Kgs 13:1-5; 2 Kgs 1:9-12, etc.), Judaism (2 Macc 3:22-30), and to later Christian literature (Acts 5:1-11; 9:1-9; *Infancy Gospel of Thomas* 3:1-3, etc.), but are completely absent from Jesus' public ministry as accounted in the four Gospels, except for this one story. This glaring discontinuity with Jesus and continuity with the Old Testament and Jewish and Christian literature suggest that the story was created by a pre-Markan author to illuminate the meaning of the Temple story.[39]

The criteria of coherence and discontinuity, applied here to judge the historicity of the fig tree story, are, however, not definite at all, and the discontinuity and continuity pointed out by Meier can be explained otherwise. Our discussion below will show that the fig tree story has enough reason to break coherence with Jesus' other deeds as well as to be continuous with the Old Testament miracles. Furthermore, the criterion of embarrassment may direct us toward an opposite conclusion. It is not likely that early Christians would invent a story that could have caused embarrassment for the early church.[40] I will not attempt to prove or disprove the historicity of the story here, since I regard such proof or disproof as much more a matter of personal tendency than a pure academic affair.[41] I regard proof or disproof of historicity as neither profitable nor necessary for understanding the Markan story.

---

ricity without great success. For a recent discussion of the criteria, see Meier, *Marginal Jew*, 1:167-95. He presents five "primary" criteria (embarrassment, discontinuity, multiple attestation, coherence, and rejection and execution) and five "secondary" criteria (traces of Aramaic, Palestinian environment, vividness of narration, tendencies of the developing Synoptic tradition, and historical presumption).

39. Meier, *Marginal Jew*, 2:894-96.

40. Meier's reply to this point (*Marginal Jew*, 2:987 n. 71) does not suggest an impossibility but only an improbability. In fact, he concedes (1:167-68) that "the function of the criteria is . . . to inspect various probabilities, and to decide which candidate is most probable. Ordinarily, the criteria cannot hope to do more."

41. In my view, traditional western critical discussions of this issue are often too skeptical; cf. C. Blomberg, *The Historical Reliability of the Gospels* (Leicester: Inter-Varsity, 1987), 246-47.

A Historical Event

A number of scholars admit that the incident actually happened and attempt to account for the problems of the story by suggesting that the original incident was distorted by misunderstandings of the disciples, by Mark's modification, or by a false transmission of the story. T. W. Manson, for example, argues thus. This incident took place not at Passover time but in the autumn when the leaves would be beginning "to change colour, but when one might still expect to find a few figs left over from the main crop." Finding no figs, "Jesus said something in Aramaic which could mean: 'Let no one ever eat fruit from thee again' or 'No one shall ever eat fruit from thee again' or 'One will never eat fruit from thee again.'" Manson further postulates that while Jesus meant his statement either in the second sense — that is, that the day of the Lord or the destruction of Jerusalem would occur before the next fig harvest — or in the third sense — that is, that Jesus himself would die before the next fig harvest, Peter and the other disciples wrongly understood it in the first sense, that is, as a curse. Manson goes on to speculate that some combination of circumstances perhaps hastened the shedding of the leaves, so that the next day Peter and other disciples, seeing the tree from a distance, supposed that the words of Jesus, misunderstood as a curse, had taken effect.[42]

This suggestion certainly has the advantage of accounting for Jesus' search for figs out of season and for his curse. But this suggestion also has some crucial weaknesses. (1) It is purely based on speculations without any concrete evidence. (2) As Robin points out, "it involves ignoring the Markan chronology in locating the incident immediately before the Passover."[43] As a matter of fact, it is inconceivable to imagine that Mark would have relocated the incident before the Passover even by adding the awkward comment of v. 13d ("for it was not the season for figs"). (3) It does not help us understand the story as presented by Mark;[44] it rather damages the flow of the story without any real evidence.[45] Then it is quite evident that

42. Manson, "Cleansing," 279-80; a similar suggestion is found in Bartsch, "Verfluchung," 256-60; cf. Böttrich, "Feigenbaum," 345-48.

43. Robin, "Fig Tree," 278.

44. R. T. France, *The Gospel of Mark*, NIGTC (Carlisle: Paternoster, 2002), 440-41.

45. Cf. Derrett, "Fig Trees," 254. Perhaps Manson's suggestion above may account for Jesus' historical behavior, but it does not afford any real account for Mark's story itself.

this view is also neither a convincing nor a satisfactory account for the problems raised by our pericope.

Other scholars who admit the historicity of the story suggest that we regard Jesus' behavior as "an acted parable" and interpret it symbolically.[46] This way of interpretation is supported even by those who are not interested in the historicity of the story.[47] In fact, this approach is primarily concerned not with the historicity of the story or its development before Mark but with its present form and function in Mark. It simply admits that the incident is a destructive miracle and that Jesus' statement in v. 14 is a curse. Then it attempts to find the reason for the miracle and the curse in terms of symbolic behavior in the light of the Old Testament. It also notes that such a symbolic meaning is highlighted by Mark through his sandwich structure. This approach not only seems faithful to the text itself but also provides a most satisfactory account for the problems raised. In the next section we will turn to these issues.

Keys to the Problems

Scholars who are interested in the story's function in Mark rather than its origin before Mark tend to see the story's Old Testament background and its sandwich structure in Mark as the crucial keys to the meaning of the story in Mark.

The Old Testament Background

After the study of Telford, it is almost unanimously accepted that the Old Testament provides one of the crucial keys to the proper understanding of the Markan fig tree story. Since the Old Testament formed a central part of the daily environment of the first-century Christians,[48] study of the Old

---

46. E.g., Cranfield, *Mark*, 356; Robin, "Fig Tree," 279-81; W. L. Lane, *The Gospel According to Mark*, NICNT (Grand Rapids: Eerdmans, 1974), 400-402; France, *Mark*, 439-41.

47. E.g., Hooker, *Mark*, 261; Schweizer, *Mark*, 230; Telford, *Temple*, 237. For a different view, however, see Evans, *Mark*, 158.

48. This tenet has already been well expressed by C. H. Dodd in his classic book, *According to the Scriptures: The Substructure of New Testament Theology* (London: Nisbet, 1952), 132; cf. Telford, *Temple*, 129-32. In addition to the Old Testament, Judaism and some part of

Testament background then seems imperative. So we will examine the importance of the Old Testament for the proper reading of the story.

Two aspects of Old Testament background are pointed out as important. First is the prophets' use of symbolic actions in their proclamation of the destiny of Israel or other nations (e.g., Isa 20:1-6; Jer 13:1-11; 19:1-3, 10-11; 27:1-15; 28:10-17; Ezek 4:1–5:4).[49] To those acquainted with such actions, Jesus' behavior could readily be understood as a symbolic action with a prophetic character.[50] In this case the withering of the fig tree may have symbolized the coming doom of Israel. Then Jesus' search for figs from a tree out of season may be the sort of thing we could expect, "for an element of the unexpected and incongruous, which would stimulate curiosity, was a characteristic feature of the symbolic actions of the O.T. prophets."[51]

Second, the fig tree, along with the vine, is one of the most notable trees in the Old Testament. The fig tree is mentioned in descriptions of the fertility of the Promised Land (Num 13:23; Deut 8:8). The fig tree or fig appears as an image in the prophetic books,[52] very often in passages with eschatological import. Telford points out that the twin motifs of the blessing and judgment of Israel are common to these passages.[53] The fig tree is prominently associated with the peace and prosperity of the messianic age. The blossoming or fruit-bearing of the fig tree appears as an image in passages which depict Yahweh's eschatological blessing (Mic 4:4; Hag 2:19; Zech 3:10; cf. 1 Macc 14:12; Deut 8:7-8; 1 Kgs 4:24-25). Conversely, the withering of the fig tree or the destruction of its fruit appears as an image in passages which depict Yahweh's coming judgment of Israel (Isa 28:3-4; Jer 5:17-18; 8:13; Hos 2:11-13; 9:10-17; Joel 1:2-12; Amos 4:4-13; Mic 7:1-6; Hab

---

the New Testament may be background for the story. Though it may be useful to study all these backgrounds, the limited space does not allow us to do so. A comprehensive study of them is found in Telford, *Temple,* chapters 6 and 7. Telford also provides a study of the Greco-Roman background of the story in his recent article, "More Fruit."

49. Cf. D. I. Block, *The Book of Ezekiel, Chapters 1–24,* NICOT (Grand Rapids: Eerdmans, 1997), 164-70. Other cases are also found in 1 Kgs 11:29-39; 22:11; 2 Kgs 13:14-19; Jer 16:1-9; 32:1-44; 35:1-19; 43:8-13; 51:59-64; Hos 1:2-9; 3:1-5; Zech 6:9-15.

50. Cf. Cranfield, *Mark,* 356; Lane, *Mark,* 400; J. A. Brooks, *Mark,* NAC 23 (Nashville: Broadman, 1991), 180-81.

51. Cranfield, *Mark,* 356.

52. According to Telford, *Temple,* 133, the fig tree imagery occurs eighteen times in the prophetic books: Isa 28:4; 34:4; Jer 5:17; 8:13; 24 passim; 29:17; Hos 2:12; 9:10; Joel 1:7, 12; 2:22; Amos 4:9; Mic 4:4; 7:1; Nah 3:12; Hab 3:17; Hag 2:19; Zech 3:10.

53. Telford, *Temple,* 134.

3:17). As Telford properly observes, very often the reason given for God's wrath is "cultic aberration on the part of Israel, . . . her condemnation for *a corrupt temple cultus and sacrificial system*" (Jer 5:17-18; 8:12-22; Hos 2:11-13; 9:10-17; Amos 4:4-13).[54] Mark's readers, who would have been schooled to recognize such symbolism, would readily have understood Jesus' cursing of the fig tree as an eschatological sign prefiguring the solemn judgment of Israel and particularly the destruction of the corrupt Temple.[55]

Along with this general understanding of the Old Testament background, the connection with Mic 7:1-6 is particularly suggestive.[56] The whole passage describes the prophet's disappointed search for the first ripe fig, for which he hungers, after the summer fruit harvest, as he beholds the decayed state of the nation and its leaders. Jesus' search for a fig out of season (Mark 11:13b) and Mark's comment that "it was not the season for figs" (11:13d) may well indicate Jesus' disappointment at the state of Israel and the Temple. Whereas the Messiah has already arrived and visited the Temple, searching for spiritual fruits (cf. 11:11), the Temple and its leaders have not been prepared for his coming and have failed to meet his expectations. His verdict on the braggart fig tree (11:14) is then nothing but a verdict on the failure of Israel and the Temple.[57] It becomes thus quite probable that Jesus' searching for figs out of season and his cursing of the fig tree are not real problems as generally supposed, but rather a symbolic way of pronouncing the messianic disappointment at the state of Israel and the coming judgment of the Temple. And Mark's comment explains the real reason for Jesus' disappointment, namely the unreadiness of Israel and the Temple.[58]

---

54. Telford, *Temple*, 135. Along with this idea, it is noteworthy that Israel is often identified with the tree in general, which is planted in the Promised Land and on the Temple mount in particular (cf. Exod 15:17; Ezek 17:3-10, 22-24). It seems natural then, on the one hand, that the tree would blossom and bear fruits, if the Temple were functioning as it should, and, on the other hand, that cultic aberration would bring a curse on the tree and destruction to the Temple; cf. Telford, *Temple*, 137-42.

55. Telford, *Temple*, 136, 163; cf. Telford, "More Fruit," 300-304.

56. Robin, "Fig Tree," 280-81; J. N. Birdsall, "The Withering of the Fig Tree (Mark xi.12-14, 20-22)," *ExpT* 73 (1962): 191; Lane, *Mark*, 401-402; Telford, *Temple*, 150-52; cf. France, *Mark*, 441. Telford (*Temple*, 142-56) suggests five passages (Jer 8:13; Isa 28:3-4; Hos 9:10, 16; Mic 7:1; Joel 1:7, 12). After a long investigation, however, he concludes that "no one 'fig' verse seems to have provided a starting-point for Mark's story"; he rather thinks that "the contribution of a number of passages, rather than any single one, is more in view" (156).

57. Cf. France, *Mark*, 441.

58. Evans's suggestion (*Mark*, 156-57) on the basis of Cotter's comment regarding

It seems now quite clear that the Old Testament background studies so far account for the problems raised by our pericope quite meaningfully, without unsatisfactory conjectures of a legend or of a historicized parable. On the one hand, the Old Testament background studies in general show that Jesus' cursing of the fig tree was not an unjust and illogical response to it but rather an intentional eschatological sign prefiguring the destruction of the corrupt Temple. On the other hand, Mic 7:1-6 in particular may well provide the theological clue to Jesus' search for the fig out of season, his cursing of the fig tree, and the reason for the comment in Mark 11:13d.

The Sandwich Structure

A careful reader of Mark's Gospel will notice that the so-called "sandwich structure" is Mark's characteristic literary convention. This convention breaks up a story by inserting a second story into the middle of it, and creates an A1-B-A2 schema. The B unit is not so long that the reader fails to link A2 with A1, which need one another to become a complete story. A2 usually includes a word, phrase, or theme at its beginning which recalls A1.[59] According to Edwards, in Mark's Gospel the sandwich structure occurs some nine times: 3:20-35; 4:1-20; 5:21-43; 6:7-30; 11:12-21; 14:1-11; 14:17-31; 14:53-72; 15:40–16:8.[60] Of these nine cases, the structure is preserved only five times in Matthew and four in Luke. This shows Mark's distinct preference for this sandwich technique. Not a few scholars, therefore, recognize that Mark uses the sandwich technique with a particular goal in mind. Edwards offers a convincing suggestion: the B unit "*nearly always provides the key to the theological purpose* of the sandwich" and interprets the separated A units.[61]

Mark's using of *gar* is interesting and useful, though not conclusive. He suggests that the *gar* of v. 13d explains why Jesus went to see if he might find edible figs (11:13a), rather than why he found nothing except leaves (11:13c). This suggestion solves not only the chronological problem but also Jesus' seeming illogical behavior. Nevertheless, it does not seem to be a most natural way of reading the *gar* clause.

59. Cf. H. C. Kee, *Community of the New Age: Studies in Mark's Gospel*, NTL (London: SCM Press, 1977), 54; Edwards, "Sandwiches," 193, 197.

60. Edwards, "Sandwiches," 197-98. For a different list see Kee, *Community*, 54-56 (2:1-12; 3:1-6; 3:20-35; 5:21-43; 6:6b-30; 11:12-25; 14:53-72; 15:6-32).

61. Edwards, "Sandwiches," 196.

Mark 11:12-25 is one of the more apparent sandwiches.[62] The Temple story (unit B) does, in fact, reveal the inherent meaning and purpose of the fig tree story (units A1 and A2). As we have seen, Jesus' cursing of the fig tree is an acted parable showing the messianic disappointment at the corrupt state of the Temple and prefiguring its coming judgment. Thus the fig tree story by itself is already related to the issue of the Temple. Mark's sandwich structure then makes this inherent symbolic meaning much clearer and confirms the results of our background studies, namely that the fig tree story needs to be understood in relation to the state of the Temple.

But it is often admitted that not only does the Temple story provide the interpretive key to the fig tree story, but also the fig tree story provides the key to the Temple story.[63] The incident in vv. 15-19 is traditionally called the "cleansing" of the Temple.[64] But since the cursing and withering of the fig tree foreshadow the destruction of the Temple, Jesus' actions in the Temple are not to be understood simply as a removal of impurities and restoration to a true function. It is to be seen more as a symbolic/prophetic action of pronouncing the eschatological doom of the Temple (cf. 13:2; cf. also Jer 7:11-14).[65] Just as the leafy fig tree without fruits is cursed and with-

62. As we have seen, it seems most probable that the sandwich structure here is the result of Mark's redaction. In this case Mark's intention in inserting the Temple story (11:15-19) into the middle of the fig tree story (11:12-14, 20-25) may be more positive.

63. Cranfield, *Mark,* 357; Anderson, *Mark,* 263; Edwards, "Sandwiches," 208; H. Waetjen, *A Reordering of Power: A Socio-Political Reading of Mark's Gospel* (Philadelphia: Fortress Press, 1989), 182; Brooks, *Mark,* 180; Evans, *Mark,* 158; France, *Mark,* 436.

64. For example, R. H. Hiers, "Purification of the Temple: Preparation for the Kingdom of God," 82-90; he argues that "Jesus went to Jerusalem in order to prepare that city and the Temple [by purifying or cleansing it] for the coming of the Kingdom" (90). Cf. J. Roloff, *Das Kerygma und der irdische Jesus. Historische Motive in den Jesus-Erzählungen der Evangelien* (Göttingen: Vandenhoeck und Ruprecht, 1970), 95-97; P. M. Casey, "Culture and Historicity: The Cleansing of the Temple," *CBQ* 59 (1997): 306-32.

65. B. Gärtner, *The Temple and the Community in Qumran and the New Testament* (Cambridge: Cambridge University Press, 1965), 105-11; R. J. Mckelvey, *The New Temple* (Oxford: Oxford University Press, 1969), 60-66; Telford, *Temple,* 261; E. P. Sanders, *Jesus and Judaism* (London: SCM Press, 1985), 69-76; J. Neusner, "Money-Changers in the Temple: The Mishnah's Explanation," *NTS* 35 (1989): 287-90; Edwards, "Sandwiches," 207-8; E. P. Sanders, *The Historical Figure of Jesus* (London: Penguin Press, 1993), 42, 254-57; D. Seeley, "Jesus' Temple Act," *CBQ* 55 (1993): 263-83; France, *Mark,* 438; cf. H. D. Betz, "Jesus and the Purity of the Temple (Mark 11:15-18): A Comparative Religion Approach," *JBL* 116 (1997): 455-72. Sanders (*Judaism,* 69-76) argues extensively that Jesus' behavior in the Temple is to be regarded not as an act of purification but as symbolizing destruction; Sanders's arguments,

ers, so the aberrant Temple full of cultic activities but without spiritual fruits is doomed to destruction. As R. J. Mckelvey remarks, "By embedding the cleansing in the story of the cursing and withering of the fruitless fig tree Mark shows that he understands the action of Jesus to mean nothing less than the abrogation of the Temple and cult."[66] Like the fig tree the Temple is about to be condemned and to wither away "to its roots" (11:20).[67] Even though we admit the historicity of the fig tree story and the Temple story and the Markan (and Matthean) chronology locating the incidents immediately before the Passover together, it seems now quite clear that the problems raised by the fig tree story are not real, but rather function as stimuli for the readers to seek the deeper level of meaning of the story. If Mark's sandwich structure is his own creation, what he is doing with this literary convention may well be an attempt to help his (probably Gentile) readers to see this deeper, inherent but symbolic meaning of the story more easily and clearly, which would be readily understood by Jewish readers who were more familiar with the Old Testament. This might ex-

---

however, have some problematic areas, especially as regards the authenticity and historicity of the Temple story, and they are discussed comprehensively by C. A. Evans, "Jesus' Action in the Temple: Cleansing or Portent of Destruction?" *CBQ* 51 (1989): 237-70. For a response to Evans's arguments, see Seeley, "Temple Act," 265-70. Evans himself, however, does not deny the possibility of understanding the story as a prophecy of the Temple's doom; see especially 269: "the cleansing idea does not oppose the main point for which Sanders had argued. Criticism of Temple business activities, coupled with a warning (or threat) of destruction, coheres well with the prophetic Scriptures, with Jesus' own prediction of the Temple's destruction (Mark 13:1-2), and with the charge brought against him at his trial (Mark 14:58)." More recently Evans argues for the possibility more positively; see his *Mark,* 158: "the thrust of Jesus' action and teaching in the Temple is prophetic in terms of Jer. 7:11-14, with its reference to the coming destruction of the Temple as God's judgment. . . ."

66. Mckelvey, *Temple,* 65.

67. As a matter of fact, it is noteworthy that the Temple theme is not only sandwiched between the two fig tree episodes, but itself acts as a wider sandwich covering the whole unit, with mentions in v. 11 and vv. 27ff. That is to say, the fig tree story is itself enveloped in the Temple theme as well as vice versa. This fact strengthens the link between the two stories all the more.

The limited space of the present chapter does not allow us to discuss the relation between the fig tree story and the mountain-moving saying of 11:22-25. Our understanding of the story above, however, encourages us to understand the mountain in those verses as a symbol of the Temple mountain, and its removal into the sea as a symbolic image signifying the utter destruction of the Temple. For a lengthy discussion of this matter, see Telford, *Temple,* 95-127.

plain why Matthew does not adopt Mark's sandwich structure in his redaction, if he used Mark's Gospel itself as his source.

A Korean Perspective

What Is a Korean Perspective?

Should a Korean reading of Mark 11:12-25 be different from what we may call a "western"[68] reading? My initial response to this question is positive. As H.-G. Gadamer points out, a reading of biblical texts involves "two horizons," namely the horizon of the biblical text and the horizon of the reader. The meaning of a text is determined in the course of relating the reader's horizon to that of the text.[69] That is to say, the reader's understanding of a text is bound up with the reader's horizon. A different reader's horizon brings forth a different understanding. In this case a Korean reading may naturally be different from a western reading, though the degree of difference may depend on how much the Korean horizon is different from the western horizon.

The Korean horizon, however, is too broad and vague to define. Therefore, I will describe my own horizon as a Korean to make the discussion more concrete. I belong to one of the conservative Presbyterian denominations[70] and teach in one of the conservative Presbyterian seminaries. Korean conservative Presbyterians confess the ultimate authority of the Bible as the inspired word of God and believe in the infallibility[71] of

68. "Western" here is a general term representing North American and European, in opposition to "eastern," including Korean.

69. H.-G. Gadamer, *Truth and Method*, 2d ed. (London: Sheed and Ward, 1993), 277-379; cf. A. C. Thiselton, *The Two Horizons* (Exeter: Paternoster, 1980), 10-17, 304-10.

70. The Presbyterian church constitutes about two-thirds of the Christian population in Korea, and most Presbyterian denominations in Korea tend to be conservative in their theological stance. *The 1991 Korea Christian Yearbook* (Seoul: Christian Literature Press, 1991 [in Korean]) reports that Presbyterians have 24,539 out of a total of 35,869 churches. Cf. also Y. J. Kim, *A History of the Korean Church* (Seoul: The Korean Society for Reformed Faith and Action, 1992 [in Korean]), 356-58.

71. The distinction between "infallibility" and "inerrancy" is a matter of definition. I prefer "infallibility" in the sense of "entire trustworthiness" to "inerrancy," which needs much qualification. See I. H. Marshall, *Biblical Inspiration* (London: Hodder and Stoughton, 1982), 73. This is, however, by no means an agreed position of the Korean conservative Presbyterian church.

the Scriptures.[72] Therefore, we generally accept the historicity of biblical accounts.[73] Most of our seminaries are denominational and are usually expected to share these beliefs.[74] In such a situation academic activities in these seminaries are to reflect that expectation. As a result of this, in a number of the leading Presbyterian seminaries in Korea, historical-critical methods can be used only with great care and discernment. As a teacher in these seminaries, I am not free from this general environment.

Like most other teachers in Korean seminaries, I received my theological education not only in Korea (B.A.) but also in the western world[75] (B.A., M.A., and Ph.D.). So my theological thinking is inevitably very western. I am much more open to the western historical-critical methods than the Korean church traditionally is.

Nevertheless, my way of using these methods may not be exactly the same as that of western critical scholars. When I am working in such a conservative environment, my interpretation of the biblical texts needs to reflect the church's tendency, its concern, and its expectations sensibly and in such a way as to meet its needs, questions, and problems meaningfully though critically. This is how I communicate my interpretation with my church. In reading the Gospels for my church, therefore, the critical discussions of the historicity, sources, and origin of the Gospel stories are not primary interests,[76] especially when the arguments are not conclusive, as is often the case, and do not contribute to the understanding of the stories.[77] Usually these discussions bring no real meaning to my church but rather provoke it to close its mind to further discussion.[78] So for me methodol-

72. Cf. *The Westminster Confession of Faith* 1.1-10. This confession is still adopted more or less in its original form by most Korean conservative Presbyterian denominations as their standard of faith.

73. For the interrelation between the infallibility of the Scriptures and the historicity of biblical accounts, see Marshall, *Inspiration*, 59.

74. The conservative beliefs described above may not be characteristically Korean. But the denominations' strong expectation for the seminaries may surely be characteristically Korean.

75. I studied in London for four years and in Oxford for three years.

76. As mentioned above, in my view critical discussions of these issues are often too skeptical.

77. As a matter of fact, this tendency may not be characteristically Korean. Not a few exegetically-oriented western scholars show such a tendency.

78. The hermeneutical crisis caused by the distance between historical-critical re-

ogy is not an ideology; it is an instrument in search for the true reading of the Gospels. I give, therefore, more weight to those methodologies which are really effective and profitable for reading the Gospels in the Korean church today than to others.[79]

Reading Mark 11:12-25 from a Korean Perspective

The discussion above regarding the historicity and origin of Mark's pericope has not, in fact, provided any definite conclusions. Nor is it very helpful either for solving the problems of the pericope or for providing a meaningful understanding of it. Most discussions related to historicity and origin of our pericope so far are based on pure speculation and turn out to be unsatisfactory. In such a situation, in relation to our pericope, it does not seem to be sensible to focus our discussions on historicity and origin, especially considering the Korean church's tendency and concern. Therefore, in our discussions above, my main concern has naturally been not with the story's origin or historicity but with the function of the story as it stands within Mark's Gospel. Whatever the origin of the story, it has been my ultimate concern to recognize what Mark has done in his redactional scheme. In fact, this kind of concern is not particularly Korean. It is also expressed by some western scholars such as Telford.[80] But my concern may be much stronger than that of the western scholars.

Secondly, as regards the Synoptic problem, it is extremely difficult to determine which option of the two hypotheses (the two-source hypothesis and the Griesbach hypothesis) provides the more probable account of the problem. Both have persuasive arguments both for and against. Though the great majority of scholars favor the two-source hypothesis, in this pericope the Griesbach hypothesis provides a less complicated and therefore more readily understandable account of the problem. So I wonder whether any decision is truly helpful or even required for the proper reading of the pericope. As a matter of fact, it seems possible and realistic to leave the Syn-

---

search and the church's interests is well pointed out by U. Luz, *Matthew in History: Interpretation, Influence, and Effects* (Minneapolis: Fortress Press, 1994), 5-13.

79. Cf. Evans, *Mark,* lvii: "The true test of any hypothesis is its effectiveness." His point of effectiveness, of course, is not related to the Korean church's context but to the western biblical academic circle.

80. Telford, *Temple,* 156, 233, 237-38.

optic problem unsettled, but to confirm that the sandwich structure is the result of Mark's redaction, as even the majority of scholars favoring the two-source hypothesis admit. In this case Mark may have deliberately subordinated the chronological order to the effective communication of the theological significance. Conservative Christians might feel uncomfortable with this explanation, since for them such a view of Mark's redaction may seem to result in a chronological error. But they may need to be reminded that if "Mark was not at this point intending to write in strict accordance with chronology, it is perverse to label non-chronological order as an 'error.'"[81]

Thirdly, scholars who are interested in the story's function in Mark rather than in the story's origin before Mark tend to see the story's Old Testament background as a crucial key to the meaning of the story in Mark. As a matter of fact, to the twenty-first-century reader, whether western or Korean, these background studies have a very important place in reading Mark's Gospel through the eyes of first-century readers, since the Old Testament formed a central part of the daily environment of the first-century Christians. Our background studies have shown that two aspects are important. (1) Prophets in the Old Testament pronounce the destiny of Israel by means of their symbolic actions. In the light of this, Jesus' withering of the fig tree may well be considered a symbolic action pronouncing the coming doom of Israel. (2) The withering of the fig tree appears as an imagery in passages which depict Yahweh's coming judgment of Israel. Very often the reason given for God's wrath is the corruption of the Temple cultus and sacrificial system. Then Mark's readers, who would have been acquainted with the above symbolism, would readily have understood Jesus' cursing of the fig tree as a sign prefiguring the messianic judgment of Israel and particularly the destruction of the corrupt Temple. It seems then quite clear that the Old Testament background studies help today's readers to account for the problems raised by our pericope quite meaningfully, without unsatisfactory conjectures of a legend or of a historicized parable.

Fourthly, our concern with the story's function in Mark also invites us to consider the sandwich structure of our pericope, which is Mark's characteristic literary convention. The Temple story, as usual in the Markan sandwich stories, is expected to provide the key to the interpretation of the fig tree story and in fact does so. According to our investigations, the fig tree story by itself is already related to the corrupt state of the

81. France, "Chronological Aspects," 40.

98

Temple. Mark's sandwich structure then makes this inherent symbolic meaning much clearer, and confirms the results of our background studies. In the case of the present sandwich structure, however, it is often admitted that not only does the Temple story provide the interpretive key to the fig tree story but also vice versa. In that case, the Temple story needs to be understood in the light of the fig tree story. Jesus' behavior in the Temple then is not simply to be seen as the cleansing activity in terms of a removal of impurities and restoration to a true function, but is more to be seen as a symbolic action prefiguring the eschatological doom of the corrupt Temple. This character of the present sandwich structure links the two stories much closer, and brings the inherent symbolic meanings of the stories to the surface very efficiently. If Mark's sandwich structure is his own creation, as is generally agreed, what he is doing with this literary convention may be an attempt to help his (probably Gentile) readers to see this deeper, inherent but symbolic meaning of the story more easily and clearly. A proper recognition of this structure then may also help twenty-first-century Korean (i.e., Gentile) readers very effectively.

From our investigation above, the Old Testament background studies and the literary investigation regarding the sandwich structure have turned out to be the most reliable and profitable methodologies in reading the Markan fig tree story. This may be true not only for the present writer, who belongs to a conservative Korean Presbyterian church, but also for most western scholars. Discussions regarding the Synoptic problem have turned out to be necessary but inconclusive. I am comfortable in leaving the problem unsettled, though not a few traditionally critical western scholars may not be comfortable with such a state. Discussions regarding historicity and origin have turned out to be neither satisfactory nor profitable, and therefore, for the present writer, not necessary. This may be the case for some exegetically-oriented western scholars. For many traditionally critical western scholars, however, they may be still very important and crucial academic issues. These summary observations may answer our initial question, "What is a Korean reading of Mark 11:12-25?" and may illustrate how much it is different from western reading(s). A conservative Korean reading may not be far from an exegetically-orientated western one, though it uses traditional historical-critical methods with much more care and discernment. But it is distinctively different from a traditionally critical one, especially in its approaches to the historicity and origin of the story and also to the Synoptic problem.

Salvation Today: Reading Luke's Message for a Gentile Audience

ALLAN MARTENS

It is tantalizing to speculate what Theophilus, presumably the first reader of Luke's Gospel, may have thought about the document addressed to him (Luke 1:3). Was he pleased with the way Luke told his version of the story about Jesus, particularly since he already knew certain elements of the story (1:4) and must certainly have been aware, as Luke acknowledges, that there were many other accounts already in existence (*polloi epecheirēsan anataxasthai diēgēsin,* 1:1)? Was he suitably impressed with the research of Luke, who declares up front that he "has investigated everything carefully from the very first" (*parēkolouthēkoti anōthen pasin akribōs,* 1:3)? More importantly, was he actually confirmed in his faith, or at least in the "things about which he had been instructed," since this was clearly Luke's purpose for writing (*hina epignōs peri hōn katēchēthēs logōn tēn asphaleian,* 1:4)? Finally, we may wonder, what did Theophilus take from his reading of Luke to be the dominant message of the Gospel?

Since Luke's Gospel is alone among the four Gospels in mentioning a specific addressee, we may think that the identity of this addressee would help us to clarify questions that naturally arise about the character, message, and purpose of this literary work. But, alas, virtually nothing is known about Theophilus to help us with our questions. About all we can say, for sure, is that he is obviously the same individual that Luke addresses in his book of Acts (1:1). Clearly, then, Theophilus has a stake in Luke's two-volume work, which is often called Luke-Acts. Thus many scholars believe that Theophilus was Luke's patron, the one who commissioned Luke and paid for the publication and dissemination expenses connected with the Gospel. But whether Theophilus was even a Christian cannot be finally determined; all we can gather is that he had been instructed (*katēchēthēs*, 1:4) about certain matters concerning Jesus and the gospel. Some older commentators postulated that Theophilus may have been a Roman provincial governor, since Luke addresses him as "most excellent" *(kratiste)*, a term used for one of equestrian rank.[1] But the term does not indicate a precise position: it can be used as a courteous form of address to a highly placed person (cf. Acts 23:26; 24:3; 26:25), but it was also used conventionally as we might use the terms "dear" or "honored." More recently, the suggestion has been made that Theophilus was a Gentile believer who was experiencing doubt about his association with the new community, wondering whether he really belonged in this racially mixed and persecuted group.[2] This is certainly an appealing proposal, and one that fits the Lukan context, but it is still speculative.

Perhaps the only information that we can usefully take from Luke's reference to Theophilus is that he was most likely a Gentile and that, while Luke addresses him specifically, Luke has in mind a wider circle of readers, also Gentile. The Gospel, therefore, has a Gentile orientation. This is an important observation, especially if we compare this Gospel to Matthew's, which is clearly Jewish in orientation. Ironically, however, Luke's Gentile interests appear rather intermittently in the Gospel, becoming dominant only in Acts. We will take up this issue again at a later point.

Such minimal information about Theophilus and Luke's wider audience is of little real help in determining how best to read Luke's Gospel. Therefore modern readers, like ancient ones, are left with Luke's text by itself to determine the answers to the questions of the Gospel's character, message, and purpose. So today we must put ourselves in the position of Theophilus as first-hand readers of Luke's Gospel.

Despite our disadvantage of not being part of the first-century culture of Luke and Theophilus, we do have the advantage of possessing many literary-critical methods that have served to sharpen our analysis of a number of features of Luke's Gospel. Scholars have become aware of the interaction that occurs between the three constituent aspects of literary

---

1. See N. Geldenhuys, *Commentary on the Gospel of Luke*, NICNT (Grand Rapids: Eerdmans, 1951), 52-53.

2. See D. Bock, "Luke, Gospel of," in *Dictionary of Jesus and the Gospels*, ed. J. B. Green and S. McKnight (Downers Grove: InterVarsity, 1992), 498.

theory, and hence of the reading process, namely, the author, the reader, and the text. Although hard and fast lines cannot be drawn between literary-critical methods — for all must take account of the three aspects just mentioned — it is noteworthy that every method tends to focus on *one* of these three aspects. Thus the historical-critical method in general, and redaction criticism in particular, have been author-centered, with the latter method focusing on the author's intention in his selection, adaptation, and theological shaping of the traditions he has received. Reader-centered methods are those that focus on the text as constructed to achieve a particular effect on the reader. Rhetorical criticism, in its classical form as referring to "persuasive argumentation," and reader-response criticism belong to a reader-centered approach. And narrative criticism, which emphasizes the implied author and implied reader (both of which are constructs of the text itself) and analyzes how the narrative is related, is a text-centered approach. All of these methods, and others not specifically mentioned, have helped to answer the very questions that we began with above, as we pondered the response of Theophilus to Luke's Gospel.[3]

Having stated the value of literary methods for interpretation and having categorized some of these methods in general terms, it must be stated that this chapter will not be using any particular method to help us understand Luke's Gospel. Our purpose here is much more general. Uninitiated readers of Luke's Gospel and, I believe, even those more familiar with its contents want to have a general framework for understanding the Gospel. They want to know the essential message of the Gospel as it can be demonstrated by its main theme, which in turn can be seen to be supported by other themes and sub-themes. In what follows, therefore, I wish to trace out Luke's overall message, showing how a number of key themes or motifs that appear at various points in Luke's story are woven into the predominant theme.

What, then, is Luke's central theme or overall message?[4] In a phrase,

---

3. For a survey of critical methods see C. Tuckett, *Reading the New Testament: Methods of Interpretation* (London: SPCK, 1987), and J. B. Green, ed., *Hearing the New Testament: Strategies for Interpretation* (Grand Rapids: Eerdmans, 1995).

4. The question is integrally related to Luke's intention for writing. D. L. Bock follows R. Maddox in providing some suggested intentions:

(1) to explain why Jesus had not returned (Conzelmann), (2) to provide a defense brief for Christianity (Easton, Haenchen), (3) to defend Paul before Rome (Matill),

it is simply "salvation in Jesus Christ."[5] Put more expansively, Luke's purpose in writing was to present the gospel of salvation, now available in Jesus Christ, in order to confirm the faith of his readers (Theophilus in particular) and to lead to faith those interested in Christianity.[6] One may immediately respond that such a purpose and theme are not unique to Luke among the Evangelists. This is true, but a linguistic analysis of Luke shows that salvation terminology is both distinctive and central to Luke, whereas that is not the case for Matthew and Mark.

The Language and Theology of Salvation in Luke

What is perhaps most striking in this regard is that Luke explicitly uses the title "Savior" *(sōtēr)* twice in his Gospel, once for God (1:47) and once for Jesus (2:11), whereas this term is not found at all in Matthew or Mark.[7] Similarly, whereas Luke uses the word "salvation" *(sōtēria* and *sōtērion)* six times in his Gospel and seven times in Acts, this word is absent from Matthew and Mark.[8] Given these facts, the reader is now better able to appreciate the significance of the theme of salvation in the following passages. Zechariah declares in the Benedictus: "Blessed be the Lord, the God of Israel, for he has visited *(epeskepsato)* and redeemed *(epoiēsen lytrōsin)* his

---

(4) to defend Paul before the community (Schneckenberger, Jervell), (5) to combat gnosticism (Talbert), (6) to evangelize (O'Neill), (7) to confirm the Word and the message of salvation (van Unnik, Marshall, O'Toole), (8) to present a theodicy of God's faithfulness (Tiede), (9) to provide sociological legitimation of full fellowship for Gentiles and a defense of the new community (Esler).

See Bock, "Luke, Gospel of," 498. A survey of the above views appears in R. P. Martin, *New Testament Foundations*, rev. ed. (Grand Rapids: Eerdmans, 1986), 1:246-50.

5. Here we follow the emphasis of I. H. Marshall, *Luke: Historian and Theologian* (Grand Rapids: Zondervan, 1970), 84ff. More recently see his "'Israel' and the Story of Salvation," in *Jesus and the Heritage of Israel: Luke's Narrative Claim upon Israel's Legacy*, ed. D. P. Moessner (Harrisburg: Trinity, 1999), 340-57.

6. Given that all of the New Testament documents are "church books," written for the community of believers, it may be questioned whether any of them has a truly evangelistic purpose. Yet the notion of "confirming faith in a person" is not totally distinct from evangelism if we think of interested nonbelievers reading a Gospel.

7. The title is also used twice of Jesus in Acts 5:31; 13:23.

8. *Sōtēria:* Luke 1:69, 71, 77; 19:9; Acts 4:12; 7:25; 13:26, 47; 16:17; 27:34; *sōtērion:* Luke 2:30; 3:6; Acts 28:28.

people. He has raised up a horn of salvation *(keras sōtērias)* for us in the house of his servant David, . . . salvation *(sōtērian)* from our enemies. . . . And you, child, will be called the prophet of the Most High; for you will go before the Lord to prepare his ways, to give knowledge of salvation *(sōtērias)* to his people by the forgiveness of their sins" (1:68-71, 76-77). And the angel's message to the shepherds about a newborn Savior rings out in bold relief: "I bring you good news of great joy that will be for all the people: Today is born to you in the city of David a Savior *(sōtēr),* who is Christ the Lord" (2:10-11). As the aged and devout Simeon holds the infant Jesus in his arms he praises God, saying, "My eyes have seen your salvation *(sōtērion),* which you have prepared in the sight of all peoples, a light for revelation to the Gentiles and for glory to your people Israel" (2:30-32). We may also mention the proclamation of John the Baptist, who quotes Isa 40:3-5 as representing his own ministry as the forerunner of the coming Messiah: "The voice of one crying out in the wilderness: 'Prepare the way of the Lord, make his paths straight. Every valley shall be filled, and every mountain and hill shall be made low, and the crooked shall be made straight and the rough ways made smooth; and all flesh shall see the salvation *(sōtērion)* of God'" (3:4-6). Finally, in the paradigmatic story about Zacchaeus's encounter with Jesus, we see Jesus reaching out to a "sinner," and on Zacchaeus's repentance, we read these words that encapsulate Jesus' mission: "'Today salvation *(sōtēria)* has come to this house. . . . For the Son of Man came to seek out and to save *(sōsai)* the lost'" (19:9-10).

Having seen Luke's distinctive use of the nouns "Savior" and "salvation," we may now inquire concerning his use of the verb "save" *(sōzō).* Here we can say that Luke is not unique among the Synoptics, nor does he use the verb proportionately more often than Matthew or Mark.[9] In fact, Luke takes over a number of instances of the verb from his Markan source.[10] A few times he adds the verb to Mark's account, seemingly to intensify or highlight some aspect of salvation.[11] And in five cases Luke includes the verb in material that is uniquely his own.[12] The verb is sometimes used with the common

---

9. The verb *sōzō* appears seventeen times in Luke (6:9; 7:50; 8:12, 36, 48, 50; 9:24 (twice); 13:23; 17:19; 18:26, 42; 19:10; 23:35 (twice), 37, 39), thirteen times in Acts, fifteen in Matthew, and fourteen in Mark.

10. See Luke 6:9/Mark 3:4; Luke 8:48/Mark 5:34; Luke 9:24 (twice)/Mark 8:35 (twice); Luke 18:26/Mark 10:26; Luke 18:42/Mark 10:52; Luke 23:35 (twice)/Mark 15:31 (twice).

11. See Luke 8:12, 36, 50; 23:37.

12. See Luke 7:50; 13:23; 17:19; 19:10; 23:39.

meaning "deliver from danger." Thus Jesus can ask, "Is it lawful to save life or destroy it?" (Luke 6:9) or can state, "Those who want to save their life will lose it, and those who lose their life for my sake will save it" (Luke 9:24). Often the verb is used with the meaning "heal," so that Jesus can say to someone he has just healed, "Your faith has saved you" (Luke 8:48; 17:19; 18:42).

But Luke also uses the verb in a more spiritual sense that stands out by comparison with Matthew and Mark. Luke connects Jesus' saving work directly with forgiveness, belief, and repentance. So when Jesus forgives the sinful woman in the Pharisee's house, he says to her, "Your faith has saved you; go in peace" (Luke 7:47-50). In recounting Jesus' interpretation of the parable of the sower, especially in regard to the seed on the path that represents the word taken from the hearts of people by the devil, Luke adds the poignant comment by way of explanation, "so that they may not believe and be saved" (Luke 8:12). And when Zacchaeus repents by committing himself to repay what he has gained by fraud, Jesus "saves" him (Luke 19:8-10).

It is not that Matthew and Mark have no message of salvation or do not conceive of Jesus' activity as being salvific. But they use other terms to describe Jesus' work and his call on people's lives. Thus the central theme of Jesus' proclamation in Mark is, "The time is fulfilled and the kingdom of God has come near. Repent and believe in the good news" (Mark 1:15; cf. Matt 4:17; omitted in Luke 4:15). And both Mark and Matthew focus on the death of Jesus on the cross as being the primary saving event. In Mark especially, the cross is the event where Jesus' identity as Son of God and where his messianic mission are both finally clarified. Jesus' mission to go to the cross is a matter of serving others by giving his life as "a ransom for many" (Mark 10:45; cf. Matt 20:28). Matthew adds two elements to this picture. First, in his infancy narrative an angel reveals to Joseph that Jesus "will save his people from their sins" (1:21). The future reference to "saving" is fulfilled only at the cross. Second, it is only at the cross — where Jesus sheds his blood — that forgiveness of sins is accomplished (26:28; cf. Mark 1:4 with Matt 3:1-4). Moreover, for both Matthew and Mark, it is the cross that also serves as the paradigm for the call to discipleship: "If any want to become my followers, let them deny themselves and take up their cross and follow me" (Mark 8:34; Matt 16:24). By contrast, Luke uses explicit salvation terminology, he broadens the concept and time-frame of salvation as compared to the other Synoptists, and he makes this theme central to his theological presentation.

But Luke's frame of reference for salvation goes even beyond what we already noted. The whole life of Jesus, in fact, is portrayed by Luke as saving activity. As we have already seen, Jesus' mission is "to seek out and to save the lost" (19:10), so that he continuously brings salvation to those whom he encounters. Repentance (5:32; 11:32; 13:1-5; 15:7, 10, 17-21) and forgiveness (5:20-26; 7:47-50) are particularly associated with the saving activity of Jesus, being in fact grounded in the Scriptures as part of messianic prophecy (24:46-47). And so in Jesus' saving activity is realized the hope of Zechariah, as expressed for his son John: "to give his people the knowledge of salvation through the forgiveness of their sins" (1:77). But Jesus "saves others" (the phrase used by mockers as Jesus hangs on the cross, 23:35) in a multitude of ways. He accepts "sinners," as symbolized frequently by his joining them in table fellowship (5:27-32; 7:36-50; 14:15-24; 15:1-2; 19:1-10). In light of this portrayal, even Jesus' healing activity, whether for the sick (5:17, 31; 6:18-19; 7:1-10), the blind (18:35-43), the lepers (17:11-19), or the handicapped (5:18-26; 6:6-10; 13:10-17), is saving activity in a spiritual sense that goes beyond the linguistic sense already noted. Jesus also feeds the hungry (9:10-17), exorcises the demon-possessed (4:33-37, 40-41; 8:2, 26-39; 9:37-43), and associates in various ways with the "poor" or marginalized in society: tax collectors (5:27-32; 19:1-10; cf. 18:9-14), Samaritans (17:16, 18; cf. 10:25-37), Gentiles (7:1-10), children (18:15-17), widows (7:11-17; cf. 18:1-8; 21:1-4), and women in general (7:36-50; 8:40-56). In all of these activities Jesus is functioning as the "Savior" announced by the angel of the Lord (2:11)

Salvation, for Luke, therefore, is essentially *liberation:* Jesus saves people by liberating them from whatever constrains them or hinders their full enjoyment of the blessings of God. A good example of this appears in the story of Jesus healing a crippled woman (Luke 13:10-17). Jesus simply calls her forward and says, "Woman, you are set free *(apolelysai)* from your infirmity." When the synagogue ruler objects to Jesus' healing on a Sabbath, Jesus reiterates the theme of liberation: "Ought not this woman, a daughter of Abraham whom Satan bound for eighteen long years, be set free *(lythēnai)* from this bondage on the Sabbath day?" This idea of salvation as liberation or release is set forth in a remarkable way by Luke at the very beginning of Jesus' ministry as recorded in the "Nazareth pericope" of Luke 4:16-30. Overwhelmingly scholars have judged that Jesus' sermon, given in his hometown synagogue, is programmatic for Luke's understanding of Jesus' mission.[13] Je-

---

13. See J. B. Green, *The Theology of the Gospel of Luke* (Cambridge: Cambridge University Press, 1995), 76-77, for a brief discussion on the importance of this pericope.

sus here quotes Isa 61:1-2 and 58:6 and, applying them to his own mission ("Today this scripture has been fulfilled in your hearing"), claims that he has come "to preach good news to the poor, to proclaim release *(aphesin)* to the captives, and to let the oppressed go free." And so as Luke narrates his story of Jesus, he depicts Jesus as continuously saving or releasing all kinds of people from various situations. Luke makes no distinctions among physical, spiritual, or social aspects of salvation. All who encounter Jesus can receive freely the grace of God.

Besides the "save, salvation" word group, Luke also uses another word group to portray the concept of salvation. Here we encounter the words "redeem" and "redemption." We have already noted Zechariah's song in which he praises God because he has "visited *(epeskepsato)* and made redemption *(epoiēsen lytrōsin)* for his people" (1:68). In the context, redemption means the same thing as salvation, that is, deliverance from enemies. More broadly, since "redemption" in the New Testament connotes the general idea of God's liberation or deliverance, without any necessary idea of the payment of a price, redemption becomes virtually the same as "salvation," which also refers to rescue or deliverance from either physical or spiritual bondage.[14] Luke uses "redemption" once again in 2:38, where, in parallel with Simeon's reference to Israel's salvation (2:29-32), the prophetess Anna speaks about the "redemption *(lytrōsin)* of Jerusalem." Significantly, both of these stories are directly related to the appearance of the child Jesus, whom Simeon and Anna both see in the Temple. Thus the salvation of Israel that Simeon refers to and the redemption of Jerusalem that Anna speaks of are one and the same and are focused in Jesus. In Luke 21:28 there is a further reference to redemption *(apolytrōsis),* but here the eschatological deliverance is in view. Finally, an interesting occurrence of the verb "redeem" appears in the story of Jesus speaking to two disciples on the road to Emmaus. The disciples, disappointed about the events surrounding Jesus' death and not yet knowing about his resurrection, say wistfully about Jesus, "But we had hoped that he was the one coming to redeem *(lytrousthai)* Israel" (24:21). Here we find the same hope expressed by Simeon and Anna, though now more explicitly linked to Jesus. Jesus, of course, did redeem or save Israel, though not according to these disciples' nationalistic expectations. Our point in

---

14. See F. Büchsel, "λύτρον, κτλ.," *TDNT* IV.340-56, especially 351: "λύτρωσις is virtually the same as σωτηρία."

linguistic terms, however, is simply that the usage of redemption language reinforces Luke's theology of salvation rather than distinguishes one idea from another.

Salvation in Relation to the Death of Jesus

At this point the modern-day reader may begin to wonder, What about the death of Jesus on the cross? Does Luke not say anything about the saving significance of Jesus' death? It is well known among students of Luke that the Evangelist does not very clearly give salvific importance to the cross. Luke attaches God's gift of salvation to Jesus' birth (Luke 2:11), to his life and ministry (19:9-10), and to his exaltation (Acts 5:31), but never to his death.

Various explanations have been given for this phenomenon.[15] Some believe that Luke is hostile to a soteriological meaning in Jesus' death and so eliminates the traditions that evidence this. Thus, for example, Luke omits the "ransom saying" of Mark 10:45. The only two traditional formulations that have escaped Luke's vigilance are the long text of the institution of the Lord's Supper ("given *for you*. . . . This cup that is poured out *for you* is the new covenant in my blood," Luke 22:19b-20), if this is authentic, and Acts 20:28, "shepherd the church of God that he obtained with the blood of his own Son" (NRSV). Others hold that Luke was not averse to the idea of ransom/expiation *(lytron)* in Mark 10:45 as the reason for omitting this verse. Accordingly, there is nothing in the Markan saying that does not suit the Lukan soteriology. Luke, in fact, uses the cognate terms "redeem," "redemption," and "redeemer" (see Luke 1:68; 2:38; 24:21; Acts 7:35). But Luke's emphasis is on Jesus' *service* (cf. Luke 22:27, replacing Mark 10:45), which evokes the Suffering Servant of Isaiah 53. And since Luke does cite Isa 53:7-8 in Acts 8:32-33, he can be seen to add salvific import to the death of the Servant Jesus in Luke 22:27, even though the Isaiah passage is not explicit. Yet others explain the rarity of soteriological meaning attached to Jesus' death by appealing to the issue of literary genres: the two allusions to the salvific value of the cross (Luke 22:19-20; Acts 20:28)

---

15. See especially F. Bovon, *Luke the Theologian: Thirty-Three Years of Research (1950-83)*, trans. K. McKinney (Allison Park: Pickwick, 1987), 164-70; M. A. Powell, *What Are They Saying about Luke?* (New York: Paulist, 1989), 68-71.

appear in texts where believers are addressed. So Luke is not hostile to sacrificial redemption. By contrast, the sermons of Acts do not mention this mystery because they are destined for the unconverted. None of these interpretations, however, is particularly cogent.

Many interpreters, therefore, while noting the difficulties in Luke's presentation, think that Luke wanted to portray Jesus' death as that of an innocent martyr and so emphasizes the categories of service and suffering, rather than salvation. The following four Lukan features are particularly relevant: In the first place, Luke repeatedly includes references to Jesus' innocence (of the accusation of sedition, Luke 23:2, 5, 14) by Pilate (23:4, 14, 22), Herod (23:15), one of the crucified thieves (23:41), and the centurion at the cross (23:47). The last reference is significant, for it declares Jesus to be a "righteous man" *(dikaios)*. While the word can mean simply "innocent," it probably suggests the deeper sense of "righteous." For Jesus at times is called the "Righteous One" in the Lukan writings (Acts 3:14; 7:52; 22:14), and the centurion's glorifying of God would seem to indicate more than merely praise for Jesus' innocence. In all of Jesus' suffering, therefore, he is portrayed as a man of integrity to the end, a righteous sufferer.

Second, several elements in Luke's Passion story have parallels with the story of Stephen's martyrdom in Acts 7. Both Jesus and Stephen refer to the Son of Man at the right hand of God (Luke 22:69; Acts 7:56), both ask God to forgive their oppressors (Luke 23:34; Acts 7:60), and both, with their dying breaths, commit their spirits to another (Luke 23:46; Acts 7:59).

Third, in connection with Jesus' last cry of committal to his Father (Luke 23:46), which is quite different from the cry of dereliction in Mark 15:34 and is an echo of Ps 31:5, Luke imparts a greater serenity to Jesus' last moments. Jesus dies as a martyr, with more composure than in Mark, with confidence of entering paradise, and even able to converse calmly with two criminals beside him.

Fourth, Jesus in his last hours is depicted as showing magnanimous love for humanity, including his oppressors. Thus he rebukes the violence of his disciples, healing the cut-off ear of the high priest's servant (22:51), he prays for his persecutors (23:34, at least in some manuscripts), and he offers salvation to the repentant thief beside him (23:43).

All of these features have something in common with Jewish stories of martyrdom as seen in such texts as Dan 3:25; *3 Maccabees* 5:6ff.; 6:1ff.; *4 Maccabees* 17:11-16; *Martyrdom of Isaiah* 4:11–5:14; Josephus, *Antiquities*

17.6.4 (167). The implication, of course, is that Jesus' death is meant by Luke to be seen as exemplary and inspirational, rather than soteriological.

Yet the question must be asked, Did Luke intend such a picture of righteous martyrdom to be divorced from a soteriological meaning to Jesus' death? Jesus is, after all, no ordinary martyr, but the righteous Son of God. More recent interpreters have attempted to place Luke's portrayal of Jesus' death within the broader compass of Lukan christology. Robert Karris argues that in the Judaism of the first century a martyr's death could be considered redemptive.[16] According to Luke, God alone saves, but he uses the death of the innocent Jesus to do so. And Jesus' faithfulness in death serves as a model to awaken faith in others. Jerome Neyrey makes the case that Jesus' faithfulness is more than just a model of trust and that Luke ascribes soteriological significance to Jesus' death through an implicit presentation of Jesus as the "new Adam" who abrogates the effects of Adam's sin and initiates a new creation.[17] These views, however, can be critiqued as stretching a point too far.

A better conclusion to the enigma of the meaning of Jesus' death in Luke is that Luke views salvation as present in the whole Christ-event, with Jesus' death being an essential aspect of that event. Jesus' death is a saving event, but must be seen alongside many other saving events. In the first place, Luke, more than the other Evangelists, emphasizes the necessity of Jesus' suffering and death (9:22; 13:33; 17:25; 22:37; 24:7, 26-27, 44, 46-47), so that the cross must be seen as part of God's plan of salvation. Second, though Luke highlights in Acts the resurrection as the critical event in salvation, Jesus' death cannot be separated from the resurrection in the redemptive work of God. We may not simply dismiss Luke's record of Paul's words in Acts 20:28 that the church was "purchased" *(periepoiēsato)* with the blood of Jesus. In his Gospel, Luke depicts the whole Christ-event as that which brings salvation. Jesus' birth (2:11, 30), his life of service (19:9-10; 22:27), and his suffering and death "for you" (22:19, 20) together make up the divine plan of salvation. Luke 24:46-47 is a remarkable text explaining how salvation is linked to the Passion, death, and resurrection of Jesus and how all of this is grounded in the plan of God as revealed in the Scrip-

16. R. Karris, *Luke, Artist and Theologian: Luke's Passion Account as Literature* (New York: Paulist, 1985).

17. J. Neyrey, *The Passion According to Luke: A Redaction Study of Luke's Soteriology* (New York: Paulist, 1985).

tures: "[Jesus] told them, 'This is what is written: The Christ will suffer and rise from the dead on the third day, and repentance and forgiveness of sins will be preached in his name to all nations, beginning at Jerusalem.'"

Third, though Jesus' death is not so much depicted in terms of sacrifice, redemption, or the expiation of sin, but primarily in exemplary fashion as the culmination of Jesus' unconditional obedience to God, his death still has atoning effects. The substitution of Jesus for Barabbas illustrates the idea that Jesus took the place of the sinner, the innocent for the guilty (23:18-25). Further atoning effects are seen in Jesus' forgiveness of those who crucified him (23:34), in his acceptance of and promise of paradise to the penitent criminal beside him (23:43), in his impact on the centurion as revealed in his statement, "Surely this was a righteous man" (23:47), and by the repentance of the witnesses at the cross who "beat their breasts and went away" (23:48). All of these atoning effects can be seen in Jesus' ministry of bringing salvation, and here we see that they continue through Jesus' Passion until the very point of his death. In the words of John T. Carroll and Joel B. Green, "It is highly ironic that at the very moment when Jesus' incapacity to 'save' makes him the target of taunts by Jewish leaders, soldiers, and one of the criminals, he is still pursuing the work of saving others."[18]

Jesus' Mission as Determined by God's Plan of Salvation

We have necessarily focused first on *Jesus* as the bringer of God's salvation. We must now give attention to the second part of that phrase, namely, *God's salvation*. In Luke, salvation is "of God" (3:6; 18:26-27; cf. Acts 28:28) and the saving activity of Jesus is presented as the outworking of the master plan of God to initiate and accomplish salvation for all people. Ultimately it is God's design that "all flesh shall see the salvation of God" (3:6).

It is highly significant that Luke begins his prologue with a reference to "the events that have been fulfilled among us" (*tōn peplērophorēmenōn en hymin pragmatōn*, 1:1). The perfect passive participle "fulfilled" is the language of God in action, whose purpose has been accomplished but demonstrates ongoing effects. Although Jesus is not mentioned in Luke's prologue, the Gospel context makes it clear that God's purpose revolves

18. J. T. Carroll and J. B. Green, *The Death of Jesus in Early Christianity* (Peabody: Hendrickson, 1995), 72.

around and has been fulfilled in his agent and Son Jesus. According to Luke, God's purpose has a completed aspect in the mission of Jesus from his birth to his ascension, which forms the material of Luke's Gospel, but God's purpose has ongoing results, spilling over into the activity of Jesus' followers, as recorded in Acts (see 1:1: "all that Jesus *began* to do and to teach"). Yet by the end of Acts, God's purpose still had not reached its consummation (see 28:31: Paul is still "proclaiming the kingdom of God and teaching about the Lord Jesus Christ with all boldness and *without hindrance*"). Nor has God's purpose even yet come to completion today. But for now we must focus on the divine plan as Luke depicts it first and foremost in his Gospel.

If Luke refers to events that "have been fulfilled," he must also have had an eye on the promises of God, now seen as fulfilled. Indeed, this is the case. Unlike Matthew, Luke rarely uses fulfillment language for Jesus' ministry.[19] Yet in passages narrating the beginning and end of Jesus' ministry Luke does just this. In 4:21 in the "Nazareth pericope" Jesus announces that the inception of his own ministry "fulfills" *(peplērōtai)* Isa 61:1-2. And following Jesus' resurrection, in 24:44, he tells his disciples, "Everything must be fulfilled *(dei plērōthēnai)* that is written about me in the Law of Moses, the Prophets, and the Psalms." So the fulfillment in Jesus is part of the ancient plan of God enunciated in the Old Testament.

Besides these explicit fulfillment texts, however, Luke makes numerous references or allusions to the Old Testament to show God's plan.[20] We will mention only two of these by way of example. First, just as Luke cites Scripture (Isa 61:1-2) at the inauguration of Jesus' ministry, he does the same for the beginning of John's ministry (3:4-6), citing another Isaianic passage (Isa 40:3-5). Second, and also in connection with John and Jesus, Luke imbues the whole of his infancy narrative with a scriptural "feel."

---

19. The verb *plēroō*, used in the sense of fulfillment — especially of the Scriptures, but also as referring to the person of Jesus or the events surrounding Jesus' ministry — appears in Mark twice (1:15; 14:49) and in Matthew fourteen times (1:22; 2:15, 17, 23; 3:15; 4:14; 5:17; 8:17; 12:17; 13:35; 21:4; 26:54, 56; 27:9). Luke uses *plēroō* nine times, but only twice in the sense of fulfillment of the Scriptures (4:21; 24:44). But he also uses *teleō* in this sense in 18:31; 22:37.

20. See M. Rese, *Alttestamentliche Motive in der Christologie des Lukas* (Gütersloh: Gütersloher Verlagshaus Gerd Mohn, 1969); D. Bock, *Proclamation from Prophecy and Pattern: Lucan Old Testament Christology* (Sheffield: JSOT Press, 1987); J. T. Squires, *The Plan of God in Luke-Acts* (Cambridge: Cambridge University Press, 1993); Green, *Theology of the Gospel of Luke*, 24-28.

Luke writes the story in septuagintal style, which serves to ground the ful-fillment of John and Jesus in the divine plan of Israel's Scriptures.

Luke's interest in God's plan is to be noted further in a number of ex-pressive words that all have to do with the will of God. Particularly note-worthy are "purpose" *(boulē)*, "will" *(thelēma)*, and "it is necessary" *(dei)*. The purpose of God is explicitly highlighted more often in Acts than in the Gospel. For example, Peter declares in his Pentecost sermon that Jesus was handed over to the Israelites "according to the definite plan *(boulē)* and foreknowledge of God" (2:23; cf. also 4:28; 13:36; 20:27). But in one notable passage in the Gospel, in which the author includes what seems to be a parenthetical aside, Luke says, "But by refusing to be baptized by [John], the Pharisees and the lawyers rejected God's purpose *(boulē)* for them-selves" (7:30). Thus the purpose or plan of God may be opposed and re-jected. Such does not occur, of course, with Jesus, whom Luke portrays as the obedient Son throughout his life and in his death. Just before his public ministry begins, Jesus demonstrates his fidelity to God's plan by resisting the temptations of his chief opponent, the devil (4:1-13). At the other end of his ministry when Jesus faces his greatest trial, that of death on a cross, Jesus prays to God, "Father, if you are willing *(ei boulei)*, remove this cup from me; yet not my will *(thelēma)* but yours be done" (22:42).

A prominent feature of Luke's Gospel is the frequent use of "it is nec-essary," often translated as "must" *(dei)*. Forty of the one hundred one uses of this word in the New Testament appear in Luke-Acts.[21] Jesus says that he *must* be in his Father's house (Luke 2:49). He *must* proclaim the good news of the kingdom (4:43). He *must* free the crippled woman tormented by Sa-tan (13:16). He *must* stay at the house of Zacchaeus (19:5). He *must* go to Je-rusalem to suffer, be rejected, and be killed (9:22; 13:33; 17:25; cf. 24:7, 26; Acts 17:3). He *must* fulfill the Scriptures (22:37; 24:44). All these references portray the divine necessity that Jesus feels is laid upon him in fulfilling the plan of God.

From a narrative-critical approach it would be interesting to investi-gate how other characters in Luke's story of Jesus advance or hinder the working out of God's plan. Luke's story includes angels and demons, Satan and the Holy Spirit, Jewish leaders and Gentile individuals, and many more "actors," rich and poor, young and old, righteous and unrighteous. Space does not permit an investigation in these terms. Suffice it to say that God's

---

21. So D. Bock, "Luke, Gospel of," 503. The Gospel has eighteen uses of *dei*.

purpose has been accomplished in Jesus (1:1), despite hostility, and that God's purpose continues to be realized in the story of the church, which now proclaims the message of salvation in the name of Jesus (Acts 4:12).

Now we must ask whether Luke does anything more than connect in thematic terms Jesus' saving mission to God's plan. In other words, does Luke's Gospel exhibit anything structurally to demonstrate how Jesus' mission actually fulfills the divine plan?

The Structure of Luke's Gospel in Relation to Jesus' Saving Mission

Luke writes his Gospel using a geographical progression to tell the story of Jesus and the outworking of God's plan of salvation. The basic outline, moving from Galilee to Jerusalem, follows Mark, but Luke gives far greater emphasis to Jerusalem. Interestingly, the Gospel story begins and ends in Jerusalem, and in particular, in the Temple (see 1:9 and 24:52-53). What is most revealing is that Jesus' resurrection appearances all take place in and around Jerusalem, and Jesus commands his disciples not to leave the city until a later time (24:49). By contrast, Mark refers to post-resurrection reunions that will take place only in Galilee (Mark 14:28; 16:7). And Matthew recounts that the eleven disciples, in fact, went to Galilee where Jesus commissioned them on a mountain (Matt 28:16-20).

In the opening chapters, Luke relates incidents occurring in Jerusalem. Ch. 2 tells of two visits by Jesus to Jerusalem (2:22-40, 42-52), with an intervening notation that Jesus' parents traveled annually from Nazareth to Jerusalem for Passover (2:41). Following Jesus' baptism (3:21-23) and temptation (4:1-13), which also take place around Jerusalem, Jesus goes to Galilee for the first part of his ministry (4:14–9:50). Then, in the middle of the Gospel, Luke devotes ten chapters to the "Travel Narrative" (9:51–19:27), which presents Jesus slowly but resolutely making his way to Jerusalem where he will suffer rejection and death. The last section concerns Jesus' final ministry, Passion, and resurrection appearances, which all occur in and around Jerusalem (19:28–24:53).

Of primary interest for us is the Lukan Travel Narrative. This major section of Luke seems to have no obvious structure, but Luke has evidently drawn material from the Q and L traditions, placing them loosely into an order as he has seen fit. Nearly half of the material here is uniquely Lukan, and there is a high concentration of teaching, especially in parables. There are seventeen parables, fifteen of which are unique to Luke. The journey to Jerusalem does not go forward in a straight line, for Jesus can be near Jerusalem in 10:38-42 but farther north in 17:11, before finally approaching Jericho (18:35; 19:1) and arriving in Jerusalem (19:28). Clearly Luke is not concerned to recount a historical and chronological account at this point. His purpose is to emphasize that Jesus is moving toward his goal. Thus Luke makes a point of repeatedly reminding his readers that Jesus is heading toward the city of destiny, Jerusalem (9:51, 53; 13:22, 32-33; 17:11; 18:31; 19:11).[22]

For Luke the journey to Jerusalem takes place as part of the necessity of God's plan. It has a salvation-historical function. Nowhere is this clearer than in Jesus' words after he has been warned that Herod wants to kill him: "Go tell that fox for me, 'Listen, I am casting out demons and performing cures today and tomorrow, and on the third day I finish my work. Yet today, tomorrow, and the next day I must be on my way, because it is impossible for a prophet to be killed outside of Jerusalem'" (13:32-33). From these words we may note that although Jesus performs saving acts like exorcisms and healings throughout his ministry, the goal of his mission will be accomplished in Jerusalem. If we ask why it has to be Jerusalem, the answer must be that Jesus must recapitulate Israel's history, in which the prophets all died at Jerusalem.[23] This is not to deny that Jesus' journey to Jerusalem is traditional, for Luke certainly found it in Mark. But Luke infuses an additional significance to the tradition: Jerusalem is the salvation-historical center of God's plan.[24] Jerusalem, with its Temple, is the center of Israel's life

22. Marshall (*Luke: Historian and Theologian,* 152-53) states that it is extraordinarily difficult to trace clearly the themes of the travel narrative, but that the main theme is the teaching of Jesus, which alternates between instruction to the disciples and discussion with opponents. Yet, ironically, despite the repeated references to going to Jerusalem *to suffer and be rejected,* Jesus' teaching in this section is not controlled by that motif.

23. The background to this idea is known as the "deuteronomistic view of Israel's history." It perceived Israel's history as cyclical and as including the following elements: Israel was persistently disobedient, God sent prophets who were always rejected, God punished Israel, a new call for repentance was or will be issued, Israel was or will be restored if she repents, and God judged or will judge Israel's enemies. See O. Steck, *Israel und das gewaltsame Geschick der Propheten* (Neukirchen-Vluyn: Neukirchener Verlag, 1967); A. D. Jacobson, *The First Gospel: An Introduction to Q* (Sonoma: Polebridge, 1992), 72-73.

24. This statement holds true for Luke's story in Acts as well. Jerusalem is the starting point for the church's mission (1:8), it is the place where the churchwide council is held (15:1-35), and it is the city Paul visits after each "missionary journey" (15:2-4; 18:22; 21:17).

and worship (2:22, 38, 41; 4:9; 13:33). Hence, by casting Jesus' ministry in the form of a journey to Jerusalem, Luke deftly directs attention to the theme that Jesus will offer and accomplish his saving mission at the heart of the nation in accordance with the plan of God.[25]

But what will happen in Jerusalem? Will Israel accept Jesus Messiah and the salvation he brings? Will God's plan in Jesus be accomplished or will it be rejected? We get more than a hint of the outcome at the very point that Jesus enters Jerusalem, weeps over the city, and declares,

> If you, even you, had only recognized on this day the things that make for peace! But now they are hidden from your eyes. Indeed, the days will come upon you, when your enemies will set up ramparts around you and surround you, and hem you in on every side. They will crush you to the ground, you and your children within you, and they will not leave within you one stone upon another; because you did not recognize the time of your visitation from God (19:42-44).

Jews and Gentiles in God's Plan of Salvation

The ominous note of rejection, sounded in Jesus' lament over Jerusalem, does not take long to be realized, for in the very next scene Luke relates that after Jesus had cleared the Temple "the chief priests, the scribes, and the leaders of the people kept looking for a way to kill him" (19:47). The reader cannot help but ponder the question, If Jesus was fulfilling the plan of God, why was he opposed by the leaders of God's own people?

This in turn raises the issue of the place of Israel in the plan of God, according to Luke. The corollary question is, What does this mean for the Gentiles? Scholars are agreed that Luke's readers were uncertain as to how Gentile Christianity related to Judaism and that Luke wrote his Gospel, in part, to answer this question. And this is where the Gentile orientation of the Gospel shows itself most significantly. On this particular issue, however, Luke's views are expressed more clearly in Acts, and later on we will have to examine a number of passages there as well. But for now we must recount Luke's portrayal of the Jewish people in his Gospel.

25. J. D. Kingsbury, *Jesus Christ in Matthew, Mark, and Luke* (Philadelphia: Fortress, 1981), 96-97.

The Jewish People in Luke

To begin, we may note that Luke shows the gospel of salvation being rooted in Jewish piety. The first two chapters picture the best of Israel in the persons of Zechariah, Elizabeth, Mary, Simeon, and Anna. These persons are truly pious, obeying the Law in all respects and waiting for the redemption, salvation, or consolation of Israel. Of course, it is through these people that God works to effect his plan. Israel, on the other hand, needs salvation, as the Lukan canticles suggest. Moreover, the angel Gabriel says that John will turn "the disobedient to the wisdom of the righteous — to make ready a people prepared for the Lord" (1:17).

The disobedient side of Israel soon becomes evident in Luke's story. The attempt to kill Jesus in the Temple (19:47) was not the first time Jesus has faced opposition or even threats on his life. Even at his first public appearance in the Nazareth synagogue the people tried to throw him off a cliff (4:28-29). In the remainder of the story it is the scribes and Pharisees who are primarily Jesus' opponents. They accuse him of blasphemy when he forgives sins (5:21), they grumble when he fraternizes with tax collectors and "sinners" (5:30; 15:2), and they question the lawfulness of his Sabbath activity (6:2, 7; cf. 13:14). Jesus will eat with Pharisees, but often gets into conflict and reprimands his host (see 7:36-50; 11:37-52; 14:1-24). Pharisaic rejection of Jesus is rooted in their rejection of God's purpose, as demonstrated in John's baptism (7:29-30).

The theme of rejection is then played out in various ways after the clearing of the Temple. In this section Luke follows Mark quite closely, recounting the conflicts that Jesus has with the Jewish authorities (20:1-47), the conspiracy of the leaders to arrest Jesus (22:2-6), the leaders' participation in arresting Jesus (22:52), the trial of Jesus before the Sanhedrin (22:66-71), the leaders' accusation of Jesus before Pilate (23:1-5; Luke adds a trial before Herod where the leaders vehemently accuse Jesus [23:10]), and their mocking of Jesus while he hung on the cross (23:35).

No one will deny that Luke portrays the Jewish leaders as rejecting Jesus and being culpable for his death. But what role do the crowds and the nation play? Are they guilty as well? During Jesus' ministry the crowds show a mixed reaction to Jesus, but in the end they share responsibility for the death of Jesus when they ask for the release of Barabbas, a known criminal, instead of the innocent Jesus (23:18-25; cf. Acts 3:14). As for Israel, Luke may not be as bitter in his tone against the nation or the Jewish people as a whole as is Matthew, but it is difficult to deny that Luke also sees a national or corporate rejection of Jesus. Luke's parable of the unproductive fig tree (13:6-9) is often interpreted as being directed against the nation, for the fig tree is frequently a symbol of Israel in the Old Testament (cf. Isa 28:4; Jer 8:13; 24:1-8; Hos 9:10; Mic 7:1). If this is the case, then Jesus is warning not only individuals but also the nation to repent while God is still patient. Similarly, Jesus' parable of the wicked tenants (20:9-19) is addressed not only to the Jewish leaders, represented by the tenants, but by extension to the nation as well, which is represented by the vineyard. The parable is obviously an allegory based on the Song of the Vineyard in Isa 5:1-7, where the vineyard represents Israel. In addition to these parables, Jesus gives other warnings to "this generation" (7:31-35; 11:29-32), which certainly have the people as a whole in view. Finally, we may mention Jesus' lament over Jerusalem in 13:34-35 and the similar lament in 19:42-44, which are focused — despite the references to the city of Jerusalem — on the nation of Israel, which continually rejects God's messengers.[26]

A number of interpreters are reticent to say that Luke is "anti-Jewish" or "anti-Judaistic," and least of all "anti-Semitic." And there are various ways such terminology can be construed.[27] Yet we must deal with the question, How does Luke interpret the Jews' rejection of Jesus in light of the salvation-historical plan of God? But first let us examine Luke's picture of the Gentiles.

The Gentiles in Luke

It is well known that Luke has an interest in Gentiles and the Gentile mission in his Gospel. Probably the first indication of this interest appears in the announcement of an angel who brings good news that will be "for all people" about a Savior, who is Christ, the Lord (2:10-11). Here "all people" probably points to Gentiles and not just "all Jews."

26. If these passages reflect the deuteronomistic view of history, which perceived the nation's persistent disobedience and rejection of God's prophets as a theological construct, then it seems that Luke is also using this idea to say that the nation as a whole has rejected one more prophet, Jesus.

27. See, e.g., J. A. Weatherly, "Anti-Semitism," Dictionary of Jesus and the Gospels, 13-17. Here is a rather strained attempt to rid the Gospels of anti-Judaism, denying that the Evangelists see Israel's rejection of Jesus in national terms.

Following this somewhat ambiguous hint about Jesus' significance that may reach beyond Israel, Luke begins to add more references that point toward the salvation of the Gentiles. Simeon speaks of "a light for revelation to the Gentiles" (2:32) and "the falling and rising of many in Israel" because of Jesus (2:34). Luke couches the ministry of the Baptist and Jesus in terms of Old Testament prophecy that "all flesh will see the salvation of God" (3:6). When Luke records the ancestry of Jesus, he takes it back beyond Abraham, the father of the Jewish people, to Adam, the son of God (3:23-38). Surely this is meant to point out that Jesus' saving work affects all of the human race, not just Jews. Then when Jesus begins his public ministry in Nazareth, he refers to Elijah being sent to a Gentile widow and Elisha to the Gentile Naaman (4:24-27). The anger and refusal of the townsfolk to listen to such a message about God's favor to Gentiles over Jews set the course of Luke's entire two-volume work.

More anticipations of a Gentile mission appear in Jesus' ministry. Luke tells of some Jews who plead with Jesus to heal the servant of a Gentile centurion because the centurion deserves it. When the centurion himself says he does not deserve Jesus' presence but will simply accept his word of healing, Jesus responds, "I have not seen such great faith, even in Israel" (7:1-10). The mission of the seventy (or seventy-two) in Luke 10:1 is often interpreted as an anticipation of the Gentile mission, since the number seventy reflects the number of nations in Gen 10:1-32. In Jesus' parable of the great banquet (14:15-24), after the first set of invitees have refused to come to the banquet and the marginalized have indeed come, a third command (perhaps added by Luke to the original Q version) is given to compel others who are outside the town to come. Those who are outside (i.e., in "the roads and country lanes") are Gentiles, whom the master desires to come and fill his house. The parable serves as an allegory of Jewish refusal and Gentile acceptance of the banquet of salvation.

Finally, we may mention Jesus' very clear words about a post-resurrection Gentile mission: "Thus it is written, that the Messiah is to suffer and to rise from the dead on the third day and that repentance and forgiveness of sins is to be proclaimed in his name to all nations, beginning from Jerusalem" (24:46-47). These words of Jesus form the foundation for Luke's presentation of the Gentile mission in Acts. First the *proclaimer* in the Gospel, Jesus, will become the *proclaimed* in Acts, for salvation — or as Acts has it, "the word of this salvation" (13:26) — will be proclaimed in his name. Second, the Gentile mission will begin in Jerusalem, and this, indeed, takes place in Acts. Third, Jesus' statement that his suffering-death-resurrection and the proclamation of salvation to the Gentiles are grounded in the Old Testament plan of God is reiterated in various ways in Acts.

Jews and Gentiles in Acts

When we come to the book of Acts, it would appear that Luke's perspective on Jews and Gentiles in the plan of God is finally articulated. But scholars disagree widely on several issues. The underlying problem is that for Luke to tell the story of salvation to a Gentile audience, he must enter the world of Judaism. He must explain how God's plan has unfolded through the Jewish nation and its history, the Jewish Scriptures, and a Jewish Messiah to include, in the present time, Gentile people on an equal basis. Thus some scholars stress the Jewish orientation of Luke's Gospel and the Jewish sphere of activity in Acts, while others emphasize the Gentile and "anti-Jewish" features of Luke's two volumes. François Bovon observes, "For some, Acts marks the Church's progressive and ineluctable disengagement from Judaism; for others, it constantly reminds us of the Church's pretension to remain the Israel of God."[28] This statement will be appreciated more after a brief survey of some scholarly views.

Jacob Jervell, in a 1972 monograph that collected several earlier articles, argues against the widespread acceptance of a universalistic Luke who is hostile to Jewish particularism.[29] According to Jervell, (1) Luke does not write primarily for Gentiles; (2) Luke is a most ardent defender of the Jewish character of the church, for "outside Israel, there is no salvation"; (3) Luke considers the Gentile mission important, but writes about it in the context of Jewish Christianity; and (4) Luke thinks of the church, not as the new Israel, but as Israel restored. Of prime interest for us is Jervell's view that the Gentile mission in Acts did not spring out of Jewish rejection of Christianity but out of the Jewish Christian fulfillment of the prophecies of God that when Israel is restored the Gentiles will repent. Instead of

---

28. Bovon, *Luke the Theologian*, 310.
29. J. Jervell, *Luke and the People of God: A New Look at Luke-Acts* (Minneapolis: Augsburg, 1972). In these brief summaries of scholarly positions I am indebted to Powell, *What Are They Saying about Luke?* 51-58, and Bovon, *Luke the Theologian*, 323-43.

seeing Jewish rejection, Jervell sees a fabulous Jewish conversion to the gospel, as reported by the Acts summaries of growth (2:41; 4:4; 5:14; 6:7), so that by Acts 21:20 there are "myriads" of Jewish Christians who are "zealous for the law." Thus the restoration of Israel is an accomplished fact and the influx of the Gentiles proves this. In addition, there is no thought that the Gentile mission represents a break with Israel, or that the promises of God have been transferred to a substitute people. The break is not between Jews and Gentiles, but between Jews who have believed in Jesus and Jews who have not. For Jervell, Luke thinks of Israel as a family divided. But God's promises to Israel are being fulfilled for Jews who have believed in Jesus — and one of those promises is the salvation of the Gentiles.[30]

In sharp contrast to Jervell's position is the view that Luke presents a sharp break between Judaism and the church. Robert Maddox, for example, says Luke emphasizes the Jewish rejection of both Jesus and Christian missionaries, and thus God's plan of salvation.[31] The Jews have been judged by God and are excluded from the ancestral promises of God, which are now fulfilled for Gentile Christians. For Maddox, the presence of Gentiles in Luke's community has necessitated a defense against attacks from outside. Jack T. Sanders agrees with Maddox that Luke emphasizes Jewish rejection of Christianity, and he says explicitly that Luke is anti-Semitic.[32] Yet Luke's hostility is not limited to Jews, but reaches even to Jewish Christians, who are his real target. Sanders believes that Judaizers, such as are found in Acts 15:5, are a threat to Gentile Christianity. This is what motivates Luke to write his Gospel. Thus the presence of Gentiles in Luke's community has brought about a division and consequent polemics within the church.

Does Luke find that the Jews as a whole have rejected Jesus? And does Luke see the Gentile mission as motivated by Jewish rejection of Jesus? My own answer to both these questions is Yes. But both situations are also seen to be part of the plan of God, as Luke 24:46-47 has already indicated.

---

30. At least some aspects of Jervell's position seem to be reflected in the works of E. Franklin, *Christ the Lord: A Study in the Purpose and Theology of Luke-Acts* (London: SPCK, 1975), 77-115; D. Juel, *Luke-Acts: The Promise of History* (Atlanta: Knox, 1983), 109-112; and J. Fitzmyer, *Luke the Theologian: Aspects of His Teaching* (New York: Paulist, 1989), 187-95.

31. R. Maddox, *The Purpose of Luke-Acts* (Edinburgh: Clark, 1985).

32. J. T. Sanders, "The Salvation of the Jews in Luke Acts," in *Luke-Acts: New Perspectives from the Society of Biblical Literature Seminar,* ed. C. H. Talbert (New York: Crossroad, 1984), 104-28; *idem, The Jews in Luke-Acts* (Philadelphia: Fortress, 1987).

The first part of Acts deals with the question of Israel's rejection of Jesus. In Luke's record of Peter's sermon at Pentecost, the apostle says, "Men of Israel . . . Jesus of Nazareth, a man attested to you by God . . . this man, handed over to you according to the definite plan and foreknowledge of God, you crucified and killed by the hands of those outside the Law" (2:22-23). At the end of this same sermon Peter declares, in words reminiscent of Luke 24:46-47: "Repent, and be baptized every one of you in the name of Jesus Christ so that your sins may be forgiven: and you will receive the gift of the Holy Spirit. For the promise is for you, for your children, and for all who are far away, everyone whom the Lord our God calls to him" (2:38-39). In these passages it is evident that corporate Israel is responsible for Jesus' death, though this also took place according to the plan of God, and that the promise of salvation will extend to those "who are far away," a likely reference to Gentiles.

The same picture unfolds in Peter's sermon in Acts 3, where Peter accuses the Israelites of rejecting Jesus and killing him (3:13-14). Then Peter explicates Israel's general culpability, though in a curious way, and also God's plan: "I know that you acted in ignorance, as did also your rulers. In this way God fulfilled what he had foretold through all the prophets, that his Messiah would suffer" (3:17-18). Nearly the exact message is given in Paul's message in 13:27. In another passage the Christians recognize God's sovereign plan, and an even more general culpability, as they pray, "For in this city, in fact, both Herod and Pontius Pilate, with the Gentiles and the peoples of Israel, gathered together against your holy servant Jesus, whom you anointed, to do whatever your plan had predestined to take place" (4:27-28).

After the Gentile mission begins, in the latter part of Acts, the question of the motivation for the mission is addressed in three famous texts. In Antioch of Pisidia Paul and Barnabas declare to Jewish opponents: "It was necessary that the word of God should be spoken first to you. Since you reject it and judge yourselves to be unworthy of eternal life, we are now turning to the Gentiles. For the Lord has commanded us, saying, 'I have set you to be a light for the Gentiles, so that you may bring salvation to the ends of the earth'" (13:46-47). Then during Paul's ministry in Corinth, we read that he was "proclaiming the word, testifying to the Jews that Messiah was Jesus. When they opposed him and reviled him, in protest he shook the dust from his clothes and said to them, 'Your blood be on your own heads! I am innocent. From now on I will go to the Gentiles'" (18:5-6).

Finally, when Paul is in Rome and encounters opposition, he quotes Isa 6:9-10 and concludes, "Let it be known to you then that this salvation of God has been sent to the Gentiles; they will listen." Acts concludes two verses later with the statement that Paul taught for two years about the Lord Jesus Christ "with all boldness and without hindrance" (28:31). The reader cannot help but feel that Luke ends his work with the picture of the gospel passing from Israel to Gentiles. But in each of these three references Paul's announcement about transferring his missionary activity stems from Jewish recalcitrance, and in two of the references Paul's shift in focus is said to be rooted in Old Testament prophecy. So, as in many aspects of life, both the human and the divine operate together.

A Restored Israel?

Scholars debate whether Luke intends to indicate that the rejection of Israel is irrevocable. Whatever the answer is, it is not the main thrust of Luke. He has succeeded in showing how the good news of salvation has reached the Gentiles and that Gentiles receive salvation on the same basis as Jews do, that is, by faith in Jesus Christ (Acts 15:7-11; 16:31). The message of salvation is no longer tied to Israel as a nation, for God's purpose is not confined to the Jews; rather the gospel of salvation must now go to "all nations," as Jesus declared. Against Jervell, Luke does not redefine Israel to mean believing Jews, or believing Jews and believing Gentiles. Luke does not speak about Christians in Paul's terms as "the Israel of God" (Gal 6:16). Jews and Gentiles have their own backgrounds and cultures, and they remain that way. But believers from these backgrounds, according to Luke, together compose the new people of God, which is called "the church" (Acts 20:28).

Salvation and Eschatology

When referring to the topic of eschatology in Luke, it has become almost traditional to begin with a treatment of Hans Conzelmann's work, for he set the agenda for Lukan studies for many years to come.[33] He argues that

---

33. H. Conzelmann, *Die Mitte der Zeit* (Tübingen, 1954), translated as *The Theology of St. Luke* (London: Faber and Faber, 1960).

the problems of eschatology, specifically the delay of Jesus' return (the parousia), were central to Luke's theology and the motive for his writing Luke-Acts. When the parousia did not occur as the early Christians expected, this caused disillusionment and a theological crisis. In response, Luke developed a particular history of salvation, in which he sought to eradicate the anticipation of an imminent end by substituting the idea of a prolonged "age of the church." Luke regarded salvation history as now being divided into three periods: the time of Israel, the time of Jesus, and the time of the church. The parousia, the kingdom, and salvation, which together are essentially synonymous, were pushed forward into the indefinite future. Conzelmann thinks that, for Luke, Jesus brought salvation, but that salvation has been "historicized" and is now relegated to the past — to the time of Jesus. For Luke, the time of salvation is not "now," but it will be available again at the parousia. In the meantime, during this time of the church, the Spirit operates as the substitute for the possession of ultimate salvation.

Conzelmann's thesis was attractive to many at first, but has been modified to the point where few accept it in its original form.[34] First, his identification of the delay of the parousia as the motivation for Luke's Gospel has come to be viewed as too narrow an explanation. Second, his presentation of salvation history seems strained, especially since it builds on the faulty view that the delay of the parousia caused a crisis. There is evidence that the early Christians reckoned with an interval between the resurrection of Jesus and his parousia. Third, it is evident that salvation itself, rather than salvation history, is what really interests Luke.

Of prime interest to us, however, is how Luke in fact does relate salvation to eschatology. First, Luke's depiction of the timing of the parousia is diverse. Luke retains some texts (contra Conzelmann) that indicate that the end is very near. For example, Jesus tells his disciples, "Truly I tell you, this generation will not pass away until all things have taken place" (21:32; cf. 10:9, 11). On the other hand, some texts point to a delay (12:38, 45; 19:11; 21:24). Perhaps both ideas are present in the same passage in the parable of the persistent widow, when Jesus concludes, "And will not God grant justice to his chosen ones who cry to him day and night? Will he delay long in helping them? I tell you, he will quickly grant justice to them. And yet

---

34. Bovon, *Luke the Theologian*, 11-77, traces the history of scholarship regarding Conzelmann's thesis.

when the Son of Man comes, will he find faith on the earth?" (18:7-8). Perhaps both ideas of imminence and delay may be reconciled by Jesus' words "It is not for you to know . . ." (Acts 1:7) and by the thought that what Jesus wants of his people during the interval is watchfulness and faith (Luke 21:36).[35]

Second, Luke presents the kingdom of God as having both future and present dimensions (again, contra Conzelmann). Both pictures are in fact "eschatological" if we understand that, by definition, the "coming of the kingdom" is considered one of the "last things." In any case, Luke can relate Jesus' discourse about the end of the age, and record Jesus as saying, "When you see these things taking place, you know that the kingdom of God is near" (21:31). On the other hand, Luke can report an incident when the Pharisees asked Jesus when the kingdom of God was coming, to which he replied, "The kingdom of God is not coming with things that can be observed; nor will they say, 'Look, here it is!' or 'There it is!' For, in fact, the kingdom of God is among you" (17:20-21). Both present and future dimensions appear in Jesus' saying to Peter in 18:29-30: "Truly I tell you, there is no one who has left house or wife or brothers or parents or children, for the sake of the kingdom of God, who will not get back very much more in this age, and in the age to come eternal life." In this saying we may also see that salvation is the equivalent of receiving or possessing the kingdom.

Though Luke presents both future and present dimensions of salvation, he certainly lays emphasis on salvation that is available here and now. Jesus' saving ministry, which we recounted earlier, represents the inbreaking of the present kingdom. This is "realized eschatology." In a remarkable series of texts Luke draws the reader's attention to the fact that salvation is available "Today!" Conzelmann was incorrect in positing that Luke thinks of God's salvation as available only at the parousia. Surely Luke means his stories to be read existentially. And so readers are invited to apply personally the following words to their own "today" in a way that transcends the historical sense:

"Today . . . a Savior is born" (Luke 2:11)
"Today . . . this scripture has been fulfilled" (4:21)

---

35. On this theme, see H. W. Bartsch, *Wachet aber zu jeder Zeit!* (Hamburg-Bergstet: Herbert Reich — Evangelischer Verlag, 1963). Summaries are in Powell, *What Are They Saying about Luke?* 44; and Bovon, *Luke the Theologian,* 424 n. 45.

"Today . . . we have seen strange things" (5:26)
"Today . . . I must stay at your house" (19:5)
"Today . . . salvation has come to this house" (19:9)
"Today . . . you will be with me in paradise" (23:43)

Conclusion

If we may end where we started this study, we may try to answer what Theophilus might have thought about Luke's Gospel, based on our own experience of reading it. When Luke speaks of "the events that have been fulfilled among us," we now know that these events center on the coming and mission of Jesus to bring salvation. This salvation has a broad-based character so that those who encounter Jesus, whether during his life or at his death, are released or liberated from whatever prevents their full enjoyment of life and peace. Jesus' mission is carried out under the divine plan of God, according to the Scriptures, and God's purpose continues to be realized in the story of the church, which now proclaims the message of salvation in the name of Jesus. The plan of God includes all people, Jews and Gentiles alike. Though Israel as a nation has rejected God's plan of salvation in Jesus Christ, this too is part of the divine plan. The good news is that God's salvation reaches to all people. Therefore Gentiles like Theophilus can be assured that they belong in the church as much as anyone. They too have a place in God's history of salvation.

Luke's emphasis on the purpose of God in Jesus functions today as an invitation to all readers to embrace that purpose in their daily lives. Joel Green has put this practical emphasis so aptly that he bears quoting:

> Luke's readers . . . are encouraged to listen carefully to the Scriptures of Israel, to follow the course of ministry of Jesus, and so to adopt a perspective internal to the narrative itself. Having done so, Luke's readers may hear the challenge of Jesus to side with those who side with God's redemptive project, and having done so to serve it as those empowered by the Holy Spirit. This is the call of discipleship in Luke: to align oneself with Jesus, who aligns himself fundamentally and absolutely with God.[36]

36. Green, *Theology of the Gospel of Luke*, 49.

Reading John:
The Fourth Gospel under Modern
and Postmodern Interrogation

ANDREW T. LINCOLN

To turn to John's Gospel after reading the Synoptics is, as all students of the Gospels discover, to enter a very different world. The protagonist is introduced immediately as the preexistent Word who became flesh, his first followers acclaim him with messianic titles from the start, and the Temple incident is at the beginning of his career rather than, as in the Synoptics, at the end, where it serves as the catalyst that leads to his death. No longer do we find a Jesus who teaches in parables and pithy aphorisms about the kingdom of God but one who holds forth in lengthy monologues and extended disputes about his own person and his relation with his Father. Not only so, but, whereas in the Synoptics one is hard put to find Jesus even accepting a messianic designation for himself, in his discourses in the Fourth Gospel Jesus talks of himself openly as the Son of God, who is totally at one with the Father and aware of the glory he shared with the Father before the foundation of the world. At the same time he frequently employs of himself the divine self-identification "I Am." Strikingly, the language of John's Jesus has more in common with the language of the Johannine Epistles than it does with that of the Synoptics. How then does one assess the truth of such a Gospel? This is, of course, no new question. By the beginning of the third century CE, Clement had famously remarked that, conscious that the other Gospels had set forth the outward facts, John composed "a spiritual Gospel" (*Hypotyposes* 6), while Origen in his commentary on John (10.2), after noting the many places where "the careful student of the Gospels will find that their narratives do not agree," claimed that "the student, staggered at the consideration of these things, will either renounce the attempt to find all the Gospels true, and . . . will choose at random one of them to be his guide; or he will accept the four, and will consider that their truth is not to be sought in the outward and material letter."

Truth in John's Narrative: An Initial Orientation

John's Gospel itself presses this question of truth. One of its distinctive characteristics is the frequency of its use of the *alētheia* word group. The noun occurs twenty-five times in this Gospel as opposed to seven times in the three Synoptics together. The adjective *alēthēs*, "true," is found fourteen times in John as compared with twice in the Synoptics, while the related adjective *alēthinos* is featured nine times in John in comparison with once in the other Gospels.

In the most general sense, "truth" in the Gospel of John stands for the reality of God and God's revelation in Christ. But the term takes on a distinctive force in this Gospel narrative by being linked with a number of other characteristically Johannine terms, particularly the "witness" or "testimony" and the "judgment" word groups. In this connection, as I have argued elsewhere, building on the work of other scholars,[1] it forms part of what is a dominant motif, namely, that of a cosmic trial or lawsuit in which Jesus as God's uniquely authorized agent acts as both witness and judge. God's sovereign rule, depicted primarily in terms of Jesus' inauguration of the kingdom of God in the Synoptics and of Christ's lordship in Paul, is expressed in John as God's judgment of the world carried out in Jesus; and eternal life, another characteristically Johannine theme, is the positive verdict in that judgment.

Major themes and specific language from the lawsuits between God and the nations and God and Israel in the Septuagint version of Isaiah 40–55 are taken up and reworked in John's presentation. Significantly, truth is frequently paired with righteous judgment or justice in Isaiah and in the OT in general (cf. Isa 42:3; 45:19; 48:1; 59:14; also, e.g., Pss 45:4; 96:13; 119:142, 160). For Yahweh, to judge justly is to determine, declare, and demonstrate

---

1. Cf. A. T. Lincoln, *Truth on Trial: The Lawsuit Motif in the Fourth Gospel* (Peabody: Hendrickson, 2000), especially chapters 1 and 3.

the truth. So in the context of a lawsuit truth will stand for the whole process of judging, culminating in the verdict, and its specific content will be dependent on the particular issue at stake. What is the issue in John's narrative? According to 20:31, at its heart is whether the crucified Jesus is the Messiah, the Son of God, and, from the rest of the narrative discourse we can add, therefore one with God. The discourse's depiction of the relation between Jesus and God also justifies putting the issue the other way around. As it concerns God, it is whether God is the God who is now known in the crucified Jesus and whether through him God has effected a judgment that means life for the world. Truth is the affirmative judgment on these interrelated issues, as that judgment develops into a culminating verdict.

Other highlights of this Gospel's presentation of truth can only be touched on here. The prologue already intimates that this truth is summed up in Jesus. Its assertion is that, in the incarnate Logos's embodiment of the relation of God's word to the world and in his making God known, grace and truth came into being through him (1:17, cf. also 1:14, 18). John's Gospel, unlike the Synoptics, has no trial of Jesus before the Jewish Sanhedrin. This is because Jesus' public ministry has already been depicted as a trial before Israel, in which the controversy with "the Jews" takes the form of both a number of acts of judgment and a series of interrogations. The issue of truth is most to the fore in Jesus' mission to Israel in the heated contest of claims in 8:12-59. In response to accusations about his single witness being invalid, Jesus declares that both his witness and his judgment are nevertheless true because of his divine origin and destiny (8:14, 16). Later he asserts that continuing belief in his word enables people to know the truth of the issue at stake in the trial and to experience the salvific effect of its true judgment in liberation from sin (8:31, 32). As becomes clear from the parallel statement in 8:36 — "If the Son makes you free, you will be free indeed," the truth that emancipates is again God's revelation embodied in Jesus. In his farewell discourse to the disciples Jesus claims to be the truth that is life-giving (14:6) and promises to send them another Advocate, the Spirit of truth, who will guide them into all the truth (14:17; 15:26; 16:13). John's account of the trial of Jesus before Pilate, the most extensive of all four Gospels, is the central feature of the Passion narrative, functioning as a climactic expression of the broader trial motif. Again, as will be discussed more fully below, it explicitly confronts its readers with the issue of the truth, as Jesus claims, "For this I was born, and for this I came into the world, to testify to the truth," and provokes Pilate's well-known question, "What is truth?" (18:37, 38). And, of course, at the end of the Fourth Gospel as a whole, the final author asserts of the witness of the Beloved Disciple, whose authority is claimed for its writing, that "we know that his witness is true" (21:24).

Modern and Postmodern Interrogations of the Truth of John's Gospel

In his book, *Is John's Gospel True?* Maurice Casey answers the question he poses with a resounding No![2] He brings together in a lucid and rigorous way data and arguments that he believes the majority of New Testament scholars would, for the most part, accept but whose necessary implications, as he sees them, they have been hesitant to draw. But truth is not simply scholarly honesty for Casey. Clearly he also holds that there is such an entity as truth to which the Fourth Gospel fails woefully to match up. What then are his criteria for truth? Basically, they are those of reason — particularly its historical knowledge and its ethical categorical imperative (which for Casey also happens to be found in the teaching of the historical Jesus about love of neighbor). Judged by these standards, his verdict is that the Fourth Gospel fails on both counts. History, for Casey, is meant to tell us what actually happened, but, using the tools of historical criticism, he claims, it can be shown that John's Gospel is historically inaccurate and a distortion. If we want to know what happened in the life of the historical Jesus, John's Gospel can only lead us astray.[3] Casey then adds to his indictment that this Gospel is morally deficient because it is anti-Jewish and has fostered anti-Semitism, and claims that this is such a pervasive feature of this Gospel that it is irredeemable. Casey's pressing of this critical perspective with its ideal of objective knowledge and a universal ethical absolute might be said to represent a typically modern approach to the question of the truth of John's Gospel.

2. M. Casey, *Is John's Gospel True?* (New York: Routledge, 1996).

3. It is significant in this regard that both the Jesus Seminar and N. T. Wright in their very different accounts of the historical Jesus would appear to agree with Casey, since neither account uses John in its portrayal. Cf. R. W. Funk and R. W. Hoover, *The Five Gospels: The Search for the Authentic Words of Jesus* (New York: Macmillan, 1993); R. W. Funk, ed., *The Acts of Jesus: The Search for the Authentic Deeds of Jesus* (San Francisco: Harper, 1998); N. T. Wright, *Jesus and the Victory of God* (Minneapolis: Fortress, 1996).

But there are also late modern or postmodern criticisms of its truth. The focus here will be on a strand of postmodern thinking that overlaps at some points with a modern approach but is built on a different premise. Applied to John's Gospel, that premise dictates that this Gospel is no more or less true than any other grand claims to truth, because they are all simply a disguise of the will to power. Foucault has stated the case for truth as power as clearly as anyone — "Truth is a thing of this world: it is produced only by virtue of multiple forms of constraints. And it induces regular effects of power. Each society has its regime of truth, its 'general politics' of truth: that is, the types of discourse which it accepts and makes function as true. . . ."[4] Following Nietzsche, such a view sees all claims to truth as ways of asserting one's place in the world and as inevitably leading to manipulation and violence. Interestingly, Nietzsche himself referred to John's Gospel in expounding his views — "Do I still have to add that in the entire New Testament there is only *one* solitary figure one is obliged to respect? Pilate, the Roman governor. To take a Jewish affair *seriously* — he cannot persuade himself to do that. One Jew more or less — what does it matter? The noble scorn of a Roman before whom an impudent misuse of the word 'truth' was carried on has enriched the New Testament with the only expression *which possesses value* — which is its criticism, its *annihilation* even: 'What is truth?'"[5]

For Nietzsche's postmodern heirs, the bigger the claim to truth the worse the consequences. John's Gospel can be held to be a prime example. On this account, it started out as the claims of an oppressed religious minority, the Johannine Christians, who had been excommunicated from the synagogue because of their distinctive belief in Jesus. The only means of power this group had left was to assert that the one to whom it professed allegiance surpassed all the claims that had been made about Moses and about the Law and its major festivals by its parent religion turned oppressor. Such counter-claims escalated to include Jesus actually sharing the divine name "I Am" and being one with God. But then the stakes were high for a group dispossessed of their religious heritage, and, therefore, in a setting where religion and society were so closely interwoven, dispossessed

4. M. Foucault, *Power/Knowledge: Selected Interviews and Other Writings, 1972-1977* (New York: Pantheon, 1980), 131.
5. F. Nietzsche, *The Anti-Christ* in *Twilight of the Idols: The Anti-Christ* (ET Harmondsworth: Penguin, 1968), 162.

also of their social identity and status. This is a claim to truth with a vengeance from a marginalized group. With a vengeance may be truer than one might wish, it is held, if attention is paid to the rhetoric of this Gospel, placed in the mouth of Jesus, of calling its opponents murderers and liars and children of the devil. The truth claims of this Gospel, then, are part of a power conflict and indeed could be nothing other.

This is reinforced by the tragic irony of what happened to this Gospel later. With the expansion and rise in power of the Christian movement and the acceptance of this document into its canon, its truth claims changed from being those of an oppressed minority to those of the dominant religion and became weapons to use against the now marginalized religion of Judaism. Its characterization of those of the group's compatriots who declined to believe its claims simply as "the Jews" was exploited in an anti-Semitism that took this to refer to all Jews, who could now be written off. Indeed a ghastly line can be traced from this Gospel's portrayal of "the Jews" through the anti-Semitic statements of Cyril of Alexandria and Chrysostom, the medieval proliferation of anti-Semitic tracts illustrated with woodcuts of "the Jews and their father, the devil," and the inflammatory outbursts of Luther, up to the Nazi propaganda that employed the slogan "Der Vater der Juden ist der Teufel."[6]

Space permits only a brief response to such perspectives on John. The response assumes that for the most part the major conclusions of historical criticism about the Fourth Gospel are convincing, so that, for example, despite the historical substratum about Jesus with its links to the Synoptic tradition on which the narrative is built, it is not plausible to defend any consistent or detailed one-to-one correspondence between John's narrative and what is likely to have happened in the ministry of Jesus.[7] Traditions about events and controversies in the mission of Jesus have been reinterpreted in the light of the beliefs of the Evangelist and his community and the situation they faced in regard to the Jewish religious authorities of their own day. This response also accepts that there are ethical dilemmas posed by the effects of the portrayal of "the Jews" in the narrative, that interpreters and their communities have a significant role in deter-

6. Cf., e.g., R. Lowry, "The Rejected Suitor-Syndrome: Human Sources of the New Testament 'Antisemitism,'" *JES* 14 (1977): 229.

7. The most recent attempt to do so is C. L. Blomberg's *The Historical Reliability of John's Gospel* (Leicester: Apollos, 2001), which is dependent on the view that the eyewitness author was John the son of Zebedee and on strained argumentation.

mining the meaning of texts, and that therefore any truth claims of the narrative or claims made on its behalf inevitably involve issues of power. It proposes, however, that what is needed is to take a different view of truth in which truth encompasses but cannot simply be reduced to matters of historicity, ethics, or power. It proposes also that John's Gospel is most appropriately read in a way that sees this different view of truth as at the heart of its message.

Truth and Historicity

The Fourth Gospel tells its story of Jesus by fusing the debate between Johannine Christians and their local synagogue with traditions about the ministry of Jesus. If, therefore, for example, contrary to its story, the historical Jesus did not go about explicitly claiming identity with God and his followers were not put out of the synagogue during his earthly mission for making a confession about his identity, what is the truth of this narrative about truth? The focus here will be on two matters. The first is the conventions of ancient biography, of which the Fourth Gospel is a part by virtue of its taking up the genre of gospel. This discussion assumes the consensus in current New Testament scholarship that the Gospels are a subset of the genre of *bios* or *Life,* ancient biography.[8] The second matter is the function of this Gospel's language of "witness" and its implications.

Ancient biographies are not to be confused with modern ones. The Fourth Gospel emanated from an originally Jewish community. It therefore shares features of the typical way of rewriting historical tradition within Judaism where history could be creatively elaborated in order to illustrate concerns of the present but at the same time be attributed to a figure from the past. The *Testament of Levi,* for example, contains a lengthy rewriting of Israel's history which has been put into the mouth of Levi as a prophecy and in which all the main concerns of the writer and his community have been attributed to Levi and his sons.

But the Fourth Gospel's narration of the life of Jesus is in Greek and at the same time fits the broad parameters of Greco-Roman biography. This genre was flexible and operated within a continuum that stretched

---

8. Cf. especially R. A. Burridge, *What Are the Gospels? A Comparison with Graeco-Roman Biography* (Cambridge: Cambridge University Press, 1992).

from ancient history writing on the one side through to the ancient novel or romance on the other. Arnold Momigliano, in *The Development of Greek Biography*, wrote that "the borderline between fiction and reality was thinner in biography than in ordinary historiography,"[9] a judgment from which it should not be inferred that "ordinary historiography" did have a thick borderline between fiction and reality. What is implied for our purposes is that it would be an error to judge John's biography, written some sixty years after its subject's death, by the canons even of ancient historiography, let alone of modern historical study. Patricia Cox would agree, "In antiquity biography . . . had its own unique characteristics and sustained historical veracity was not one of them. To impugn the integrity of a Greco-Roman biography on the basis of factual discrepancy is to misconceive the literary tradition of the genre to which it belongs."[10]

Plutarch in his *Lives* is an example of a biographer who adhered somewhat more closely to the conventions of ancient historiography. Yet a recent study of Plutarch argues that in his biographies, as in ancient history writing, invention or free composition was a central feature. What counted was the plausibility of the portrait, and to achieve this Plutarch was willing "to help the truth along." For Plutarch as a biographer with a historical bent what we view as fabrications would fall into the category not of true or false but of "true enough." What counted as historical truth was not, then, what could be authenticated by evidence but what was agreed in prevailing convention to be adequately plausible.[11]

Whereas lives of politicians and military leaders, such as those produced by Plutarch, naturally tended to stay closer to history writing, lives of philosophers and religious leaders or holy men were more idealized and often used by adherents of a philosophy or a religious tradition as propaganda against competitors. In such biographies the writers' overall convictions are even more in play in their portraits of their subjects. From early on writers such as Xenophon and Aristoxenus used legendary traditions, invented characteristic traits, and fabricated anecdotes, which they employed in a mix with more authentic material in producing portraits of

9. A. Momigliano, *The Development of Greek Biography* (Cambridge: Harvard University Press, 1971), 56.

10. P. Cox, *Biography in Late Antiquity: A Quest for the Holy Man* (Berkeley: University of California Press, 1983), 5.

11. C. B. R. Pelling, "Truth and Fiction in Plutarch's *Lives*" in *Antonine Literature*, ed. D. A. Russell (Oxford: Clarendon, 1990), 19-52.

philosophers that functioned as claim and counter-claim between rival philosophical schools. Accounts of events and discourses became the vehicle for the biographers' ideals taking graphic form within a historically framed narrative, thereby creating verisimilitude.

All this should make clear why the term "history-like," thought by some to be a weasel word avoiding hard questions of historical truth, is in fact entirely appropriate when used of ancient biographical narratives such as the Gospels. It reminds us of the wide range of connotations of truth that should be in play when an attempt is made to evaluate the Fourth Gospel's claims in terms of its genre and therefore of the mutual expectations of author and readers about such claims. It means that we should expect that, in line with other ancient biographers, the Fourth Evangelist has composed a narrative that was an interpretive superstructure built around some core events in his traditions. We should also expect that, if ancient readers were both disinclined and usually unable to disentangle the two, although it remains part of our historical study to attempt to do so, it will be much more difficult to distinguish these elements with any certainty than scholars sometimes think, especially from our distance in time. But it should also be clear that, in regard to the truth of the narrative in its own terms, such an attempt at disentanglement misses the point.

As noted at the beginning, according to its penultimate verse (21:24), this particular ancient biography of Jesus claims to be based on the testimony of the Beloved Disciple. The narrator, representing the community from which the Gospel emanated, adds, "and we know that his testimony is true." It has been thought by some that the final claim about the Beloved Disciple's testimony means that interpreters are obliged to take the whole narrative as the straightforward historical report of an eyewitness. But what we know about ancient historiography and biography, where claims to eyewitness status could function as a device for adding verisimilitude to one's work, should give pause. There are indications that something similar is in play here.[12] The Beloved Disciple is explicitly introduced only in the last part of the narrative and given special insight into the significant last events of Jesus' life but without his insight affecting the progress of the action. Most hold that he appears to be an idealization of the founding figure behind the Johannine community who has been read back into the last

12. For a fuller discussion of this issue, see A. T. Lincoln, "The Beloved Disciple as Eyewitness and the Fourth Gospel as Witness," *JSNT* 85 (2002): 3-26.

part of the narrative in order to give this interpretation of the tradition authority. Just as Johannine views about Jesus have been attributed to Jesus in his earthly mission, so Johannine insights about the events surrounding his death and resurrection have been attributed to the Beloved Disciple as the ideal witness. What is more, the language of witnessing is, not unnaturally, frequently associated with seeing in this narrative, but from the start seeing and testifying do not carry their straightforward everyday sense of eyewitnessing. They are part of the overall *metaphor* of a trial, as three early references will suffice to indicate. In this matter, as in others, the prologue sets the tone and guides readers' expectations. In 1:7, 8 John the Baptist is said to testify to the light so that all might believe. Clearly this first use of the witness terminology has in view a pointing to the significance of Jesus' identity as the embodiment of the divine light and all that it symbolizes. It presupposes the Baptist's acquaintance with Jesus but it does not refer to a physical seeing of a light or the reporting of any historical fact. When later in the prologue the narrator, representing the community, testifies that "we have seen his glory" (1:14), this does not mean that Jesus had something like a halo that all could observe but refers to testimony to what was believed about Jesus' status.[13] Again when Jesus, as representative of the community, declares in dialogue with Nicodemus, "we speak of what we know and testify to what we have seen" (3:11), it turns out that this is a reference to heavenly things (3:12), realities not accessible to normal human sight but requiring the sort of spiritual sight that only comes with being born from above (3:3). Seeing and hearing are both equivalents of believing in this Gospel's discourse, and so testifying to what one has seen and heard is the equivalent of testifying to one's belief.

But even if witness language should not be assumed to be referring to eyewitness testimony, is not the picture that has been drawn complicated by, in particular, John 19:35? There, after the narrator has recounted that one of the soldiers pierced Jesus' side with a spear and at once blood and water came out, he adds, "And the one who saw has testified, and his testimony is true, and that one knows that he tells the truth, so that you also may believe." Here, at the level of the narrative itself, witness terminology is linked to a reference to what could be seen with one's eyes. At the historical level, it might be said that, although this substantial elabo-

---

13. Cf. N. R. Petersen, *The Gospel of John and the Sociology of Light* (Valley Forge: Trinity, 1993), 20.

ration on Mark 15:44 is completely unknown to any other tradition about Jesus' death, there is nothing intrinsically impossible about its claim. But the most likely candidate for this witness about whom the narrator speaks in the third person is the Beloved Disciple, who has just been mentioned as present at the crucifixion (19:26), and here, as elsewhere in the narrative (cf. especially 13:23-28), his role appears to constitute a particular literary device. The reference to his eyewitnessing is parenthetical; the narrative flows smoothly without it. This eyewitness also is not a real participant in the action; his seeing and testifying is not for the benefit of other characters but for the readers. This is in fact the one point in his whole telling of the story where the narrator in the persona of this ideal witness stops and explicitly addresses the readers. As a literary device, the Beloved Disciple's role here allows the narrator to draw the implied readers into the story line, inviting them to share the perspective of this witness that Jesus' death was life-giving. His literal eyewitnessing can be held to be functioning within the extended trial metaphor and as lending the account verisimilitude. Its truth claim must be related first of all to what is implied by the statements of 19:35 within its narrative's universe of discourse. In this light the truth being asserted is that the condemnation of death that Jesus experienced results in the positive verdict of life. So the primary function of this eyewitnessing, in the same way as the earlier language about seeing and testifying, is to stress belief in the significance of what has happened to Jesus. Its truth is emphasized so strongly because the decisive moment in the lawsuit motif is God's verdict in the death of Jesus. The Beloved Disciple's witness, which at this point stands both within and outside the story line, is to the belief that the divine judgment has taken place in Jesus' death and results in life being made available. This positive verdict of life is expressed symbolically through the blood and water flowing from Jesus' side. What Paul simply asserts theologically, namely, that the death of Jesus issues in life for believers (1 Thess 5:10), Matthew depicts in narrative symbolism with the bodies of the saints being resurrected at the point of Jesus' death (Matt 27:52, 53), and John portrays here in terms of blood and water coming from the crucified Jesus. This takes up the language from earlier in the narrative about the life of the Spirit emanating from Jesus — "out of his belly shall flow rivers of living water" (7:38). That, in turn, takes up the exodus tradition about water from the rock in the desert. And John's account of the significance of Jesus' death incorporates not only the exodus tradition but also its Jewish interpretation in which Moses struck the rock twice, and the first time it gushed blood and the second time water flowed out (cf. Targum *Pseudo-Jonathan* Num 20:11; *Midrash Rabbah* on Exodus 17). Testimony in this Gospel is primarily confessional and the truth claims about this Gospel's testimony are not to its circumstantial accuracy ensured by eyewitness testimony but to the explanation of God's purposes for human existence implied by its narrative witness.

In analyzing ancient biography the modern categories of "fact" or "fiction" set up a false dichotomy. This observation coheres with the findings of both the philosopher of religion, Paul Ricoeur, in his work on narrative, and the theologian, Hans Frei, in his study of biblical narrative. Ricoeur argues that historical narrative contains elements of fictionalization and fictional narrative contains elements of historicization.[14] Frei conceives of the Gospel narratives as both history-like and fiction-like. For him they are "at once intensely serious and historical in intent and fictional in form."[15] But their meaning or point is the story they tell — fictive elements and all. The theological corollary of Frei's view is that it is this story that is to be acknowledged as true. There are no superior criteria of truth to which one must appeal to determine the truth of such a narrative about the identity and significance of Jesus.[16]

Truth and Anti-Judaism

Casey usually formulates his second indictment in terms of this Gospel being anti-Jewish, but he can also claim that the Gospel is at the center of the deceit that constitutes Christian anti-Semitism.[17] Post-Holocaust awareness and Jewish-Christian dialogue have rightly made this topic inescap-

---

14. See P. Ricoeur, *Time and Narrative* (Chicago: University of Chicago Press, 1988), especially 3:180-92.

15. H. W. Frei, *The Identity of Jesus Christ: The Hermeneutical Bases of Dogmatic Theology* (Philadelphia: Fortress, 1975), 15.

16. On this point, see especially B. D. Marshall, *Trinity and Truth* (Cambridge: Cambridge University Press, 2000), 108-40, who argues for the unrestricted epistemic primacy of the Gospels' narrative identification of Jesus. As Marshall claims, "the narratives which identify Jesus are epistemic trump; if it comes to conflict between these narratives and any other sentences proposed for belief, the narratives win."

17. Cf. Casey, *Is John's Gospel True?* 228.

able.[18] Its seriousness for Christian reevaluation of the Gospel can perhaps be judged from the response of Richard Hays, who would on most matters of interpretation be thought to be at the conservative end of the spectrum of New Testament scholarship. Yet in his major book on New Testament ethics, he concludes that in its view of Judaism the Fourth Gospel distorts the Christian gospel and is a "theologically misconceived development."[19] This difficult and delicate issue featured in both the modern and postmodern critiques of John mentioned above, and both this and the following section are relevant as part of a response.

First, this Gospel's use of the term "the Jews." Some have suggested that its negative use refers only to the Judeans or to the Judean religious authorities. But this does not fit all the data. The term is also employed of Galileans or the crowds. Instead, the *sense* of the term is the broad one of Jews in contrast to members of other ethnic groups, but in its negative use its *referent* can vary, sometimes particularly having the authorities in view and, frequently, like the depiction of nearly all the characters in the narrative, having a representative function. The Jewish opposition to Jesus in the narrative is the vehicle for the views, attitudes, and actions of those Jews in the author's locale who have rejected the testimony of Johannine Christians about Jesus as Son of God, who have put them out of the synagogue for their beliefs, and may even have killed some of their number (cf. 9:22; 12:42; 16:2). But in the narrative such Jews are also representatives of the unbelieving world as a whole. The term "the Jews" then has an ethnic sense, but its referent transcends ethnic categories. This representative and not purely ethnic function can be seen on the surface of the narrative, as just two of many possible examples will show. In 13:33 Jesus, a Jew, says to his disciples, themselves Jews, "as I said to the Jews, so now I say to you. . . ." Then in 18:35 Pilate, the Roman governor, asks the ironic question, "I am not a Jew, am I?" to which the answer he expects is a negative one but the answer the reader is supposed to supply is in the affirmative. In his response to Jesus, Pilate proves himself to be a Jew in the special negative sense of this narrative's discourse, namely one who belongs to the world that does not believe in Jesus.

18. For a recent full-scale discussion of the topic from various perspectives, see R. Bieringer, D. Pollefyt, F. Vandecasteele-Vanneuville, eds., *Anti-Judaism and the Fourth Gospel: Papers of the Leuven Colloquium, 2000* (Assen: Royal van Gorcum, 2001).

19. R. B. Hays, *The Moral Vision of the New Testament* (San Francisco: HarperCollins, 1996), 434.

Those who put Johannine Christians out of the synagogue clearly held that the latter were in some sense no longer true Jews, particularly because of the status they assigned to Jesus in relation to God. It is a fair inference that in the light of such a dispute the Evangelist, while still holding that salvation is "of the Jews" (4:22), accepts the reality of Jewish Christians' situation, concedes the disputed name "Jews," and now gives it a primarily negative twist to mean unbelieving as opposed to believing Jews.

What is most offensive to our contemporary sensibilities is the fierceness of the Fourth Gospel's polemic in this debate. In particular, in John 8, which is often considered the *locus classicus* of Christian anti-Semitism, Jesus accuses his opposition of trying to kill him and on this basis asserts, "You are from your father the devil, and you choose to do your father's desires. He was a murderer from the beginning . . ." (8:44). Such rhetoric needs, however, to be heard in its first-century context, where it is unlikely to have sounded significantly different to Jewish ears from some of the fierce indictments made of Israel in its own Scriptures. Indeed, nearly all of the accusations Jesus makes in John 8 were made by Yahweh against Israel in Isaiah. Among the indictments in Isaiah, Yahweh had told Israel that its ancestor was a transgressor (Isa 43:27), that from birth it, too, had been a rebel (48:8), that it was involved in idolatry (44:9), and that such idolatry was participation with the devil (cf. LXX Isa 65:11: "you are those who have left me, and forget my holy mountain, and prepare a table for the devil"). Intra-Jewish polemics continued in this vein, so that *Testament of Dan* 5:6, "your prince is Satan," is an accusation of Dan against his children who, he believes, are abandoning the Lord, and one rabbi can call his brother "the firstborn of Satan" for giving a ruling with which he disagreed (Babylonian Talmud *Yebamot* 16a). This was typical of ancient debate in general, where such language functioned as a way of labeling one's opponents as opponents.

And of course this is reflected elsewhere in early Christian argumentation, where Jesus can tell Peter, "Get behind me, Satan!" (Mark 8:33), or Paul can call other Jewish Christian missionaries false apostles, deceitful workers, and servants of Satan (2 Cor 11:13-15). So this sort of language was employed of those who would have considered themselves Christian believers but whose stance various New Testament writers found objectionable.

This is the case with the polemic of John 8. "You are from your father the devil" is addressed not to unbelieving Jews in general but to Jews who have believed in Jesus (cf. 8:31, 32) but have not continued in their belief in a way the Evangelist finds satisfactory. When the test came and persecution and death became real options, they appear to have remained in the synagogue instead of identifying with those who made the full Johannine confession. From the Evangelist's perspective, they would have been thought of as betraying both Johannine Christians and Jesus by their stance. Loose characterizations of the language of John 8 as the polemic of hatred and as inducing violence should, then, be resisted. In its original context it is the language of reproach in the face of violence. It employed conventions recognizable within Jewish tradition and was intended to convey in strong terms that those who opposed violently the message of Jesus and were now acting similarly toward his followers were doing evil and that their behavior reflected that of the diabolical agency, who, within the Jewish worldview, was considered "a murderer from the beginning."

The dualism of this Gospel, in which "the Jews" are associated with this world, the flesh, or, on this one occasion, the devil, while believers are not of this world and are linked with the Spirit and God, is not an ontological dualism. This is where Hays,[20] among others, goes astray in his reading. The rhetoric in which the dualism is couched is not about a person's essential nature or the origin of his or her being. The very first reference to the world in an unfavorable sense makes clear the nature of the dualism. The coming of the Logos into the world created through him produces a division, whereby some believe but "the world did not know him" and "his own did not receive him" (1:10-12). "Not knowing" and "not receiving" are both volitional and part of the unbelieving world's alienation from its source of life. Later in the narrative the ethical (e.g., 3:19, 20) and epistemological (e.g., 12:35, 44-46) aspects of this dualism are to the fore. It has to do with two different systems of values that lead to different criteria for judging and knowing. What is more, it is clear that the negative side of such dualism applies to all who do not believe in Jesus, whether they are Jews, Samaritans, Greeks, or Romans. It is this distinction at the deeper level between belief and unbelief that determines on which side of the dualism a person is to be found in John's narrative — and ethnic Jews are, of course, found on both sides. And, for this Gospel, the divided state of affairs is meant to be temporary, since the whole point of God laying rightful claim on the created world in the lawsuit is to overcome the alienation that

---

20. Hays, *Moral Vision,* 427, 433.

has brought it about. Accordingly, in reading this Gospel's polemic, it should be remembered that the similarly fierce indictments by the prophets or by the *Testament of Dan* were also not ontological statements but judgments aimed at producing repentance. Similarly, in John's perspective, the note of condemnation of those who do not believe functions as a warning against choosing to exclude oneself from the God of Israel's life-giving purposes for humanity. For the Fourth Gospel it is perfectly compatible to see a division taking place within Judaism and humanity as a whole over the claims of Jesus and still to hold that the God of Jesus loves the world. After all, in one of this Gospel's most striking and best-known formulations — John 3:16, God is said to love the alienated and hostile world and to desire to provide life for it through the divine self-giving in the Son.

These observations indicate that the narrative's labels and rhetoric have a totally different purpose than condemnation of Jews as Jews. If we accept the widely held definition of anti-Semitism as hatred of the Jewish people as a group because they are Jewish, then the charge that this Gospel is anti-Semitic is anachronistic and clearly untrue. But once the text was employed in a setting quite separate from the rivalry of this specific Jewish family context, there could never be the same warrant for the debate about the significance of Jesus taking this particular form. Instead it is incumbent on any responsible interpreter of John's Gospel to make absolutely clear that what is said about "the Jews" in the narrative was never meant to be taken as referring to all Jews either then or since that time. Given how the characterization has in fact often been taken, this may sound like much too little terribly too late. But clarifying the object of our indictment — the Fourth Gospel in its original context or some aspects of its later Christian use — and suggesting that such use need not be the inevitable result of this Gospel becoming Christian Scripture remains significant if we are concerned about truth.

There are some who, in reaction to what has happened in the history of interpretation, wish to modify the Fourth Gospel's fundamental message about the decisiveness of Jesus as the criterion of truth. However, there is, it seems to me, an inevitable scandal of particularity about that message. The mission and person of Jesus in the midst of Israel and the proclamation of his early followers within and beyond Israel brought about and continue to bring about a division between belief and unbelief. Unless, with Casey, one regards the pervasive early Christian belief that Jesus was more than a Jewish prophet and in some sense one with God as a huge distortion of the truth,[21] then the central debate, without its first-century polemical conventions and no longer restricted to its particular ethnic participants in the Evangelist's location, will remain the same. It seems highly questionable whether Christians can be true to their tradition and in particular its roots in this Gospel, if they are willing to give up on its distinctive truth claim about God's decisive revelation in Jesus. Allegiance to such a claim by no means precludes Christians from dialogue with Jewish communities and with others who dispute the claim. It does entail that they will engage in such dialogue both with repentance for the sins of the past and with something substantial about which to dialogue. At the same time the misuse of this Gospel's discourse means that contemporary Christian readers have no option other than continual vigilance lest its clear-cut categories of "believers" over against "the world," instead of making sense of an exclusion by others, become employed to write off others, whoever they may be, as excluded from a just God's offer of well-being and life.

Truth and Power

Whatever stance is taken on the Fourth Gospel's alleged anti-Judaism, might not this issue still indicate, after all, as a late modern or postmodern perspective would claim, that a narrative like the Fourth Gospel with its story about God's lawsuit with the world that has truth as its explicit content has to be just another master narrative inducing marginalization, exclusion, and oppression? Such a view and its indictments should not, however, be accepted too quickly. For one thing, those who hold it have their own dilemmas. Their claim is inevitably part of its own broader metanarrative.[22] According to *their* grand narrative, power produces what passes for truth and this truth then becomes the means by which the powerful wield more power. But once this is accepted as the explanation of truth, then not only are any supposed criteria for judging between truth claims undermined, because they too are

21. Cf. Casey, *Is John's Gospel True?* e.g., 61-62, 219, 229.

22. As J. R. Middleton and B. J. Walsh, *Truth Is Stranger Than It Used to Be* (Downers Grove: InterVarsity, 1995), 77, write, "The postmodernist is . . . caught in a performative contradiction, arguing against the necessity of metanarratives precisely by (surreptitious) appeal to a metanarrative."

socially produced, but we are left to the competing claims of rival groups with their own smaller truths that themselves produce violence. The earlier quotation from Nietzsche reveals that there is a cost to leaving open the question of truth or explaining it in this way, a cost to its victims. The person who treats the question about truth with contempt has no compelling reason not to treat human life with contempt, as Nietzsche's horrendous throwaway line, "One Jew more or less — what does it matter?" illustrates. We need to be alert not only to the dangers but also to the potential for human well-being bound up with claims to truth, including that of the Fourth Gospel, which sees truth embodied in Jesus.[23] What may well be needed, then, in the face of postmodern suspicion of metanarratives is not the discarding of all such grand stories but instead, as others have suggested,[24] one that witnesses to a transcendent truth from its own inevitably particular perspective, recognizing the relation of its truth claim to issues of power, while at the same time decisively subverting violence.

Like the Synoptics, John's Gospel is about a victim of violence. Yet one of the features that distinguishes this Gospel is that it so explicitly makes the death of the victim the criterion for truth. While power is entailed in truth claims, the real issue is what sort of power and how it is to be exercised. The placement of the strongest statement about Jesus' mission — "For this I was born, and for this I came into the world, to testify to the truth" (18:37) — is highly significant. It comes, of course, in the Roman trial as the assertion to which Pilate's question about truth is the response and when, as he knows, Jesus is about to be sentenced to death. It comes not only in a setting that involves a struggle for power but also in the midst of a dialogue about power. Jesus has just said that his kingship or power is not of this world (18:36). It is exercised and displayed in this world but it has its source elsewhere. It is therefore not to be categorized from within Pilate's this-worldly value system where power means political dominance, diplomatic maneuvering, and strategic treaties. This means that there can be a radical reevaluation of human power. So when Jesus says that if his kingdom were of this world, his followers would be fighting to keep him

23. I am indebted here and in what follows both to the article by T. Söding, "Die Macht der Wahrheit und das Reich der Freiheit. Zur johanneischen Deutung des Pilatus-Prozesses (Joh 18,28–19,16)," *ZTK* 93 (1996): 35-58 (for this point, see Söding, 36) and to its excellent development in M. Volf, *Exclusion and Embrace* (Nashville: Abingdon, 1996), especially 264-71.

24. See especially Middleton and Walsh, *Truth Is Stranger*, 87-107.

from being handed over to "the Jews" (18:36), he is saying that his kingdom's power is not such as to be co-opted by the destructive forces of this world's cycle of violence. Both the programmatic use of force against an oppressive system by an insurrectionist like Barabbas (18:40) and the attempt to wield the sword in self-defense by a follower like Peter (cf. 18:10, 11) are ruled out as part of Jesus' kingdom program.

The way power is exercised in Jesus' kingdom is symbolized instead by his apparent weakness over against the apparent strength of Rome's political system. Jesus makes clear that his way of exercising power is in fact dependent on his role within a different frame of reference, his role as witness to the truth. That witness becomes the arbiter of the nature, purpose, and use of power. In the confrontation between Jesus' witness to the truth and this world's religious and political power, the recourse by the representatives of the world's power to crucifying the truth will demonstrate the weakness of power, and Jesus' willingness to give his life will demonstrate that the power of truth is a quite different sort of power. The weakness of his witness to truth becomes the vehicle for the power of self-giving love. It could not be clearer that in this narrative love and the refusal of violence are essential to its notion of truth.

The fulfillment of Jesus' task of witnessing to the truth is signaled by his final words on the cross — "it is completed" (19:30). The truth is established, true judgment in the lawsuit is given, in and through Jesus' death. By absorbing the violence of the negative verdict of death, Jesus, as noted above in the discussion of the language of witness, becomes the source of life, as blood and water flow from his side (19:34). The symbols of the blood and the water have been explained earlier in the narrative discourse (cf. 6:53, 54 and 7:38, 39). They point unmistakably to the positive verdict of life for humanity through the death of the victim. This reinforces the pattern of the larger scriptural narrative to which John's story relates itself.

As has been mentioned, there are echoes in particular of the remarkable account of the Meribah incident in Exodus 17. The place name picks up on the use of the Hebrew term *rib*, lawsuit, which features in 17:2, where the people are said to bring a suit or file a complaint against Moses. Their accusation against Moses is that he has betrayed them by bringing them to their present plight and they are prepared to sentence him to death by stoning. Moses discerns that the real question at stake is not so much his leadership but "Is the Lord among us or not?" (17:7); it is the Lord whom they are testing and putting on trial. In this situation Yahweh tells Moses to go on ahead of the people and to take with him the rod of judgment with which he struck the Nile. But instead of Moses being judged, Yahweh will stand trial and will stand on the rock to receive the sentence of judgment the people wished to carry out on Moses. And it is when Moses strikes the rock and the true judge takes the penalty the rebellious people deserved that provision is made for them and a stream of life-giving water gushes out from the rock.

Now here in the Fourth Gospel in the person of the incarnate Logos this God is depicted as taking the final consequences of being willing to be tried and judged. As Jesus as witness and judge absorbs the violent judgment of humans in this world instead of passing on its destructive consequences, he opens up the possibilities of new life. The power of the ultimate arbiter of truth is exhibited in the weakness of suffering and death. Jesus embodies the truth of divine judgment while subverting the notion that truth is simply power.

With this as its founding narrative, the community from which the Fourth Gospel originated, whatever its temptation to reciprocate the hostility of the world, was continually reminded that the death of Jesus is the radical openness of God toward the hostile other. Its members could now never forget that they themselves were part of the antagonistic world for which God had given God's self and so were not free to view themselves as an innocent "us" against an evil "them" but had themselves needed the Judge's positive verdict. There could be intense, highly charged debate precisely because of their concern for the truth and for taking seriously their differences with others. But there could be no question of the perpetuation of the destructive cycle of violence through manipulation, intimidation, and hatred of those with whom they disagreed. That would be to succumb to the notion of truth as self-serving power. The whole thrust of the Gospel narrative they acknowledge as true renounces such values for an entirely different set. The suffering and death of Jesus as *the* witness is to be the paradigm for bearing their own witness to the truth.

Appropriating the Truth:
The Witness of Word, Spirit and Community

This essay's subtitle is "The Fourth Gospel under Modern and Postmodern Interrogation." It is significant that a typical device of the Fourth

Gospel is to have interrogators find themselves under interrogation. This is what happens in the case both of Jesus' opponents during his public mission and of Pilate during his trial. This is also what is meant to happen with the Gospel's readers and their views about truth. Readers enter and experience the narrative world of this Gospel and then return to their own world with the possibility of an alternative perspective on it. This world of the Gospel's story asks them to reformulate their values and questions from within its own point of view, to take its criterion as the measure of truth. That truth, it has been suggested above, is not to be confused with the factual accuracy of each detail of the Gospel but is the message of its overall narrative that witnesses to the significance of a just God's disclosure of the divine verdict of life for humanity through the crucifixion and resurrection of one particular Jew, Jesus of Nazareth. The Fourth Gospel underlines the inevitable circularity of such a claim to truth. If its God exists, then by definition there can be no higher court of appeal to which the claim can be submitted. Jesus' witness to truth is, therefore, self-authenticating — "even if I testify on my own behalf, my witness is true" (8:14) — and the witness of this Gospel to Jesus is self-authenticating — "we know that his testimony is true" asserts the community about the Beloved Disciple's witness (21:24). In the end the witness of this narrative, incomplete and culturally conditioned as it is, has to suffice.

Later Christian readers acknowledged its ring of truth as John's Gospel took its place within the canonical fourfold gospel. Such readers have continued to find that its claim to truth is compelling and that the appropriate response toward this sort of claim is faith seeking understanding. In the words of the Johannine Jesus, "Anyone who resolves to do the will of God will know whether the teaching is from God or whether I am speaking on my own" (7:17). This Gospel's claim is that the truth about the relationship between God and humanity is embodied in a particular person, Jesus of Nazareth. Recognizing that truth, therefore, entails a relationship to this person, a commitment in which basic trust is also what enables critical engagement.

But another essential factor is at work in this process of the Gospel's readers becoming convinced of the truth of its witness to Jesus. This Gospel claims that its perspective on truth has been brought about by the Spirit, the Spirit of truth (14:17; 16:13, 14). God's involvement in the world has not ceased with the death and resurrection of Jesus. Instead, the Spirit as the divine agent acts to promote the cause of God and Jesus. The truth witnessed to by the Fourth Gospel involves the triune God. "When the Advocate comes, whom I will send to you from the Father, the Spirit of truth who comes from the Father, he will testify on my behalf" (15:26). The Spirit presses home the divine verdict, overturning the world's values and its criteria for truth and judgment (16:8-11) and mediating the experience of the positive verdict of life. Yet the power of new life in the Spirit in no way bypasses the weakness of the cross. The promise of the life-giving waters of the Spirit flowing from the belly of Jesus (7:38) anticipates the crucifixion scene in which water flows from the wounded side of Jesus. It is *this* Spirit of truth who enables readers to accept the narrative's invitation to affirm its truth by participating in its continuing story within the community of those who are willing to eschew coercion and hatred and to risk following the witness of Jesus' suffering love.

In this way John's story becomes an extended metaphor by which to live, as human witness to the truth is demonstrated in the non-identical repetition of the divine love that refuses to impose its own witness by force but, with all the attendant costs, is willing to allow the other to remain other. For the Fourth Gospel this love is primarily to be displayed through a community of witness. Indeed, the credibility of any continuing witness to the truth of the narrative is bound up with the quality of this community's life. In praying that his disciples and those who will believe through their witness be sanctified in the truth (17:17-19), Jesus makes clear that the truth at stake hinges on this loving and unified community, as he asks, "that they may all be one . . . so that the world may believe that you have sent me" (17:21, cf. also 17:23). To be followers of the sent one, who was in a relation of loving intimacy with the one who sent him, is to produce evidence that substantiates the truth of the sent one's cause by embodying unity in love. Since the truth that has been established in the narrative is the oneness between Jesus and God, it is not surprising that the witness to that truth should entail the oneness of the witnesses.

For readers of John's Gospel who respond to its claims with a faith seeking critical understanding, historical consciousness, ethical idealism, and issues of power and ideology will continue to require serious negotiation but will not provide the determinative criteria of truth by which they judge this Gospel. Instead, the Spirit of truth enables them to appreciate fully the irony of Pilate's "What is truth?" question, when the one of whom he asks it has earlier announced, "I am . . . the truth" (14:6), and then to be willing to have their lives shaped by the narrative's paradoxical and subversive notion that the one who embodies the truth of the divine judgment is himself judged. The Spirit's witness in and through the Gospel of John, then, is to the truth displayed in the victim of this world's violence who, with pierced hands and side, offers the positive verdict of life, and who offers it through a community of loving service not to any one group that can lay exclusive claim to it but to a world to which all belong, whatever their ethnic origin.

The Gospels in Early Christianity:
Their Origin, Use, and Authority

Lee Martin McDonald

It should not be surprising that the early Christians frequently made use of and eventually cited by name the writings that we now call the canonical Gospels. Given the fact that Jesus was the final authority, that is, the final *canon* for the church, it would be strange if the early church had ignored the various witnesses to his life, ministry, death, and resurrection that were in circulation in the first two centuries of the church's life. The literature that focused on Jesus' words and deeds was welcomed in the churches probably from its early production, and the authority of this tradition was widely acknowledged in the churches, whether in canonical or non-canonical Gospels. The sources that were used to produce the canonical Gospels were primarily oral traditions that were eventually written down and perhaps edited over a period of time to produce what the church later called "Gospels." These Gospels were utilized in the church's worship and catechetical instruction, its defense of the "gospel" in the pagan world, and in its response to the heretical challenges it faced by the end of the first century and beyond. Moody Smith is correct when he concludes that those who wrote the Gospels initially did so with the idea of producing an authoritative guide to the Christian faith for the churches and also with the idea of continuing the biblical story. He adds that the continuation of the biblical story is a further distinguishing feature of the New Testament writings in general in that they generally continue or presuppose the biblical story of salvation history for the people of God and that they interpret that history.[1] Von Campenhausen agrees and says the Evangelists intended from the beginning that what they wrote be read in the churches.[2]

Scholars have long been aware that the way that the Gospels were crafted also displays the church's long use of these materials in their oral transmission prior to their being written down. Christians were not devoid of teaching materials before the Gospels were produced in the churches. Indeed, the teaching ministry of the church existed from its very beginning,[3] and the skills employed by the Jews of the first and second centuries to transmit or teach faithfully and orally their many religious traditions were also used in the church to transmit and teach its story and religious traditions. The earlier and still quite valuable contribution to this study by Birger Gerhardsson supports this and he shows in considerable detail and with many examples how those traditions were passed on in the churches.[4] To those who contend that the early followers of Jesus were not sophisticated enough to utilize such methods or were simply unaware of them, Gerhardsson observes that there are three common erroneous views among scholars about Christian origins that must be called into question: (1) that there was no positive relationship between Pharisaic teachers on the one side and Jesus and the early church on the other; (2) that Jesus, his disciples, and other leaders of the early church were, and remained, simple and unlearned men of the people; and finally, (3) that the "spontaneous charismatic aspect of Jesus and early Christianity ruled out acceptance of traditional forms, conscious technique and reasoned behaviour."[5]

This, of course, does not mean that the Gospels were understood as sacred Scripture either in their oral transmission or when those traditions were put into written form. Because of their subject matter, namely the words and activity of Jesus, it was clear early on, however, that these writ-

---

1. D. M. Smith, "When Did the Gospels Become Scripture?" *JBL* 119 (2000): 3-20, here pp. 8-9.

2. H. von Campenhausen, *The Formation of the Christian Bible* (Philadelphia: Fortress, 1972), 122-23.

3. Notice how teaching was an important ingredient in the churches from the beginning (Acts 2:42; 6:2-4; 28:31; 1 Cor 12:28; Rom 12:7; Eph 4:11, etc.).

4. See his *Memory and Manuscript: Oral Tradition and Written Tradition in Rabbinic Judaism and Early Christianity* with *Tradition and Transmission in Early Christianity* (reprint, Grand Rapids: Eerdmans, 1998).

5. Gerhardsson, *Transmission in Early Christianity*, 23.

ings would be taken seriously by the churches for whom they were produced — and they were! The widespread appeal of this tradition in the
church, even in its oral stage of development, can be seen even in the New
Testament writings themselves.[6] As we will see presently, there is considerable evidence for the widespread acceptance of this tradition both in its
oral transmission stage, for example in Paul's letters, Acts, 1 Peter, and
James, but also in the writings of the church Fathers when they depended
on both the oral and written transmission of that tradition about Jesus.[7]

How did the church receive the canonical Gospels? The canonical
Gospels have the place of priority in all of the surviving lists and catalogues of Scriptures in the fourth and fifth centuries and generally in the
order currently found in our New Testaments, namely, Matthew, Mark,
Luke, and John.[8] As we will soon see, however, this does not mean that by
the fourth century the whole church unanimously accepted the canonical
Gospels and no others as its sacred gospel literature. There continued to be
a number of churches that preferred noncanonical writings such as the
Diatessaron, as well as other non-canonical Gospels like the *Infancy Gospel
of James* or the thirty other non-canonical Gospels. Those writings and
others continued to have a significant impact on the churches of the
fourth and fifth centuries. As we will see later, the Syrian churches especially, but not exclusively, gave priority to the use of Tatian's harmonization of the canonical Gospels over the use of the individual canonical Gospels. Tatian's use of the canonical Gospels to produce his harmony, of
course, underscores the value that he attributed to them.

The focus in this paper will be on how the churches of the first and

6. For a useful discussion of the influence of the sayings of Jesus in their oral or pre-
written stage of development in the writings of Paul, see the still valuable volume by D. L.
Dungan, *The Sayings of Jesus in the Letters of Paul* (Philadelphia: Fortress, 1971).

7. For many examples of this influence, see the very important work of H. Koester,
Ancient Christian Gospels: Their History and Development (Philadelphia: Trinity, 1990) and
his earlier work, *Synoptischen Überlieferung bei den apostolischen Vätern* (Berlin: Akademie-
Verlag, 1957), and the massive and foundational work of E. Massaux, *The Influence of the
Gospel of Saint Matthew on Christian Literature before Saint Irenaeus,* ed. A. J. Bellinzoni,
trans. N. J. Belval, S. Hecht (Macon: Mercer University Press, 1986). Along with these, B. M.
Metzger, *The Canon of the New Testament: Its Origin, Development and Significance* (Oxford:
Clarendon, 1987), also offers many examples of the early church's use of the New Testament
writings, especially the canonical Gospels.

8. These are listed in L. M. McDonald, *The Formation of the Christian Biblical Canon*
(revised edition, Peabody: Hendrickson, 1995), 274-76.

second centuries welcomed and utilized the gospel traditions that had been handed down to them in both oral and written form. This period of time is foundational for their future in the church and it is possible to observe some development in their reception even if the transitions may be incomplete due to the scantiness of the sources available. We can trace something of the developing influence and acceptance of the gospel tradition and how this tradition, after being put in written form, was accepted in the churches and recognized as Scripture at the earliest by the end of the second century. Initially the gospel traditions were received as reliable reports of the sayings and deeds of Jesus and only later were they received in their place of priority in the canon of New Testament Scriptures. The references or allusions to these works in the second century are specifically to the sayings and deeds of Jesus, but mostly to the sayings of Jesus. Generally speaking, through the first two-thirds of that century, there are few references to the books themselves or their authors. Eusebius (c. 320-30) indicates that Papias (ca. 130-40) knew of the traditions of Jesus in books produced by Mark and Matthew, and indicates that he made use of 1 John, 1 Peter, and the *Gospel of Hebrews* (*H.E.* 3.39.14-17), but he also observes that Papias still preferred the oral traditions instead of those that were written. While Christian writings were known and used in the churches in the early second century, they were considered by some, at least Papias, to be secondary to the oral traditions circulating in the churches or the voices of those who had heard the apostles. In the now famous statement, Papias wrote: "For I did not suppose that information from books would help me so much as the word of a living and surviving voice" (*H.E.* 3.39.4). The names of the producers of the Gospels were unimportant until later in the second century, beginning with Irenaeus.

From the time when the Gospels were written until the middle of the second century at the earliest, apostolic authorship had not yet emerged as one of the significant features of the new Christian writings.[9] The canonical Gospels were produced anonymously, but in the middle to late second century apostolic names, or names of men who assisted apostles (Mark and Luke), were attached to these writings to lend credibility to their reports. What it was that led to the adding of apostolic names to the New

---

9. See, for example, Clement of Rome, who in *1 Clement* 37.3-4 shows awareness of the language of 1 Cor 15:23 and 1 Cor 12:21 respectively, but makes no mention of Paul as the author even though he knew it, as he demonstrates in *1 Clement* 47.1-3.

Testament literature (the Gospels, but perhaps others like 1 John and Hebrews) is not clear, but it probably started when both the eyewitnesses and those who had heard them had died. This was roughly the same time that pseudonymous writings in the names of the apostolic community began to appear throughout the second century. The name of an apostle was apparently intended to validate the reliability of the information in the pseudonymous writings. As New Testament scholars know, the early dating and reliability of Mark and Luke have in part been supported precisely because their work was *not* attributed to apostles. Could these non-apostolic works have survived had they been produced in the second century, when apostolic names were the order of the day? Their widespread acceptance before that time speaks to the widespread tradition (Synoptic) that is contained in them. Eventually Matthew and John were acknowledged by the churches to be apostolic in origin, but this was long after their use in the churches, as the long list of references to sayings of Jesus in these works in the Apostolic Fathers attests. The interpreting, presuming, and continuing of the biblical story, and especially the story and significance of Jesus, appear to be important ingredients in the New Testament Gospels and in many of the Epistles.[10]

The Bible is not a collection of writings that simply posits the revelation of God into loosely connected texts, but rather it sets forth a story in which the revelation of God unfolds historically and is proclaimed and explained. While there were extra-canonical Gospels that posited the sayings of Jesus as revelation without a context or narrative for understanding them,[11] that is not the case in the canonical Gospels and the book of Acts.

The value of the Gospels as reliable reports of the church's sacred traditions about Jesus was soon recognized in the churches, and several books

10. Smith, "When Did the Gospels Become Scripture?" 17-18, in part makes this point. Along with the Gospels, several of Paul's letters were also read publicly in various churches (Col 4:16), and this suggests that they too were received as authoritative writings of some sort early on, perhaps by Paul himself. Notice, for example, Paul's authoritative tone in many passages in his letters, which suggests that he viewed his writings as authoritative if not prophetic (1 Cor 5:3-5; 6:1-6; 7:10-11, 17-20, 40; 11:23-34; Gal 5:1-4, passim). The author of 2 Peter (perhaps ca. 90-100 or as late as ca. 150-80) also acknowledged Paul's writings as Scripture (3:15-16), and his comments may be reflective of what many churches believed about the letters of Paul by the end of the second century.

11. For example the *Gospel of Thomas*, the *Dialogue of the Savior*, and perhaps also the revelations found in the *Apocryphon of John* and the *Sophia Jesu Christi*.

were probably circulating among the churches at least within a few decades of their production if not sooner. By the end of the second century, they were also beginning to be received by many Christians as authoritative Scripture. In what follows, I will focus only on the canonical Gospels in their transition from the oral tradition that lies behind them to their status as sacred Scriptures in many churches by the end of the second century.

The Gospel Tradition in the Early Church

The initial authority attributed to the canonical Gospels in the early churches was doubtless because they told the story of Jesus, the Lord of the church. This is why the early church writings appealed to the sayings of Jesus themselves rather than to the apostles or to the books they reportedly produced. The widespread and early reception of the canonical Gospels in the churches was due to the fact that they continued a popular tradition that had long been circulating in those churches. The tradition (written or oral) that lies behind the Synoptic Gospels was widely received in the churches years before the actual production of those Gospels. The information in them was also compatible with the basic outlines and teachings of the Gospel of John and with much of the rest of the New Testament writings.

David Dungan argues, unlike what some scholars claim, that Paul was significantly interested in the sayings and the traditions about Jesus. He contends that even when Paul does not specifically refer to the words and deeds of Jesus, he nevertheless assumes their familiarity among his readers. He makes this claim on the basis of examination of two important Pauline passages (1 Cor 7:1-7 and 9:4-18), but he points to several other Pauline texts as well to illustrate his point. Dungan concludes from these texts that "the alleged contrast between Pauline Christianity and that branch of the early Church which preserved the Palestinian Jesus-tradition that finally ended up in the Synoptic gospels is a figment of the imagination. In fact, they were one and the same branch. . . ."[12]

While Dungan finds many similarities between Paul and the Synoptic tradition, especially Matthew, he agrees that there are no parallels in that tradition to support Paul's stand on the Law. He adds that "the reason

---

12. Dungan, *Sayings*, 150.

Paul did not appeal to any sayings of Jesus in support of his stand on the Torah was because there weren't any"![13] He also shows throughout his work that Paul "stands squarely within the tradition that led to the Synoptic gospels, and is of one mind with the editors of those gospels, not only in the way he understands what Jesus (the Lord) was actually commanding in the sayings themselves but also in the way he prefigures the Synoptic editors' use of them."[14]

Koester agrees with Dungan and shows that, even though Paul's references to sayings of Jesus are rare, he nonetheless makes several allusions to the Synoptic sayings. For example, Paul's discussion of divorce in 1 Cor 7:10-11 is quite similar to that of Jesus in Mark 10:11-12. Paul also makes it clear when he does not have anything "from the Lord" on a particular matter (1 Cor 7:25). The argument for financial support for the apostles in 1 Cor 9:14 is similar to Luke 10:7 (Q), and Paul's reference to the Lord's Supper in 1 Cor 11:23-26 is very close in substance to Mark 14:22-25. Koester also shows Pauline parallels to other Synoptic traditions, observes that they fit a particular pattern related to church life and order, and adds that these sayings are concentrated in Romans 12–14, 1 Corinthians 7–14, and 1 Thessalonians 5.[15] He concludes that the parallels are either church-order materials from the Gospel of Mark or sayings from Luke's Sermon on the Plain material. Only in the case of 1 Cor 9:14 is the Synoptic parallel from a different context.[16] Paul was thus familiar with largely oral tradition that was commonly circulating in the first-century churches and was later preserved in the Synoptic Gospels.

The Synoptic tradition also has significant parallels in 1 Peter and James.[17] There are numerous Synoptic parallels and citations in the writings of the second-century church Fathers, as we can see in the extensive

13. Dungan, *Sayings*, 150.

14. Dungan, *Sayings*, 139.

15. These include Rom 12:14 (Luke 6:27 [Q]); Rom 12:17 and 1 Thess 5:15 (Luke 6:29 [Q]); Rom 13:7 (Mark 12:13-17); Rom 14:13 (Mark 9:42); Rom 14:14 (Mark 7:15); 1 Thess 5:2 (Luke 12:39 [Q]); 1 Thess 5:13 (Mark 9:50); and possibly also Rom 12:18 (Mark 9:50) and Rom 14:10 (Luke 6:37 [Q]).

16. Koester, *Ancient Christian Gospels*, 52-54.

17. 1 Peter: 4:14 (Luke 6:22); 3:9, 16 (Luke 6:28); 2:19-20 (Luke 6:32-33); 3:14 (Matt 5:10); 2:12 (Matt 5:16b). 2 Peter: 1:16-18 (Mark 9:2-8; Matt 17:1-8; Luke 9:28-36). James: 1:5 (Luke 11:9 par. Matt 7:7); 2:5 (Luke 6:20 par. Matt 5:3); 4:2-3 (Matt 7:7, 11); 4:9 (Luke 6:21 par. Matt 5:4); 4:10 (Luke 14:11 par. Matt 23:12); 5:1 (Luke 6:24-25); 5:2-3 (Matt 6:20 par. Luke 12:33); 5:12 (Matt 5:34-37). These are listed in Koester, *Ancient Christian Gospels*, 64-65, 71-73.

discussions and listings in Edouard Massaux's massive collection of these references.[18] The sayings of Jesus, whether oral or written, were "canonical," that is they were supremely authoritative in the early church, but where they were located, namely in the Gospels that were produced by the apostles, was of little consequence until around the middle of the second century.

What we can infer from the available second-century evidence is that in many cases the word order in the allusions to or citations of the sayings of Jesus in the Synoptic traditions are so close in word selection and order in the early church Fathers that a dependence on the Synoptic Gospels is likely. In many other cases, however, the words are similar but not exact, and this may suggest that the writers were borrowing loosely from that tradition or that there was a common oral tradition about Jesus circulating in the early church known to both the Evangelists and the second-century Fathers. There are by far more parallels with Matthew in the second-century writings than with Mark, Luke, or John. A few of the more obvious examples of parallels to Matthew are in the footnote below, but the reader will find many more in Massaux's collection.[19]

Clement of Rome (ca. 95), for example, cites mostly the Old Testament Scriptures but shows an awareness of Matthew and several other New Testament writings, especially Paul's letters. He generally does not cite them by name or author, except in one case in which he clearly states that Paul is the author of 1 Corinthians and he goes on to refer to 1 Cor 1:10ff. The passage is instructive because he also calls Paul's letter a "gospel." He writes: "Take up the epistle of the blessed Paul the Apostle. What did he first write to you at the beginning of 'the gospel' *(tou euangeliou)?*

18. Massaux, *The Influence of the Gospel of Saint Matthew.* See the very useful lists of all of the parallels and citations of the canonical Gospel literature in his indexes of references to the New Testament in all three volumes (see 1:166-72; 2:351-66; and 3:250-58).

19. *1 Clement:* 16.17 (Matt 11:29); 24.5 (Matt 13:3-9); 46.8 (Matt 26:24; 18:6). *Barnabas:* 4.14 (Matt 22:14); 5.8-9 (Matt 9:13); 7.9 (Matt 27:28). Ignatius: *Smyrneans* 1.1 (Matt 3:15); *Philadelphians* 3.1 (Matt 15:13). *2 Clement:* 3.2 (Matt 10:32); 4.2 (Matt 7:21); 6.2 (Matt 16:26). Polycarp, *Philippians:* 2.3 (Matt 5:3, 10); 12.3 (Matt 5:16, 44, 48). *Martyrdom of Polycarp:* 4 (Matt 10:23); 6.2 (Matt. 10:36; 27:5); 7.1 (Matt 26:55; 6:10); 8.1 (Matt 21:7); 11.2 (Matt 25:46); and 14.2 (Matt 20:22-23). There are too many examples in the second century to list here, but they are listed by Massaux (see n. 18 above and Massaux, *Influence* 1:58, 83, 121; 2:25, 52, 164, 242, 262, and 293; 3:9, 102, 115, 119, 132, 143, and 181). Another quite useful listing and discussion of the Apostolic Fathers' parallels with the New Testament is found in Metzger, *The Canon of the New Testament,* 39-73.

With true inspiration *(ep' alētheias pneumatikōs)* he charged you concerning himself and Cephas and Apollos, because even then you had made yourselves partisans" (*1 Clement* 47.1-3, adapted from LCL).[20] The New Testament writers are generally not mentioned by name *as writers* in the first half of the second century, except for this exception and the one referring to Papias noted above (*H.E.* 3.39.14-17). Again, the sources where the church Fathers obtained this tradition about Jesus at that time were either widely known or perhaps unimportant to them, possibly both.

The pseudo-Clementine letter (ca. 130-40), also known as *2 Clement,* was written three or four decades after *1 Clement* and has several close similarities in content and word order with Synoptic Gospels.[21] This, of course, suggests some dependence. In several instances, the mixed language of the allusions or references varies considerably from that found in the canonical Gospels, and dependence cannot be clearly determined.[22] Five others were apparently cited from memory since they are not as close in word parallels, but they are close in subject matter.[23]

Our point here is that in the early part of the second century, there are many parallels between the Synoptic tradition, whether oral or written, and the early church Fathers. As we will note below, however, there are also some important parallels with John's Gospel. It is obvious that the Synoptic tradition was well known in the Christian communities of the second century. The many allusions to and direct citations of the Synoptic tradi-

20. It may seem odd that Clement appealed to Paul's writings more than to the Synoptic tradition and even stranger that Paul is later ignored by Justin in favor of the Synoptic tradition. There is not one clear reference to Paul in Justin's writings, but Clement acknowledges the inspiration of Paul's writings (*1 Clement* 47.1-2). What changed between the time of Clement and Justin is that Marcion appealed almost exclusively to Paul to justify his rejection of the Jewish Scriptures and traditions, but Justin, unlike Marcion, was equally anxious to root Christian faith squarely within the tradition of Israel and its Scriptures. Since Paul was used by Marcion to support his anti-Jewish bias, it is not surprising that Justin ignored Paul and appealed to the tradition that Marcion apparently rejected.

21. *2 Clement* 13 (Matt 5:7; 6:14; 7:1, 2) and 46 (Matt 26:24; 18:6; Mark 14:21; 9:42; Luke 22:22; 17:1, 2).

22. For example, we observe three such references in *2 Clement* that are strikingly close parallels to the Gospels but without the above sharpness, namely, 2.4 (Matt 9:13; Mark 2:17); 3.2 (Mark 10:32); 6.1 (Matt 6:24; Luke 16:13; Matt 16:26; Mark 8:36).

23. See, for example, *2 Clement* 2.7 (Luke 19:10); 4.7 (Matt 7:21); 8.5 (Luke 16:10-12); 9.11 (Matt 12:50; Mark 3:35; Luke 8:21); 13.4 (Luke 6:32, 35).

tion in the second century testify to the widespread acceptance of that tradition in the early churches.[24]

From Oral Traditions to "Memoirs"

While it may seem strange to us, given the place of priority of the apostles in the New Testament and early church Fathers, several important books of the New Testament were produced anonymously, namely, the Gospels, Acts, Hebrews, and 1 John. In the mid-second century, when both the eyewitnesses and those who had heard them were gone, apostolic authorship became an important matter in the church. At that time, numerous pseudonymous gospels, acts, and even letters were produced in apostles' name. A fairly comprehensive collection of these pseudonymous writings with significant comment is in Schneemelcher's *New Testament Apocrypha*.[25] Many scholars contend that some of the early church's pseudonymous literature actually made it into the New Testament canon because it was attributed to apostles. Such literature, however, was produced when the practice of attaching apostolic names to literature had grown in significance in the churches (ca. 130-50).

When the canonical Gospels were written, apostolic authorship had not yet emerged within the church as one of the most significant features of Christian writings, and that probably accounts for why the canonical Gospels were produced anonymously. Initially, matters of authorship were not important features of early Christian writings.[26] When the notion emerged that apostolic authorship added credibility to the various traditions about Jesus that were circulating in the churches, then the names of

24. It is worth noting that the early church Fathers cited the sayings of Jesus more accurately than they did the various narrative materials in the Gospels. This could mean that the sayings were circulating at first and for a longer period of time without the narrative in which they are found or that the church Fathers of the second century saw the former as more valuable and handed on more carefully what was considered authoritative in the churches.

25. W. Schneemelcher, ed., *New Testament Apocrypha*, trans. R. McL. Wilson (revised edition, Louisville: Westminster/John Knox, 1991-92). In German: *Neutestamentliche Apocryphen* (Tübingen: J. C. B. Mohr, 1989-90).

26. Note that when Papias speaks of the Gospels (Eusebius, *H.E.* 3.39.15-16), he discusses Mark's first and Matthew's second even though he considered Matthew to be the author of "oracles" of Jesus. In neither case does he call these productions "Gospels."

apostles who remembered the words and deeds of Jesus were commonly noted and appealed to for guidance in church life and its witness.[27] This development also lies behind Irenaeus's notion of apostolic succession.[28] His point was that those who were closest to Jesus would likely tell a more accurate story about who he was, what he said and did, and what was done to him than would those who were not eyewitnesses. Those eyewitnesses would most likely also pass on that sacred tradition to their successors. While he preferred the use of the apostolic writings in his argument, he also acknowledged the importance of the apostolic tradition handed on in the churches. He writes: "For how should it be if the apostles themselves had not left us writings? Would it not be necessary in that case to follow the course of the tradition that they handed down to those to whom they handed over the leadership of the churches?" (*Adversus haereses* 3.4.1, adapted from ANF). Until Irenaeus, however, the focus of authority in the churches was generally on the apostles as a group and not on the individual apostles who reportedly produced the Gospels. This growth in the importance of apostolic authority was accompanied in the churches by references to the "memoirs" or "remembrances" of the apostles. In Justin, for instance, it is not clear which writings he had in mind since, as we will note below, he cites or alludes to more gospel traditions than the canonical Gospels. Priority began to be given to certain writings precisely because of their supposed apostolic origin. Evidence for the widespread approval of "apostolic" literature in the churches by the latter half of the second century can be seen in the use and citation not only of canonical literature but also of extra-canonical literature produced under apostolic names, such as the *Gospel of Thomas,* the *Infancy Gospel of James,* the *Acts of Paul,* the *Gospel of Peter,* the *Acts of Andrew,* and many others.[29]

The Gnostic communities also appealed to "remembered" knowledge from the apostles. The "remembrances" of the apostles was the source of a secret knowledge that the Gnostics claimed was passed on by the apostles to certain individuals in the church. In turn, those individuals "remembered" these words and committed them to writing. The implication

27. The authority of the apostles was clearly acknowledged in the church's earliest traditions (cf. 1 Cor 12:28 and even Gal 1:15-17; 2:9; cf. Eph 4:11 and Acts 2:42; 6:2, 6; 8:1), but attaching authorial names to the story of Jesus to show the reliability of the reports was a later phenomenon.

28. See *Adversus haereses* 3.3.3.

29. See Schneemelcher, *New Testament Apocrypha,* for additional examples.

of this was, of course, that the writings that contained the "remembered" words of the apostles became recognized as authoritative teachings in their churches. Koester shows that the word "remember" was a decisive term for the trustworthiness of oral tradition and that it played an important role in establishing the credibility of other literature. For example, in the *Apocryphon of James* (ca. 130-50 CE), the author claims that ". . . the twelve disciples [were] all sitting together at the same time and *remembering* what the Savior had said to each one of them, whether in secret or openly, and [putting it] in books." This emphasis on the apostles is also found in the Gnostic *Letter of Peter to Philip*, where what the apostles said by way of instruction from Jesus is repeated frequently to clarify its significance for faith (133, 136, 138-140). Koester offers other examples of remembering and transmitting those remembrances in the churches.[30]

Justin, writing from Rome (ca. 160), refers to the apostolic tradition thusly: "For the apostles in the memoirs composed by them, which are called Gospels, have thus delivered to us what was enjoined upon them: 'that Jesus took bread, and when He had given thanks, said, "This do you in *remembrance* of me, this is my body"; and, after the same manner . . .'" (*1 Apologia* 66.3, adapted from ANF, italics added). For Justin, the "memoirs" were writings of the apostles and these were gradually becoming known as "Gospels." In other words, they were reliable written reports of the good news about Jesus, and written documents were considered more reliable than the oral traditions that were circulating in the churches. Justin shows that the Gospels or the "memoirs of the Apostles" *(apomnēmoneumata tōn apostolōn)* as he calls them were used to establish doctrine (*Trypho* 100.1) and also to relate the story of Jesus' Passion. For instance, when introducing quotations from Luke 22:42, 44, he writes, "For in the memoirs which I say were drawn up by His apostles and those who followed them, [it is recorded] His sweat fell down like drops of blood" (*Trypho* 103.8, ANF). He also appeals to the canonical Gospels when explaining the apostolic testimony regarding the Eucharist, and acknowledges that "the Apostles commanded them: that Jesus, taking bread and having given thanks, he said . . ." (*1 Apologia* 66.3, ECF). After these opening words, Justin cites Mark 14:22-24, which is similar to 1 Cor 11:23-25, as a description of what was said in the Eucharist. He also describes

---

30. Koester, *Ancient Christian Gospels,* 34. The text he cited is taken from NHC 1.2, 7-15.

the reading of the Gospels in Christian worship, either alongside of or used alternatively with the Old Testament writings. In his account of a typical worship service in the Christian community, he claims that "on the day called Sunday there is a meeting in one place of those who live in cities or the country, and *the memoirs of the apostles or the writings of the prophets are read as long as time permits*" (1 *Apologia* 67.3, ECF, italics added).

Koester observes that Justin does not use any previously established philosophical memoirs to make the Gospels more acceptable to others, but rather he makes use of a compound of the common verb "remember" (*mnēmoneuein/apomnēmoneuein*) to say that what was remembered and passed on was also reliable. This word and its cognates, Koester claims, were "often used in the quotation formulae for orally transmitted sayings of Jesus."[31] While Justin uses this term only twice in his *Apology*, as noted above, he uses it thirteen times in his *Dialogue with Trypho*.[32] Apparently Justin employs the term "memoirs" to lend credibility to the Gospels when he uses them to support his arguments against Trypho.

All of this presupposes that Justin himself accepted the Gospels as reliable history, but it is not clear that he accepted them as sacred Scripture. While the "memoirs" were read in worship along with the Prophets — a short step to recognizing their scriptural status, he nevertheless does not call them "Scripture," nor does he place them on an equal footing with the Prophets. Koester maintains that even though Justin uses the formula "it is written" in reference to Gospel quotations, this does not mean "it is written in Holy Scripture," but rather "it is recorded in a written document that Jesus said," as in the case of *Trypho* 100.1.[33] Koester supports this view by showing that sometimes quotations from the Gospels are also referred to as "acts" *(akta)* (1 *Apologia* 35.9 and 48.3; cf. also 38.7), in which cases the Gospels are referred to as reliable witnesses to what Jesus did or said. Justin valued the Gospels for their reliability and believed that they documented

---

31. Koester, *Ancient Christian Gospels,* 33-34, 38-39. Observe also the Papias tradition in Eusebius, *H.E.* 3.39.3-4, 15 in reference to Mark, and *H.E.* 3.39.15-16 in reference to Mark and Matthew. Note the times that he uses "remembered" in this text.

32. See his *Dialogue with Trypho* 100.4; 101.3; 102.5; 103.6, 8; 104.1; 105.1, 5, 6; 106.1, 3, 4; 107.1. It is noteworthy that Justin refers to Papias's statement about Mark "remembering" Peter's words (see Eusebius, *H.E.* 3.39.3-4, 15) and refers to "Peter's Memoirs" when he cites Mark 3:16-17 in *Dialogue* 106.3.

33. Koester, *Ancient Christian Gospels,* 41.

the historical fulfillment of prophecy and therefore also the truth of the Christian faith. He draws frequently on Matthew and Luke in his summary of the life of Jesus beginning with his birth (see *1 Apologia* 31.7). But again, he does not generally cite the Gospels by their authors. That comes later with Irenaeus.

The focus on apostolic authorship at the beginning of the third century clearly shifts to individual apostolic authors. This can be seen in the fact that Tertullian (ca. 200) gave priority to John and Matthew over Luke and Mark (notice the order) because the latter were not written by apostles. "Of the apostles, therefore, John and Matthew first instill faith into us; whilst of apostolic men, Luke and Mark renew it afterwards" (Tertullian, *Adversus Marcionem* 4.2.2, ANF). He likewise criticized Marcion for using only the Gospel of Luke instead of one by an apostle. He writes: "Luke, however, was not an apostle, but only an apostolic man; not a master, but a disciple, and so inferior to a master — at least as far subsequent to him as the apostle whom he followed was subsequent to the others" (*Adversus Marcionem* 4.2.5, ANF). Tertullian received Luke and Mark, but he did not place them on the same level as Matthew and John. He held the apostolic witness to be more important in the church than non-apostolic writings. In a short time, acknowledgement of the reliability of and authority of apostolic documents in telling the story of Jesus led some churches to acknowledge their scriptural status also. We will return to that later.

From Memoirs to Gospels

For centuries the church has referred to those writings in the New Testament that describe the ministry, Passion, and resurrection of Jesus as "Gospels," and it is easy to forget that these literary compositions that we now know by that name were not so designated when they were first produced. Initially the term referred to good news as "glad tidings," but in the second century it was used of a genre of literature.

The term "gospel" *(euangelion)* is used regularly in the Greek OT (LXX). In Luke 4:18, 19, Jesus cites Isa 61:1, 2 to speak of the "glad tidings" that God is about to bring to his people through his ministry. In Rom 10:15 Paul cites Isa 52:7 to tell of the blessings of those who bring the Good News to others. This is not unlike how the term was used in the Greco-Roman world when it was used to speak of the news of the birth of Caesar Augustus (Octavian), the Roman emperor.[34] When the "gospel" is proclaimed by Paul, and in most of the rest of the New Testament, what is normally proclaimed is the grace of God that comes to the believer through the activity of God in Jesus. In the New Testament, especially in Paul, the term "gospel" had first of all to do with the substance of the proclamation about God's saving work in Jesus Christ (see, for example, Rom 1:3-4, 15-16; 1 Cor 15:3-5; 1 Thess 1:10; 2:9). In the Gospels themselves, however, the term is variously used for the "good news" of the announced kingdom of God that takes place in the ministry of Jesus that also includes the story of his Passion and resurrection. If Acts 10:34-43 is taken as a summary of an early proclamation in the church, as is likely, Peter preaches the "gospel" by telling the story of Jesus and calling for a response of faith and extending an invitation for forgiveness. He begins this summary of the story of Jesus with the words "You know the message he [God] sent to the people of Israel, proclaiming the good news *(euangelizomenos)* of peace through Jesus Christ, who is Lord of all." It may be that this early tradition was circulating long before Mark adopted it in his Gospel. In Acts, the "gospel" or "good news" is equivalent to "proclaiming the kingdom" (10:34-43; 20:24-25; cf. 28:31).[35] Where the term "gospel" is used in Acts, it generally refers to the proclamation about Jesus and generally has a call for faith and repentance.[36] The term is not found in John's Gospel, but the basic contours of what John had to say are certainly compatible with the Synoptic Gospels even if the

34. The well-known inscription at Priene that speaks of the birth of Augustus is in part as follows:

> . . . and since Caesar through his appearance has exceeded the hopes of all former good messages *(euangelia)*, surpassing not only the benefactors who came before him, but also leaving no hope that anyone in the future would surpass him, and since for the world the birthday of the god was the beginning of his good messages *(ērxen de tǫ kosmǫ tōn di' auton . . . euangeliōn hē genethlios hēmera tou theou)* [may it therefore be decided that . . .].

This translation and Greek text are cited in Koester, *Ancient Christian Gospels*, 3-4. See also the various uses of *euangelion* in G. Friedrich, "εὐαγγελίζομαι, κτλ.," *TDNT* (Grand Rapids: Eerdmans, 1964), 2:707-37.

35. Surprisingly, Acts passes on a saying of Jesus not found in the canonical Gospels (Acts 20:35). Koester, *Ancient Christian Gospels*, 58-59, also notes that Paul, using the formula "as it is written," quotes a text in 1 Cor 2:9 that only roughly approximates Isa 64:4. *Gospel of Thomas* 17, written sometime in the first half of the second century, cites the same saying as Paul, but attributes it to Jesus.

36. Acts 8:12, 25, 40; 13:32; 14:7, 15, 21; 15:7; 16:10; 17:18; 20:24.

design of his particular Gospel shares only about eight percent in common with the Synoptics. For example, John, like the Synoptics, tells of Jesus beginning his ministry in conjunction with John the Baptist's ministry, of his ministry in Galilee and Jerusalem, even if the order is different, and of his Passion and resurrection. These traditions overlap considerably in the Synoptics and John.

Eventually, the term "gospel" came to refer to a particular kind of literature that focused on the story and significance of Jesus at roughly the same time when the notion of "memoirs" or "remembrances" of the apostles was circulating in the churches. Given the scarcity of available witnesses from that period, we cannot be certain when "gospel" began to refer to a literary production, but it is likely that this happened sometime around the middle of the second century. There are in the early part of the second century a few somewhat vague uses of the word "gospel" that may well suggest written documents. In the *Didache*,[37] for instance, the writer admonishes his readers: "And reprove one another not in wrath but in peace as you find in the Gospel, and let none speak with any who has done a wrong to his neighbor, nor let him hear a word from you until he repents. But in your prayers and alms and all your acts perform as you would in the Gospel of our Lord" (15.3-4, LCL). There is also a phrase in the pseudonymous 2 *Clement* (ca. 140-50) in which the author introduces words from Jesus in Luke 16:10-12 with the words, "for the Lord says *in the Gospel*" (8.5). Similarly, we see another example in the *Martyrdom of Polycarp* (ca. 160-70) of the use of the term "gospel" for a written document. Speaking of those who deny their faith under threat of persecution, the author writes: "For this reason, therefore, brethren, we do not commend those who give themselves up, *since the Gospel* does not give this teaching" (4.1, LCL, italics added).

---

37. While it is impossible to date the *Didache* with precision, it is unlikely that it was written before 90 or after 120. It shows the early conflicts between local church leaders and the wandering charismatic prophets in the church (11-13) and an early structure and worship order (14-15). Some scholars believe that the *Didache* depends on the *Epistle of Barnabas* (ca. 140) because of the considerable similarity in the way both make use of the two ways tradition (*Didache* 1-6; cf. *Barnabas* 18-20). This similarity, however, may be explained by an appeal of both writers to a common oral or written tradition. The wording is not so close as to betray dependence. While it may be that the *Didache* was written as late as the middle of the second century, as Massaux proposes in *Influence of the Gospel of Saint Matthew* 3:1, this seems unlikely given the status of church worship and order in it (see *Didache* 14-15).

The notion of a written Gospel may possibly be traced to Mark's opening comments at the beginning of his story of Jesus: "The beginning of the gospel of Jesus Christ, the son of God" (Mark 1:1). With that opening, he proceeds to tell the story of Jesus' activities beginning with his fulfillment of the Scriptures (Mal 3:1 and Isa 40:3). He also tells of Jesus' healing ministry, his exorcisms, his teachings, and finally his death and resurrection.[38] While Mark may have initiated or perpetuated in written form the "Gospel" genre, Luke did not restrict himself to that pattern. Luke continued his story of how God advanced the work that he began with Jesus through the influence and spread of the "gospel" (the Christian proclamation) in the non-believing communities beginning in Jerusalem and eventually arriving in Rome.[39] While all four canonical Gospels essentially tell the story of Jesus and his significance for faith, only Mark begins his story of Jesus using the term "gospel." The other Gospels did not follow that example.

We might also add that, even though there are some notable similarities between the ancient biographies and the canonical Gospels, there are no exact parallels in the sense that ancient biographies were not produced anonymously and they generally did not focus on one short moment in the person's life as in the case of the Gospels, which do not tell the whole story of Jesus, but focus primarily on his ministry, Passion, and resurrection. More importantly, unlike other ancient biographies, these Gospels circulated in an oral tradition for a considerable period of time before being produced in written form. Even Philostratus's *Life of Apollonius of Tyana*, Xenophon's *Memorabilia*, and even Suetonius's *Lives of the Caesars* are not comparable. Stanton agrees that these ancient sources "all contain a memorable beginning and ending with climactic moments, dramatic scenes and vividly drawn characters," but they still have no parallels elsewhere in antiquity.[40]

---

38. G. N. Stanton, *The Gospels and Jesus* (New York: Oxford University Press, 1989), 30-33, makes this point.

39. Acts was written as the second part of a two-part work which does not fit neatly within the traditional "Gospel" genre or *Gattung*. There is no evidence for when the two volumes were separated or were circulated separately except that Acts was not a part of Marcion's collection (ca. 140-50), but Luke-Acts was originally a single work of two volumes. Acts did not serve Marcion's purposes well, and so either he separated it from Luke or, more likely, the two volumes were already separated when he made use of the Gospel. It is not clear that he was even aware of the existence of Acts.

40. Stanton, *The Gospels and Jesus*, 28, but also 15-33. This conclusion has been chal-

By roughly 120-30, it appears that the term "gospel" *began* to be used in reference to the written stories about Jesus and his teaching, without losing its earlier meaning as a reference to the content or substance of the message of God's salvation in Jesus the Christ.[41] But how did "gospel" become a genre for the story of Jesus? We have suggested that it may have its roots in early Christian preaching and the Gospel of Mark (1:1) and perhaps in the writing down of the early Christian proclamation (Acts 10:34-43), but who was responsible for this change in the greater church? Koester suggests that Marcion began this practice as a result of his misunderstanding of the meaning of the term. Since Justin, the earliest writer to make such an explicit reference to Gospels as literary productions, did not use "gospel" to describe the kerygma of the church, nor did he show an awareness of the kerygmatic structure of the Gospel writings, it is not likely that this notion began with him. Koester argues that Marcion understood the tradition of Paul's gospel (Rom 2:16; 16:25; 2 Cor 4:3; cf. Gal 1:11; 1 Thess 1:5; 2 Thess 1:8; 2:14) to be the substance of that gospel reproduced in the Gospel of Luke. As a result, Koester claims, he equated the two.[42] He observes that Justin wrote a treatise against Marcion, called *"Stigma Against All Heresies"* (referred to in *1 Apologia* 26.8), and was therefore likely to know about Marcion's equating Paul's gospel with Luke's written Gospel.[43] Among the Gospels, Marcion accepted only the Gospel of Luke and excised what did not please him, namely the Jewish element. He also received

---

lenged by R. A. Burridge in *What Are the Gospels? A Comparison with Graeco-Roman Biography*, SNTSMS 70 (Cambridge: Cambridge University Press, 1992). For further discussion of this topic, which will not be entered into here, see C. H. Talbert, *What Is a Gospel? The Genre of the Canonical Gospels* (Philadelphia: Fortress, 1977); P. L. Shuler, *A Genre for the Gospels: The Biographical Character of Matthew* (Philadelphia: Fortress, 1982); and D. E. Aune, *The New Testament in Its Literary Environment* (Philadelphia: Westminster, 1987), 17-76. For an interesting perspective on this matter, see also P. Cox, *Biography in Late Antiquity: A Quest for the Holy Man* (Berkeley: University of California Press, 1983).

41. Surprisingly, Clement of Rome, in an unusual text, calls on his readers in Corinth to remember Paul's words about divisions in the church (1 Cor 1:10-12), but in so doing, he writes: "take up the epistle of the blessed Apostle Paul. What did he write to you at the beginning of the gospel *(tou euangeliou)*?" (*1 Clement* 47.1-2). This may be the first time that "gospel" is used in reference to a New Testament writing, and it is in reference to an epistle of Paul and not the genre that was eventually called "gospel," namely the canonical Gospels!

42. Koester, *Synoptische Überlieferung*, 6ff., as well as his more recent *Ancient Christian Gospels*, 35-36.

43. Koester, *Ancient Christian Gospels*, 35-36.

the writings of Paul (without the Pastorals) and denied that the apostles had faithfully told the story of Jesus. He rejected the traditions about Jesus that were passed on in their names (Matthew, Mark and John?). He accepted Paul's thesis that Christ was the end of the Law, but unlike Paul he believed that this meant a rejection of the Scriptures of Israel.

The notion of "Paul's gospel" being written down in Luke's Gospel appears clearly for the first time in Irenaeus where he shows both understandings of the word "gospel," namely the proclamation of the early church and the identity of a written book. Irenaeus begins the preface to *Adversus Haereses* 3 as follows: "For the Lord of all gave to His apostles the power of the Gospel through whom also we have known the truth, that is, the doctrine of the Son of God." In the opening lines of 3.1 he states, "We have learned from none others the plan of our salvation, than from those through whom the Gospel has come down to us." This is followed by Irenaeus stating that the gospel has also come in written form and, after mentioning that Matthew and Mark handed down the gospel in written form, he says that "Luke also, the companion of Paul, recorded in a book the Gospel preached by him" (3.3.1, ANF). Eusebius likewise passes on this tradition and indicates that the "gospel" that the early church proclaimed was also put in writing. Speaking of Luke's two-volume work, he writes:

> Luke . . . had careful conversation with the other Apostles [besides Paul], and in two books left us examples of the medicine for souls which he gained from them — the Gospel, which he testifies that he had planned according to tradition . . . , and the Acts of the Apostles which he composed no longer on the evidence of hearing but of his own eyes. And they say that Paul was actually accustomed to quote from Luke's Gospel since when writing of some Gospel as his own he used to say, "According to my Gospel." (*H.E.* 3.4.6-7, LCL)

Did the story about Luke's recording Paul's gospel in his Gospel originate *before* the time of Marcion and consequently influence him, or did Marcion's practice influence this tradition? It is difficult to tell, but the tradition was obviously passed on in the churches and was repeated by Irenaeus and Eusebius, as noted above. Whether this may also have some roots in *1 Clement* 47.1-2, cited in note 41 above, is not clear. Given the dating of the above-noted references from the *Didache* and *2 Clement*, however, this may not be the case. Since these writings probably precede

Marcion and suggest the notion of a *written* Gospel as well, the tradition may antedate Marcion. Perhaps as a result of Marcion's misunderstanding, he produced a list of books to read in his churches that included the Gospel of Luke and ten letters of Paul.[44] While he may have rejected all Christian literature except the Pauline corpus, his followers seem to have been more open to reading additional Christian literature in their churches.[45] In the second century, at least up to the last quarter of that century, the Gospels were used primarily in the churches as reliable historical reports of the sayings of Jesus and were not generally called "Scripture" nor made equal to the Prophets — even if they were placed alongside them and read in the churches. By this act they were on their way to becoming the new "Scriptures" of the church.

Justin (150-60) speaks of "the apostles in the memoirs which are called Gospels" (*1 Apologia* 63.3) and cites rather freely or loosely from Matthew and Mark.[46] He probably knew all four canonical Gospels,[47] but

44. He omitted the Pastoral Epistles from his collection, but added the Letter to the Laodiceans. It is possible that the latter is the same as the canonical letter to the Ephesians.

45. It is remarkable that after the time of Marcion, some of his churches appear to have made use of Matthew's Gospel. Origen quoted a Marcionite interpretation of Matt 19:12 in his *Commentary on Matthew* (15.3). It is not certain that this comment came from Marcion, but it is instructive that the community he left behind was not unaware of Matthew. G. Hahneman suggests that Marcion, contrary to popular scholarly opinion, may not have rejected the other canonical Gospels (Matthew, Mark, and John). For example, Ephraem Syrus (ca. 306-73) claimed that the followers of Marcion had not rejected Matt 23:8 (Ephraem, *Song* 24.1), and Marcus, a Marcionite, directly quotes John 13:34 and 15:19 in Adamantius, *Dialogue* 2.16, 20. It could be, as Hahneman claims, that the Marcionites did not reject all the Christian writings so much as they edited them for use in their churches. He cites references that point to Marcion's followers including a collection of psalms and admitting verses from the other canonical Gospels into their Scriptures. See G. Hahneman, *The Muratorian Fragment and the Development of the Canon* (Oxford: Clarendon, 1992), 90-92, who cites as evidence here both Adamantius, *Dialogue* 2.18, and Tertullian, *Adversus Marcionem* 4.5. It is likely that the later Marcionites also read Tatian's *Diatessaron* in their churches. See the arguments of R. Casey, "The Armenian Marcionites and the Diatessaron," *JBL* 57 (1938): 185-92. This all suggests, of course, that the contours of Marcion's "canon" may not have been so firmly fixed as was once thought and that he may not have produced the earliest fixed "biblical canon," as von Campenhausen, *Formation*, 152-53, and others after him have argued. For further discussion of this, see McDonald, *Formation*, 154-61.

46. For example chs. 4 (Matt 22:14), 5 (Matt 9:18), 6 (Matt 20:16), 12 (Matt 22:45), and 20 (Mark 10:23-24).

47. It is likely that he knew of the Gospel of John even though this is widely disputed. The most significant parallel comes in *1 Apologia* 61.4-5, which is an almost word-for-word

he largely made use of the Synoptics. Interestingly, when he refers to Jesus being born in a cave, he thus alludes to *Protevangelium of James* 18-19. He likewise shows awareness of the Arabic *Gospel of the Infancy* 2-3 in *Trypho* 88 and 89 as well as *Gospel of Thomas* 13. Additionally, he cites the *Acts of Pilate* 6–8 (*1 Apologia* 48). It is not always clear what writings Justin had in mind when he spoke of the "memoirs of the apostles" or the "Gospels." Since most of Justin's Gospel citations and allusions are from the Synoptics, with some parallels to the Gospel of John, he probably had these four in mind most of the time, but he also included others besides, as we have seen. Justin used the term "gospel" to refer to written stories about Jesus, but it is not certain that he had only the canonical Gospels in mind when he did so.

From Reliable Reports to Sacred Scripture

Irenaeus (ca. 170-80) was the first to promote a four-Gospel canon, and he also signaled an important transition in the church when he referred to the New Testament writings as *Scriptures*. He was not the first to do so, but from his time onward, this became common practice in the churches and was universal by the fourth century. He was also the first church teacher to designate the Christian writings as a "New Testament" and an "Old Testament." What he included in these collections is not clear from his extant writings but was supplied by Eusebius later, perhaps by observation of the New Testament writings that he cited (*H.E.* 5.8.2-8). When the term *canon* came to mean a fairly precise collection of sacred writings in the fourth century, the canonical Gospels were given the place of priority in all of the collections and generally placed in the same order that they are found in today. Along with Irenaeus, there was a growing trend toward the end of the second century to recognize Christian writings as Scripture. It is difficult to pinpoint precisely when this occurred, but the early writings that received this designation were predominantly the canonical Gospels.[48]

---

quotation of John 3:3-5, but see other parallels that are close but not exact in *1 Apologia* 6.2 (John 4:24); 32.9-11 (John 1:13-14); 33.2 (John 14:29); 35.8 (John 19:23-24); 52.12 (John 19:37); 63.15 (John 1:1); *2 Apologia* 6.3 (John 1:3). See Massaux's discussion of these parallels in *The Influence of the Gospel of Saint Matthew*, 3:46-47.

48. See my discussion of such references in *Formation*, 142-54, in which I point to the growing tendency in the second century toward recognizing and calling certain New Testa-

Irenaeus believed that the four canonical Gospels and other unspecified New Testament literature,[49] along with an unspecified collection of
Old Testament writings, were normative Scriptures for the churches, and
he unambiguously called these writings "Scripture."[50] Although Irenaeus
promoted the necessity and authority of the four canonical Evangelists,
those four and no more, he also argued something that no one before him
had claimed, namely, that the Christian message is somehow incomplete if
only one written Gospel (or fewer than four) is used.

Luke appears to have used earlier "accounts" (Luke 1:1-4), but he
tried to improve them, at least in the case of Mark, seeking to produce a
"more orderly account." John, who must surely have known the Gospels of
Mark and Matthew, offers a significantly different picture of Jesus' life,
message, death, and resurrection. He does not suggest that his Gospel
needs the other Gospels to support his claims or even to supplement
them.[51] Although Irenaeus may have seen the need for four "pillars" of
Gospels for the church, it is difficult to establish that the Evangelists themselves or anyone before Irenaeus saw such a need.[52] Indeed, there is ample
evidence to show that even after Irenaeus, there was a considerable variety
of acceptance of the canonical Gospels in the churches not only at the end
of the second century, but even later.

In defense of his view that the church should use only the four canonical Gospels, Irenaeus employed arguments that by today's standards
are certainly strange. Indeed, the manner in which he tried to limit the authoritative gospel literature to the four canonical Gospels was not the most
convincing line of reasoning, even in the ancient world! He writes:

---

ment writings Scripture. In the last quarter of that century, that does indeed take place, but
generally that is not the case before then.

49. Eusebius made a calculation of this literature in the fourth century and claimed
that Irenaeus accepted as Scripture Matthew, Mark, Luke, John, Revelation, 1 John, 1 Peter,
Shepherd, and Wisdom. Paul is listed, but his individual writings are not identified. See
Eusebius, *H.E.* 5.8.2-8.

50. See *Adversus haereses* 1.9.4; 2.26.1, 2; 3.1.1, etc.

51. That is not the intent of his concluding remarks in John 20:30, though the hyperbole in the later Johannine appendix in 21:25 may warrant that speculation.

52. H. Y. Gamble, *The New Testament Canon* (Philadelphia: Fortress, 1985), 24-25, also
makes this argument and adds that Matthew and Luke must not have had a very high view
of their sources (especially Mark), since they took such liberties in adding to and altering the
sources they used.

It is not possible that the Gospels can be either more or fewer in number than they are. For, since there are four zones of the world in which we live, and four principal winds, while the Church is scattered throughout all the world and while the "pillar and ground" of the Church is the Gospel and the spirit of life, it is fitting, therefore, that she [the Church] should have four pillars, breathing out immortality on every side, and vivifying men afresh. From this fact, it is evident that the Word, the Artificer of all, who sits upon the cherubim and who contains all things and was manifested to men, has given us the Gospel under four aspects, but bound together by one Spirit. . . .

But that these Gospels [the four canonical Gospels] alone are true and reliable and admit neither an increase nor diminution of the aforesaid number, I have proved by so many such arguments. (adapted from *Adversus haereses* 3.11.8-9, ANF; cf. 3.1.1)

We should not conclude from this, however, that all four canonical Gospels and only those Gospels were widely received as Scripture everywhere in the last part of the second century. That was clearly not the case. Irenaeus's acceptance of the four canonical Gospels alone was not generally shared by his contemporaries or even by many Christians at a later time. Clement of Alexandria, for instance, cites sources in his *Stromateis* from several noncanonical writings. Eight times he refers to the *Gospel of the Egyptians*, three times to the *Gospel of the Hebrews*, and three times to the *Traditions of Matthias*. He also introduces one of his references to the *Gospel of the Hebrews* with the formula "it is written" *(gegraptai)*. During a debate with a Gnostic, Clement quotes the *Gospel according to the Egyptians:* "When Salome inquired how long death should have power, the Lord (not meaning that life is evil, and the creation bad) said: 'As long as you women give birth to children'" (*Stromateis* 3.6.45). He even acknowledges that "we do not have this saying [of Jesus to Salome] in the four traditional Gospels, but in the *Gospel according to the Egyptians*."[53] He accepted the *Epistle of Barnabas* as apostolic and quoted from it in an authoritative manner (*Stromateis* 2.6; 2.15.67; cf. *Barnabas* 1.5; 2.3). Clement also cited *1 Clement*, the *Shepherd of Hermas*, Sirach, Tatian's *Against the Greeks*, the *Preaching of Peter*, the *Apocalypse of Peter*, and even the *Sibylline Oracles*.

53. These sources are cited by Metzger, *The Canon of the New Testament*, 132, 171.

Irenaeus's "those four and no more" was not widely accepted in his day, as we have seen. In fact, it is difficult to find other witnesses in the second century who make such an unqualified claim. For example, Bishop Serapion of Antioch (ca. 200), when asked by the Christians in Rhossus for permission to read the *Gospel of Peter* in the church, agreed at first to let it be read. He would not have done so presumably if he had already accepted Irenaeus's notion of a closed four-Gospel canon. It was only after reading for himself the *Gospel of Peter* at a later time that Serapion saw that it denied the humanity of Jesus, and so he reversed his earlier decision. He did so not on the basis of a widely accepted closed Gospel canon, but on the basis of a canon of truth that was circulating in the churches. Eusebius preserves for us his letter of reversal:

> For I myself, when I came among you, imagined that all of you clung to the true faith, and, without going through the Gospel put forward by them in the name of Peter, I said, "If this is the only thing that seemingly causes captious feelings among you, let it be read." But since I have now learned from what has been told me that their mind was lurking in some hold of heresy, I shall give diligence to come again to you. Wherefore, brethren, expect me quickly. . . . (Eusebius, *H.E.* 6.12.4, adapted from LCL)

This concern for the truth — the widespread understanding of the truth of and about Jesus — was significant in the church's decision about what literature to read in its worship. What did not conform to that tradition was rejected and considered "heresy."

Another group roughly contemporary with Irenaeus, the so-called "Alogi," a group of heretics[54] in Asia Minor (ca. 170), opposed the use of Hebrews and both the Gospel and the Revelation of John in their churches. Likewise, Irenaeus wrote that the Ebionite Christians did not accept the divinity of Jesus, held to the Jewish traditions and Law, and "use the Gospel according to Matthew only, and repudiate the Apostle Paul, maintaining that he was an apostate from the Law" (*Adversus haereses* 1.26.2, ANF).[55]

---

54. According to Epiphanius, *Haereses* 51, they denied the divinity of the Holy Spirit and the Logos, hence the name, "Alogi." The name also means "unreasonable" and they were likewise accused of being so.

55. Eusebius says that they used the *Gospel of the Hebrews* (*H.E.* 3.27.4). Epiphanius, *Haereses* 30, claims that they received the Gospel of Matthew, but called it the Gospel of the Hebrews.

Finally, Justin's famous pupil Tatian (170-80) used all four canonical Gospels in his famous *Diatessaron,* a harmony of the Gospels, but he also included traditions from non-canonical Gospels as well. He not only tried to smooth out some of the differences among the canonical Gospels, he also eliminated the genealogies and ascension of Jesus.[56] His *Diatessaron* was originally called the "Gospel of the Mixed" according to Ephraem (died ca. 373).[57] The only piece of the *Diatessaron* that remains, however, is a small fragment that shows the nature and extent of Tatian's harmonizing work:

> [. . . the mother of the sons of Zebed]ee (Matt. xxvii.56) and Salome (Mark xv.40) and the wives [of those who] had followed him from [Galile]e to see the crucified (Luke xxiii.49b-c). And [the da]y was Preparation; the sabbath was daw[ning] (Luke xxiii. 54). And when it was evening (Matt. xxvii.57), on the Prep[aration], that is, the day before the sabbath (Mark xv.42), [there came] up a man (Matt. xxvii.57), be[ing] a member of the council (Luke xxiii.50), from Arimathea (Matt. xxvii.57), g[o]od and ri[ghteous] (Luke xxiii.50), being a disciple of Jesus, but se[cret]ly, for fear of the [Jew]s (John xix.38). And he (Matt. xxvii.57) was looking for [the] k[ingdom] of God (Luke xxiii.51.c). This man [had] not [con]sented to [their] p[urpose] (Luke xxiii.51a). . . .[58]

56. Petersen suggests that the other sources in the *Diatessaron* included the Jewish Christian *Gospel of the Hebrews* and possibly also the *Gospel of the Egyptians.* Cf. W. L. Petersen, "Tatian's *Diatessaron,*" in Koester, *Ancient Christian Gospels,* 430. Petersen cites important early witnesses that these sections were dropped from the *Diatessaron.* See especially Theodoret (ca. 396-466 and bishop of Cyrrhus), *Haereticarum fabularum compendium* 1.20. Also, if those writings had been considered by Tatian and his community to be inviolable Scripture, it is a wonder why he himself excluded the genealogies of Matthew and Luke as well as Luke's ascension story.

57. Ephraem was a church Father of the Syrian church who wrote a commentary on the *Diatessaron,* in which he points out that Tatian, like Justin and Clement of Alexandria, used more than the four canonical Gospels in his work.

58. Metzger, *The Canon of the New Testament,* 115. Metzger correctly argues that Tatian regarded the four canonical Gospels as authoritative; "otherwise he would not have dared to combine them into one gospel account." There is no evidence, however, that Tatian regarded only the four canonical Gospels as authoritative. We might add, however, that his views were not like those of the church of a later era when changing and eliminating texts from the Gospels would have been unthinkable.

The influence of Tatian's *Diatessaron* was known as far to the east as China and as far to the west as England and was cited authoritatively as recently as the fourteenth century. It is likely that it was originally produced in Syria, where Ephraem wrote a commentary on it, and it was translated many times over. Eusebius speaks of the continuing use of the *Diatessaron* in the fourth century in the West (*H.E.* 4.29.6). It was also widely used in the Syrian churches well into the sixth century but began to yield to the influence of and preference for the Syriac Peshitta, which included the individual canonical Gospels. Nevertheless, it was not ignored after that, but had considerable influence for several centuries. It existed in Greek, Latin, Old High German, and many other languages.[59] Because he also founded a movement of rigorous ascetics that rejected marriage and the use of wine, it is not surprising that Tatian incorporated other writings in his *Diatessaron* to support such views. Unlike Justin, who also produced a harmony of the Gospels that focused mostly on Matthew and Luke with some parallels to Mark and fewer still to the Gospel of John, Tatian appears to have accepted all four canonical Gospels equally, but he also included the *Gospel of Peter* and perhaps other traditions.[60]

The point here is that there were few in Irenaeus's day who limited the number of Gospels to be read in the churches to the same four that Irenaeus read. It appears likely that it was more common that the canonical Gospels were received and read alongside of several non-canonical Gospels through the end of the second century. Although many scholars have argued that Irenaeus's views of the four-Gospel canon reflected the status of things in all churches of his day, that is simply not the case. The acceptance of that view took more time. It is likely that Irenaeus was defending the use of John's Gospel, which was under attack in his time, and the point of his argument was to gain the acceptance of John, but that is not certain. It is noteworthy that the *Muratorian Fragment,* a fourth-century document,[61] simply lists the four canonical Gospels with no defense. Earlier in that century, Eusebius (ca. 320-30) also listed the four ca-

---

59. See W. L. Petersen, *Tatian's Diatessaron: Its Creation, Dissemination, Significance, and History in Scholarship,* Supplements to Vigiliae Christianae 25 (New York: Brill, 1994), 1-2. Also see his "Tatian's Diatessaron" in Koester, *Ancient Christian Gospels,* 403-30.

60. See Koester's evidence and extensive discussion of this in *Ancient Christian Gospels,* 365-402.

61. See the detailed arguments for this dating in Hahneman, *The Muratorian Fragment,* and summarized in McDonald, *Formation,* 209-20.

nonical Gospels as a closed unit, placing them in the place of priority in his "recognized" *(homolegoumena)* sacred collection. He describes them collectively as "the holy tetrad of the Gospels" *(H.E.* 3.25.1), but the four Gospels had not yet achieved this prominence at the end of the second century, and that is why Irenaeus defended them so vigorously.

Conclusion

In the first century, the Synoptic tradition about Jesus was widely accepted and circulated among the churches, first in oral transmission and subsequently in the written canonical Gospels. Throughout the second century, the church Fathers made regular use of one or more of the canonical Gospels, but in addition they often cited several other sources, including some of the non-canonical Gospels that were later excluded from the churches' sacred collections. Long ago, Gould noted that the surviving literature from the second century cited, along with the canonical Gospels, several extra-canonical sources "freely and without apology." Regardless of this practice, he observes that the picture of Jesus was not remarkably changed by that, and in fact, as a consequence of it, he concludes that "the historicity of the story of Jesus presented is more triumphantly established by the corroborative testimony than by the absence of other witnesses."[62] In his subsequent discussion, he shows examples of the use of the noncanonical sources in the early church Fathers. For our purposes, the first and second centuries were foundational in the acceptance of the canonical Gospels as authoritative writings in the church. They even reached the status of Scripture for many Christians at that time. The second-century churches regularly cited with approval the testimony of the canonical Evangelists, at first as reliable reports of the words and deeds of Jesus, but eventually as the bedrock of authority in the churches. Those churches received in an authoritative manner other testimonies that were eventually excluded from the New Testament canon.[63]

In the fourth century, when the four canonical Gospels were widely

---

62. E. P. Gould, *A Critical and Exegetical Commentary on the Gospel According to St. Mark,* ICC (Edinburgh: Clark, 1869), xxxiii-xxxiv. He cites several useful examples of this in the discussion that follows on pp. xxxiv-xl.

63. Gould, *Mark,* xxxiv-xlii.

acknowledged in the majority of churches, we cannot yet say that only those Gospels and no others had received recognition and acceptance in the churches. Even after the four canonical Gospels had reached their remarkable widespread acceptance in the churches by no later than the fourth century, we cannot conclude that no other writings were acknowledged or read in the churches. Some extra-canonical Gospels that were not included in the biblical lists or catalogues of the fourth and fifth centuries continued to have an influence on the churches long after the four canonical Gospels were in the place of priority in the Christian biblical canons of the fourth and fifth centuries. For example, the *Infancy Gospel of James* had considerable influence on fourth- and fifth-century churches. This book significantly affected the results of the Council of Ephesus in 431 when decisions were made about Mary's status, that is, her relation to Jesus the Son of God. The council concluded that she was the "mother of God," the *theotokos*, and the church found support for this teaching in the *Infancy Gospel*. Following this time, that apocryphal Gospel exerted considerable influence on Christian art and piety. As Mary was venerated, groups within the church turned to this writing for inspiration and guidance.[64]

Other non-canonical Gospels filled various voids in the New Testament texts such as details on the stories of Jesus' birth, childhood, family members, resurrection, and ascension. In another genre, a *Letter to the Laodiceans* was produced under Paul's name (see Col 4:16) as well as an apocryphal book of acts that describes Paul's appearance and his ministry in Iconium, although the focus of that document is on a young woman named Thecla *(The Acts of Paul and Thecla)*. The early church seemed anxious to leave nothing to the imagination and in the second and third centuries Christians produced many such pseudonymous or apocryphal writings to fill voids in the New Testament literature. Attaching an apostle's name to such literature aided its acceptance in the churches, and also lets us know that apostolic authorship added credibility to the churches' emerging Christian Scriptures.

There were also sayings of Jesus not included in any of the canonical Gospels circulating widely in the churches of antiquity. This collection now numbers some 266 sayings of Jesus, but probably only about eight or

---

64. See R. F. Hock, "The Favored One: How Mary Became the Mother of God," *BR* 17 (2001): 13-25, and V. Limberis, "The Battle over Mary," *BR* 17 (2001): 22-23.

nine are likely to be authentic.[65] These sayings are popularly called "agrapha" today and they clearly functioned in an authoritative manner in the churches that received them and passed them on to other Christians. The "agrapha" were, after all, sayings of Jesus, the Lord of the church.

That discovery brings us back to our starting point, namely that all writings of the New Testament and early Christianity have a derived authority from the church's one true Lord, even Jesus the Christ. All writings of the early church that were believed to convey faithfully the story of Jesus and his significance for faith were welcomed in the early church and utilized in its life and mission. When there was doubt about what writings faithfully told the story and significance of Jesus the Christ, various criteria were employed to decide. These criteria included first of all the coherence of the writing with what was already commonly received in those churches. Soon after that, apostolic authorship became the standard norm for determining the credibility and authority of a written document. By the fourth century, other criteria were also employed by the church to decide the question, but that discussion would take us beyond the second century and the scope of this paper.[66]

---

65. These are discussed in detail in W. D. Stroker, *Extracanonical Sayings of Jesus* (Atlanta: Scholars, 1989), who offers the text of 266 of these sayings without evaluating their contents or attributing authenticity or inauthenticity to them. See also O. Hofius, "Unknown Sayings of Jesus," in *The Gospel and the Gospels*, ed. P. Stuhlmacher (Grand Rapids: Eerdmans, 1991), 336-60; D. J. Theron, *Evidence of Tradition* (Grand Rapids: Baker, 1980), 96-99; J. Charlesworth and C. A. Evans, "Jesus in the Agrapha and Apocryphal Gospels," in *Studying the Historical Jesus: Evaluations of the State of Current Research*, ed. B. Chilton and C. A. Evans, NTTS 19 (Leiden: Brill, 1994), 479-533.

66. These criteria are discussed in McDonald, *Formation*, 228-49.

Reading the Gospels Canonically:
A Methodological Dialogue
with Brevard Childs

AL WOLTERS

There can be little doubt that Brevard S. Childs (born 1923) is one of the giants of twentieth-century biblical scholarship. His "canonical approach" to Scripture studies has had a significant impact on the discipline, especially among scholars who do not wish to divorce their scholarship from their recognition of the Bible as the Word of God. At the same time, his refusal to isolate what is commonly called the "theological" dimension from the academic study of Scripture has provoked sharp disagreement on the part of many of his colleagues in the guild, notably James Barr.

Childs's new approach first attracted widespread attention in 1974, when he published his commentary on Exodus in the Old Testament Library series. This commentary was something of a landmark in the discipline, constituting both a challenge to mainline critical scholarship and a manifesto. It had the telling subtitle *A Critical, Theological Commentary*.[1] On the one hand, this commentary was "critical," meaning that it positioned itself in the mainstream of modern historical criticism with respect to Exodus, but on the other hand it was "theological," meaning that it sought to discern the religious relevance of the canonical shape of the biblical text, and to that end drew freely on the work of the greats of "precritical" exegesis, Jewish as well as Christian. Thus both Wellhausen

---

1. B. S. Childs, *The Book of Exodus: A Critical, Theological Commentary* (Philadelphia: Fortress, 1974).

and Rashi, Martin Noth and John Calvin were quoted alongside each other as equally authoritative commentators on the biblical text.

Childs later worked out his overall approach in his *Introduction to the Old Testament as Scripture*,[2] a work of massive erudition, in which the title's telltale word "Scripture" signaled his determination to treat the Old Testament, not just as a collection of the religious writings of an ancient people, but as the authoritative canon of the contemporary people of God. This work would have been enough to establish his reputation as a major figure in biblical studies. However, in 1985 he published another significant work in which he broke out of his disciplinary specialty in Old Testament studies. This was an introduction to the New Testament in which he showed himself to be conversant with an astonishing range of New Testament scholarship as well and applied the principles of his canonical approach to it.[3] Since then, Childs has published two further hefty tomes illustrating his overall approach, one on Old Testament theology, the other a *Biblical Theology of the Old and New Testaments*.[4] It is probably fair to say that the latter volume represents the maturest statement of his views.

I am myself an Old Testament scholar who occasionally strays into New Testament studies, and I have long been intrigued by Childs's canonical approach to biblical scholarship. Moreover, being a committed Christian with a high view of biblical authority, I am particularly fascinated by the way in which Childs seeks to integrate the "critical" and the "theological" in Scripture studies. What I propose to do in the present context is to enter into dialogue with Childs by exploring how he applies his approach to a particular issue in Gospel studies and by probing the broader philosophical and worldview assumptions which seem to me to be implicit in his treatment. Needless to say, because I am basing my remarks very largely on a detailed examination of just a small sliver of his work, the danger of giving a skewed account of his overall approach is very real. On the other hand, a focused treatment such as I propose has the advantage of relating

2. B. S. Childs, *Introduction to the Old Testament as Scripture* (Philadelphia: Fortress, 1979).

3. B. S. Childs, *The New Testament as Canon: An Introduction* (Philadelphia: Fortress, 1985).

4. B. S. Childs, *Old Testament Theology in a Canonical Context* (Philadelphia: Fortress, 1986); B. S. Childs, *Biblical Theology of the Old and New Testaments: Theological Reflections on the Christian Bible* (Minneapolis: Fortress, 1993).

the broader issues of methodology and worldview to the specifics of actual exegesis. In any case, let me say that I carry out my analysis out of an attitude of profound respect for Childs's very impressive scholarship, as well as his deep Christian commitment.

The specific exegetical topic I have in mind is his treatment of the parable of the wicked tenants in his *Biblical Theology of the Old and New Testaments,* 337-47 (cited by page number hereafter). It constitutes the second half of chapter 5, "Exegesis in the Context of Biblical Theology," the first half of which is his discussion of the binding of Isaac in Genesis 22 (the so-called Akedah). These two sections constitute the only places in the book where Childs treats a specific passage in detail. Presumably, they are meant to function as examples — one from the Old Testament and one from the New — of the way Childs's canonical approach makes a difference in the specifics of biblical exegesis.

The Argument

Childs's discussion of the parable is divided into five subsections. I will briefly summarize each of these sections, with a few initial comments of my own, before turning to a broader discussion of his methodology in general. First, however, I should point out a peculiarity in the heading of the section as a whole. Although Childs deals with the form of the parable as it is found in all three Synoptic Gospels and the *Gospel of Thomas,* his heading is "Matthew 21:33-46: The Parable of the Wicked Tenants." He does not explain why he privileges the Matthean form of the parable in this way. Perhaps it is because Matthew comes first in the canonical order. Alternatively, it may be because Matthew's version of the parable, in his view, is the most developed of the parable's canonical forms.

Synoptic Analysis

Basing himself on "a fairly wide agreement" (337), Childs assumes Markan priority and sketches the differences between the version of the parable found in Mark, on the one hand, and the Matthean and Lukan forms on the other. He notes the following points:

(a) Allusion to the "song of the vineyard" in Isaiah 5. "Explicit" in Mark, this allusion is retained in Matthew, but minimized in Luke.

(b) The servants who are sent to collect the rent. Mark mentions first three servants, the third being killed, and then "many others" who are beaten or killed. Luke mentions only three servants, none of whom is killed. Matthew mentions two successive groups of servants, both of whom are mistreated or killed.

(c) The son who is killed for the inheritance. Mark mentions the "beloved son," as does Luke, but Matthew omits the adjective "beloved."

(d) Sequence and place of the son's murder. Mark has the son murdered in the vineyard and then thrown out. Luke and Matthew have him thrown out first and then murdered.

(e) The kingdom given to another. Only Matthew has the words "The kingdom of God will be taken away from you and given to a nation producing the fruits of it" (21:43).

(f) The crushing stone. Though not found in Mark, the words "Everyone who falls on that stone will be broken to pieces, but he on whom it falls will be crushed" are found in Luke (20:18) and some manuscripts of Matthew (21:44).

Comment. It is worth pointing out that, by aligning himself with a broad scholarly consensus which accepts the priority of the Markan form of the parable, Childs is implicitly rejecting the views of two scholars whom he cites in the sequel: Dominic Crossan, who argues that the earliest form of the parable is that found in the *Gospel of Thomas,* and Klyne Snodgrass, who argues for the priority of the Matthean form.

The Demise of Allegorical Interpretation

Until the nineteenth century the parable was given an allegorical interpretation, that is, one which sees a point-for-point correspondence between the various elements of the parable and various elements of its theological meaning. However, since the work of A. Jülicher in the late nineteenth century, a sharp distinction was drawn between "parable" (which had only one point, and was characteristic of Jesus' teaching) and "allegory" (which had many, and was characteristic of later church teaching). Accordingly, Jülicher classified the story of the wicked tenants as an allegory rather than a parable, and attributed it to the early church rather than to Jesus. Later interpreters such as Dodd and Jeremias accepted Jülicher's distinction, but argued that it was possible to reconstruct a genuine parabolic kernel of this allegory which did fit Jesus' Palestinian milieu.

However, a series of other scholars (notably Fiebig, Crossan, and Flusser) successfully challenged the validity of the sharp distinction between parable and allegory. It turns out that these categories are intermingled in what can be recovered of early Jewish and Christian storytelling. As a result "no unilinear traditio-historical development [i.e., from parable to allegory] is any longer possible to maintain" (339).

Comment. The heading of this subsection is rather misleading, since the "demise of allegorical interpretation" applies only to a certain school or phase of New Testament scholarship (associated with the names of Jülicher, Dodd, and Jeremias) which has now been superseded. Besides, the story of the wicked tenants, at least in its canonical form, never ceased to be interpreted allegorically, even by Jülicher and his followers. Why then does Childs include this discussion of the fortunes of the parable-allegory distinction? Initially, it seems to function as a preparation for the next subsection by ruling out one way in which the "traditio-historical trajectory" of our parable might have been construed. As we shall see, however, this does not appear to be the case.

A Traditio-Historical Trajectory

It has been difficult to reach a scholarly consensus on the diachronic development of the parable of the wicked tenants because it depends on so many disputed issues in New Testament scholarship, notably the whole Synoptic problem and its relation to the *Gospel of Thomas.*

Two major scholarly debates are of significance here. The first concerns the earliest recoverable form of the parable. According to Crossan that earliest form is the one found in *Thomas*, which has no allegory and no appeal to the Old Testament. An analysis of the canonical form of the parable in Matthew shows up tensions in the text, which can be explained as "an allegorical layering over this original kernel." However, Crossan's proposal has been rightly criticized by other scholars as being highly subjective. Besides, like other scholarly attempts to recover an original core (allegedly going back to Jesus himself), the point of that core turns out to be either trivial (as in Crossan's case), or else a reflection of the author's own theological or ideological commitments (as with Dodd, Jeremias, Via, and Linnemann).

The second major debate concerns the cultural setting of the parable. Kümmel argued that many features of the parable make no sense in Jesus' own milieu and that it was an inferior creation of the early church. For example, a man would hardly plant a vineyard and then immediately leave it. Nor would he send his own son when his servants had been unsuccessful. Besides, the tenants would hardly think they had a chance of inheriting the vineyard if they killed the heir, and so on. In response to this, a number of scholars, drawing on rabbinic sources and Greek papyri, have argued that the parable does in fact make good sense in Jesus' Palestinian cultural context. Snodgrass concludes that "there is little question that the parable stems from the *Sitz im Leben Jesu*" (340).

On this issue of cultural setting Childs writes the following:

> One comes away from this latter debate with a sense of much exegetical frustration. On the one hand, those who have characterized the parable as artificial and artless [e.g., Kümmel] have clearly brought to bear modern literary and logical categories on the ancient text which stand in danger of skewing its meaning from the start. On the other hand, the historical scholars, usually of conservative bent [e.g., Snodgrass], have historicized the parable and brought the literary features into a historical sharpness which greatly exceeds the biblical story itself. This rationalistic refocusing of the text also runs the risk of missing the parable's point. (341)

Childs then goes on to stress that the Gospel parables clearly did undergo a complicated process of diachronic development, but that tracing that development involves a good deal of subjectivity.

> My major criticism of most critical reconstructions — whether liberal or conservative — is that no distinction is made between tracing the growth of the text's kerygmatic witness among the various Gospels, and reconstructing an allegedly non-kerygmatic, historical level apart from its reception in faith by the New Testament's witnesses. . . . [T]he crucial issue turns on the nature of the trajectory [of growth] and the failure to interpret the growth of the text within the context of the church's

kerygmatic understanding of the subject matter constituting the gospel. (341)

Comment. Childs seems to be saying that it is impossible to determine with any degree of certainty what the earliest form of the parable was and that it is beside the point to ask whether or not the parable accurately reflects the cultural conditions of Jesus' milieu. To his mind, this is all an example of "reconstructing an allegedly non-kerygmatic, historical level" of the canonical text. What needs to be done instead is to interpret the growth of the text in the light of the church's understanding of the gospel.

I find it difficult to understand Childs here. I can see no reason why either Kümmel or Snodgrass — to mention just these two — should be understood as reconstructing a "non-kerygmatic, historical level" of the parable divorced from the church's understanding of the gospel. In fact I rather suspect that they would both stress the very opposite. Furthermore, if it is impossible to reconstruct the growth of the text with any confidence, how can we interpret that growth within the context of the church's understanding? Again, the title of this subsection seems rather misleading, since no "traditio-historical trajectory" has in fact been established. We wonder again about the relevance of the preceding subsection.

The Role of the Old Testament

The parable's use of the imagery of the vineyard alludes to Isaiah 5, where the vineyard functions as part of a "juridical parable." However, the vineyard image is used quite differently in this New Testament context. In fact, "the New Testament begins where the Old Testament left off."

If we do not speculate on a precanonical form of the parable but compare the parallel versions in the Synoptic Gospels (beginning with Mark), we notice that they "show a trajectory of increasing allegorical application of the story" (343). Matthew, by replacing Mark's sequence of single servants with two groups of servants, creates an analogy with the former and latter prophets of the Old Testament. Similarly, when Matthew describes the son as being killed outside the vineyard, rather than inside (as in Mark), this is done to more closely match the Gospel accounts of Jesus' suffering. Furthermore, the citation from Ps 118:22 of the "rejected stone" passage extends the reference to Jesus' exaltation at the resurrection.

Matthew's additional words "the Kingdom of God will be taken away from you" are also fully in line with his witness to *Christ*, and the concluding verse about the crushing stone is a warning to future *Christians*.

In short, "the various forms of the parables in the Gospels are all shaped from the perspective of Jesus' death and resurrection as the rejected Messiah of Israel." The exegetically important thing is not determining how much of the parable goes back to Jesus himself, but "charting the trajectory of the church's kerygmatic witness" (344).

Comment. Once again, the heading of this subsection is rather misleading, since "the role of the Old Testament" applies only to its opening paragraphs. It is also striking that Childs focuses on the trajectory that leads from Mark (assumed to be first) to Matthew, but says nothing about the trajectory that leads to Luke. Furthermore, although he rejects speculation about a precanonical form of the parable, he does speak of the "rejected stone" citation (which is found in all the canonical forms of the parable) as a later addition.

Apart from these inconsistencies, however, his main point seems to be that the developed form of the parable in Matthew is a function of Matthew's witness to Christ as the already crucified and resurrected Messiah.

Theological Reflection in the Context of Biblical Theology

The parable shows how the New Testament "rewrote the Old Testament story [of Isaiah 5] in the light of its witness to Jesus Christ. This new story of the Gospels was developed by means of a lengthy process of the early church's reflection on the meaning of the parable by extending its witness back into the Old Testament and at the same time forward to the resurrection" (344). This stands in striking contrast to the non-canonical form of the parable found in the *Gospel of Thomas*.

The relationship of the parable to the Old Testament is not just one of picking up an Old Testament image (the vineyard) and giving it a New Testament twist. It is, rather, a typological relationship, involving a conscious witness to "a common theological reality shared by both testaments" (345). In fact, the relationship can be described as "ontological," since it involves a "shared reality." "The content with which both testaments wrestle is the selfsame divine commitment to his people and the unbelieving human response of rejection, the sin of which climaxed in the slaying of God's Anointed One. In this sense, the two testaments are part of the same redemptive drama of election and rejection" (345).

Another link to the Old Testament is the second vineyard song found in Isa 27:2-6. What distinguishes this vineyard song from the first one (in Isaiah 5) is that it is set in an eschatological context and envisages God's vineyard as a future blessing for the whole world. In other words, "the Old Testament has also extended its vision of the vineyard beyond the destruction of the wicked tenants to the restored and reconciled people of God's original intent," thus confirming "the unity of the one plan of God" (345).

Childs's final comment is that it is a great mistake to read Matthew's form of the parable as championing Christianity over Judaism. Instead, we must "leave open the response to the renewed reconciliation by the exalted Christ" (345). Christians too are challenged to "receive the Kingdom of God by producing the fruits of righteousness" (346), lest it be given to another. "It is this decisive existential note which resists linking the testaments in a rigid historicized sequence from the past, but which continues to call forth a living voice from the entire scriptures of the church."

Comment. In this final subsection Childs leaves behind his discussion of "critical" issues, and concludes with a ringing "theological" statement about the unity of God's plan in both testaments. It seems to me that it is a statement which can be endorsed by Christians of virtually every confessional persuasion (although some might wish further clarification about the final comment regarding Judaism).

However, I find the very last sentence puzzling. After stressing so strongly the "ontological" continuity of Old and New Testaments, what does he mean by rejecting "a rigid historicized sequence from the past"? Does he mean that the fundamental religious reality of God's relationship to his people which is shared by both testaments somehow transcends history? I find it hard to believe that this would be Childs's view. Instead, what I suspect he means is that we should not seek to pin down that fundamental religious reality in historical terms. Throughout, Childs is very wary of linking the reality of the "theological" to anything that is open to "critical" verification.

General Reflections

Having completed our survey of Childs's treatment of the Parable of the Wicked Tenants, we turn now to some general reflections on this treatment as an illustration of his overall methodology. Our concern is not to belabor some of the minor inconsistencies and infelicities which we have briefly flagged in our comments, but to ask after the underlying principles and patterns of his approach.

The dominant impression which Childs leaves, both in his work in general and in this specific example of it, is that of a man who combines enormous erudition with orthodox Christian faith. With regard to the first point, he consistently demonstrates that he is thoroughly familiar, not only with the history of theology and precritical biblical exegesis, but also with modern historical critical scholarship. In fact, he seems to go out of his way to show his familiarity with mainstream nineteenth- and twentieth-century biblical scholarship, even when it is not immediately relevant. For example, in the section with which we are dealing, he discusses at some length the views of Jülicher and others who posit a sharp distinction between "parable" and "allegory," even though this distinction has now been generally abandoned (338-39). Similarly, he points out that the song of the vineyard in Isaiah 5 is most probably, following the analysis of G. Yee, to be classified as a "juridical parable" (342), but this point has no bearing on the exegesis of the New Testament parable.

In fact, it is possible to go even further and to ask to what extent the impressive survey of secondary literature in subsections 1-4 is of any consequence for Childs's own theological interpretation of the parable in subsection 5. I believe the answer to this question must be "very little." Even the assumption of Markan priority does not ultimately play a role in his own interpretation. It is almost as though Childs goes out of his way to show that he can play the game of biblical scholarship with the best of them, but, once he has established that, simply takes the text at its theological face value within the broad context of the Christian canon.

However, it is significant that the "face value" which he accepts is "theological," not historical. In other words, he accepts the message of the canonical shape of the text as a kerygmatic witness to the gospel, not as a historical testimony as to what actually happened. He is quite clear about the fact that the parable of the wicked tenants is largely a product of the early church, which has reworked earlier material — possibly, but not necessarily, going back to some saying of Jesus — in the light of Jesus' crucifixion and resurrection. In fact he declares himself quite frustrated with Snodgrass's argument that the parable can be fully understood as making sense in Jesus' own cultural context. It is not that he wants to refute

Snodgrass's arguments; it is rather that he rejects, as a matter of principle, any attempt to establish the historical plausibility of the Gospel narratives. The historicity of the parable — that is, whether Jesus actually told the parable in substantially the form recorded in Scripture — is fundamentally irrelevant to understanding it.

It is at this point that Childs parts with traditional Christian biblical scholarship, now usually dubbed "conservative." Although he shares a basic confessional outlook with the practitioners of such traditional biblical scholarship, he connects his faith, not with the historical trustworthiness of the biblical narratives, but with their canonical witness. What does he mean by this? Let me quote again the relevant phrases which he uses in his discussion of the Parable of the Wicked Tenants:

tracing the growth of the text's kerygmatic witness (341)

to interpret the growth of the text within the context of the church's kerygmatic understanding of the subject matter constituting the gospel (341)

recognizing that the various forms of the parables in the Gospels all are shaped from the perspective of Jesus' death and resurrection as the rejected Messiah of Israel (343)

charting the trajectory of the church's kerygmatic witness (344)

It is clear that the key concept here is the "witness" or "understanding" or "perspective" of the early *church*. It is the proper business of canonical exegesis to read the text — or rather its growth along a particular trajectory — in the light of this ecclesiastical understanding. The locus of authority has shifted from the text and its narrative claims to the kerygmatic witness of the early church. It is ultimately the testimony of the early church — or, more precisely, its *theological* testimony, since its historical testimony is not to be trusted — which must be accepted.

What is striking about Childs's treatment of the parable is that he only partially follows his own prescription for canonical interpretation. Although he readily concedes that each parable has undergone a complicated process of development, reflecting oral, written, and redactional levels, he considers attempts to trace that development highly subjective

(341). In fact, in the case of the Parable of the Wicked Tenants, as we have seen, he does not even attempt to define its tradition-historical trajectory. What he actually does is trace the development of the parable as found in Mark to the parable as found in Matthew, disregarding both the Lukan form and Snodgrass's argument that the Matthean form actually comes first.

What is even more striking is that his own concluding theological interpretation is in large part independent even of this limited form of canonical exegesis. His basic point about how the vineyard imagery of Isaiah and of the parable reflect the typological — in fact, ontological — relationship between the two testaments and "the unity of the one plan of God" (345) is one that traditional Christian biblical exegetes, not to mention ordinary believers, have accepted for centuries. In the end, it seems, not only the whole apparatus of scholarly discussion but even the basic point of a canonical approach à la Childs is unnecessary to come to a valid Christian reading of the parable.

What are we to make of this strangely unsatisfactory conclusion? What is ultimately going on in this odd juxtaposition of scholarly pyrotechnics and traditional Christian interpretation? By way of conclusion, allow me to suggest, in a few broad strokes, what I take to be the fundamental issues.

Mainline historical criticism, which dominated the academic study of Scripture throughout most of the nineteenth and twentieth centuries and which has until recently enjoyed enormous prestige in academia, is a product of the modernism of the Enlightenment, aided and abetted by the influential epistemological split between fact and value, knowledge and belief. This historical criticism, cut off in principle from religious faith, tended to undermine the historical reliability of biblical narrative. It is only quite recently, with the rise of postmodernism, that the ideological character of much of historical criticism has been widely recognized in secular academia, even though the modernist tradition continues to be very strong.[5]

Childs in principle accepted the claims of mainline historical criticism and was prepared (like his mentor Karl Barth) to give up the historicity of the Bible where critical scholarship undermined it. However, he did

---

5. See, for example, A. K. M. Adam, *What Is Postmodern Biblical Criticism?* (Minneapolis: Fortress, 1995).

challenge historical criticism on one crucial point — not on its claim to unbiased objectivity, but on its failure to deal with the objective fact of the faith of the biblical tradents. By including the factor of canonical *witness* as part of the objective givens of biblical scholarship, he believed he could retain traditional theological themes in his treatment of Scripture. He was prepared to give up historicity in exchange for canonical witness. The difficulty, of course, is that much of the witness is historical.

Coupled with this broadly philosophical background, we must take into account a basic issue of theology or Christian worldview. What I have in mind is the relationship between "nature" and "grace," that is, between human life and the world outside salvation in Jesus Christ, on the one hand, and that life and world as redeemed by Christ on the other. This is a relationship which has been construed within orthodox Christianity in a limited number of ways and has given rise to the traditional Christian viewpoints on the relationship of Christ and culture, church and world, faith and reason, theology and philosophy. It is also the fundamental issue at stake in different Christian assessments of biblical criticism. As I see it, the four basic paradigms in this connection are those which see grace as opposing, as supplementing, as flanking, and as restoring nature. What distinguishes the first three of these is that they recognize a realm of "nature" (including culture, "world," reason, philosophy, and biblical criticism), which has its own autonomy vis-à-vis "grace" (including Christ, church, faith, theology). In such dualistic Christian worldviews, natural reason — and by extension the scientific enterprise in general, including critical scholarship — stands in a relationship of either dialectical tension, hierarchical subordination, or parallel juxtaposition to Christian faith. Christians holding to one of these dualistic paradigms of the nature-grace relationship can readily make common cause with the heirs of Enlightenment modernism by simply equating the scientific rationality of the Enlightenment project with the cognitive powers of "nature" as opposed to "grace."[6]

As I see it, Childs has essentially accepted the claim of mainline his-

---

6. On the various nature-grace paradigms, see my "Nature and Grace in the Interpretation of Proverbs 31:10-31," *Calvin Theological Journal* 19 (1984): 153-66, reprinted in A. Wolters, *The Song of the Valiant Woman: Studies in the Interpretation of Proverbs 31:10-31* (Carlisle: Paternoster, 2001), 15-29, and my "Christianity and the Classics: A Typology of Attitudes," in *Christianity and the Classics: The Acceptance of a Heritage*, ed. W. Helleman (Lanham: University Press of America, 1990), 189-203.

torical criticism to be wearing the mantle of value-free scientific objectivity and autonomous rationality and has accommodated this to a dualistic Christian construal of the relationship of nature and grace. By failing to challenge, either philosophically or religiously, the ideological nature of aggressively secular biblical criticism, he has set himself the difficult — I would argue: ultimately impossible — task of defending orthodox Christian theology while in principle conceding its historical basis to biblical criticism.

In my own view, a better approach is that represented by the fourth traditional Christian paradigm of the nature-grace relationship — the view that grace enters nature in order, like a medicine, to penetrate and restore it from within.[7] This would mean an approach to biblical criticism which would openly, and from the outset, bring its religious commitment to the God of the Bible into the academic arena and unashamedly forge a Christian way of doing biblical criticism which would in many ways be at odds with mainstream biblical criticism.[8] I would see this as but one facet of the broader task of doing integrally Christian scholarship.[9]

7. On a non-dualistic Christian worldview, see my *Creation Regained: Biblical Basics for a Reformational Worldview* (Grand Rapids: Eerdmans, 1985). See also my "Confessional Criticism and the Night Visions of Zechariah," in *Renewing Biblical Interpretation,* ed. C. Bartholomew, et al., Scripture and Hermeneutics 1 (Grand Rapids: Zondervan, 2000), 96-117.

8. For a philosophical critique of classical biblical criticism along these lines, see "Two (or More) Kinds of Scripture Scholarship," chapter 12 in A. Plantinga, *Warranted Christian Belief* (New York: Oxford University Press, 2000), 374-421.

9. On the project of doing Christian scholarship, see G. Marsden, *The Outrageous Idea of Christian Scholarship* (New York: Oxford University Press, 1997).

Index of Modern Authors

Index of Subjects

allegory, 182-85
Alogi, 173
anti-Judaism. *See* Jews
Antiochus IV Epiphanes, 24
Augustinian hypothesis, 82
authority, 23, 24

Beloved Disciple, 137

Caesar, Augustus, 23-25, 163, 164
church, 14, 15

devil (or Satan), 6
disciples, similar to Jesus, 74

eschatology of Luke, 123-26

faith, 8, 9
form criticism, 35, 39-42, 49, 50

Gentiles: in Acts, 120-23; in Luke, 118-20
Gnostics, 160, 161
Gospel genre, 38-44, 133-35, 138, 165-67
Goulder's hypothesis, 82
Griesbach hypothesis. *See* Matthean
  priority

healing, 24
Herod, 10, 11
Herodians, 10, 11
historical criticism, 102, 190-92
historical Jesus research: history of, 28,
  30-37, 44, 50; criteria, 29, 30, 32-36,
  47, 49-54, 87; relevance for reading
  the Gospels, 37-53
Holy Spirit, 6, 21, 22, 147-49

Jesus: death of, 108-11; Paul's reference
  to, 156; spoken language of, 44-49
Jesus Seminar, 28, 35, 130
Jews: in Acts, 120-23; in John, 138-43; in
  Luke, 117-18
John the Baptist, similar to Jesus, 74
Josephus, 12, 111

law, 71
literary criticism, 101, 102
Luke: interpreting Luke in the light of
  Markan priority, 17-22

Marcion, 32, 158, 166-69
Mark: interpreting Mark in the light of
  Markan priority, 22-25
Markan priority, 3-9, 181, 188; relevance

Index of Ancient Sources